T0301719

Humane Entrepreneurship

Creating a New Economy, Venture by Venture

New Teaching Resources for Management in a Globalised World

Print ISSN: 2661-4774
Online ISSN: 2661-4782

Series Editor: Professor Léo-Paul Dana

The classic economic view of internationalisation was based on the theory of competitive advantage, and over the years, internationalisation was seen in various lights, as an expansion option. With the reduction of trade barriers, however, many local small enterprises face major international competitors in formerly protected domestic markets. Today, competitiveness in the global marketplace is no longer an option; it has become a necessity as the acceleration towards globalisation offers unprecedented challenges and opportunities.

This book series will bring together textbooks, monographs, edited collections and handbooks useful to postgraduates and researchers in the age of globalisation. Relevant topics include, but are not limited to: research methods, culture, entrepreneurship, globalisation, immigration, migrants, public policy, self-employment, sustainability, technological advances, emerging markets, demographic shifts, and innovation.

Published:

The complete list of the published volumes in the series can also be found at
https://www.worldscientific.com/series/ntrmgw

New Teaching
Resources for
Management in a
Globalised World
Volume 6

Humane Entrepreneurship

Creating a New Economy, Venture by Venture

Craig S. Galbraith
Curt H. Stiles
University of North Carolina Wilmington, USA

NEW JERSEY · LONDON · SINGAPORE · BEIJING · SHANGHAI · HONG KONG · TAIPEI · CHENNAI · TOKYO

Published by

World Scientific Publishing Co. Pte. Ltd.

5 Toh Tuck Link, Singapore 596224

USA office: 27 Warren Street, Suite 401-402, Hackensack, NJ 07601

UK office: 57 Shelton Street, Covent Garden, London WC2H 9HE

Library of Congress Cataloging-in-Publication Data

Names: Galbraith, Craig, author. | Stiles, Curt H., author.

Title: Humane entrepreneurship : creating a new economy, venture by venture /
    Craig S. Galbraith, Curt H. Stiles, University of North Carolina, Wilmington, USA.

Description: New Jersey : World Scientific, [2023] | Series: New teaching resources for management
    in a globalised world, 2661-4774 ; Volume 6 | Includes bibliographical references and index.

Identifiers: LCCN 2023003618 | ISBN 9789811271236 (hardcover) |
    ISBN 9789811271243 (ebook) | ISBN 9789811271250 (ebook other)

Subjects: LCSH: Social responsibility of business. | Business ethics. | Industries--Social aspects.

Classification: LCC HD60 .G33 2023 | DDC 658.4/08--dc23/eng/20230131

LC record available at https://lccn.loc.gov/2023003618

British Library Cataloguing-in-Publication Data

A catalogue record for this book is available from the British Library.

For any available supplementary material, please visit
https://www.worldscientific.com/worldscibooks/10.1142/13278#t=suppl

Desk Editors: Aanand Jayaraman/Lai Ann

Typeset by Stallion Press
Email: enquiries@stallionpress.com

Printed in Singapore

To our wives, Jacqueline Benitez-Galbraith and Sharon Stiles, and to our families.

Foreword

"How selfish soever man may be supposed, there are evidently some principles in his nature, which interest him in the fortune of others, and render their happiness necessary to him, though he derives nothing from it except the pleasure of seeing it."

That is the opening sentence from a treatise which the author (by some accounts) regarded as his greatest work. It appears to sharply contrast with one of the most famous quotes in economics; "It is not from the benevolence of the butcher, the brewer, or the baker, that we expect our dinner, but from their regard to their own interest."

In fact, the quotes are by the same person, the eighteenth-century Scottish economist, Adam Smith. The first quote is taken from his *Theory of Moral Sentiments*, the second from his *Wealth of Nations*. Much of the discussion in Smith's "Moral Sentiments" is taken up with an examination of the emotion of sympathy (which today we would more likely describe as empathy). Selfishness and empathy are both intrinsic features of the human condition and influence human behavior, so it is curious that only self-interest is taken as the unique motivating force behind traditional economics as represented by standard or neoclassical theory. Economics has often reflected such selectivity, such as through confirmation biases as discussed by Galbraith and Stiles here in their introductory chapter. The Prisoner's Dilemma is a classic example, both of economic modeling and of how empirical economics can be riddled with confirmation biases.

The basic set up of the Prisoner's Dilemma involves two prisoners being held separately on alleged crimes and not allowed to communicate. The dilemma is that if both prisoners considered only their narrow individualistic self-interest, then they would both confess and be worse off than if they were able to cooperate and stay silent. The "correct" answer in economics is, of course, that they only consider their self-interest and finish up incarcerated for an unnecessary number of years (unnecessary from an individual prisoner's point of view, though perhaps not from a social point of view).

But I once watched in horror as a lecturer attempted to demonstrate the basic foundations of economics in a first-year class by selecting two students to play a version of the Prisoner's Dilemma. The experiment collapsed when the students independently adopted the co-operative solution. How could a diehard neoclassical economist typically explain away such "anomalous" behavior? One way is to treat cooperating subjects as "naïve," which is perhaps why a number of early studies of the Prisoner's Dilemma often used second year economics students who by now had learned sufficient economics to play the "correct," non-cooperative self-interested answer.

Of course, examples of the Prisoner's Dilemma can be found and cited in many aspects of human endeavor. But this is where confirmation bias can creep into the picture. Once we allow for motives other than individualistic self-interest, then the interesting issue is how often mutually beneficial co-operative solutions can arise, almost spontaneously, out of complex social interactions. The question is why, in a world of imperfect information and limited coordination, society does not collapse into a morass of mutually dog-eat-dog, race-to-the-bottom, self-defeating and destructive, non-cooperative outcomes.

One answer is that, as Adam Smith noted, motives other than selfishness can be in play. It is a pity that his famous quote about the self-interest of the butcher, brewer and baker is often quoted out of context and without qualification — selectivity in action again. Smith goes on in the same paragraph to discuss the existence of beggars (which an unthinking proponent of the invisible hand of capitalism might dismiss as just an unfortunate by-product of a free market). But Smith does not resort to such simplistic interpretations, he instead points out that "the charity of well-disposed people, indeed, supplies (the beggar) with the whole fund of his subsistence." So, what is the well-spring of this "charity"? Smith had earlier provided the answer in the second sentence of his *Theory of Moral Sentiments*. It is, "pity or compassion, the emotion which we feel for the misery of others, when we either see it, or are made to conceive it in a very lively manner." It could well be the pity or compassion of the butcher, brewer or the baker who may have just sold a leg of lamb, a keg of ale, or a loaf at market price and now stop on their way home from work to help a fellow citizen in distress.

These entrepreneurs may pursue self-interest in one context and social consciousness in another. These may be contrasting motives, but they can be complementary, not necessarily contradictory. Adam Smith came from the county of Fife in Scotland, and another Fifer Andrew Carnegie was to demonstrate both hard-nosed entrepreneurship and enlightened social philanthropy, a trend carried on today by modern billionaires such as Bill Gates and Warren Buffett.

But as Galbraith and Stiles note in their introductory chapter, this involves examining not what it is to be a human being and the purpose of a human life, but also the nature of the institutions of human social life including economic institutions. It is a fascinating paradox that those who broadcast the virtues of free markets are quite often those least know-ledgeable as to how markets work. Market competition can — or should be — like competition in sport. We all like to see exciting, free flowing and fair competition in sport. But free flowing does not mean free from rules, on the contrary the absence of a rule book would mean that sports such as football would very quickly collapse into chaos if rules to promote and protect competition did not exist. Similarly, market competition typi-cally only works effectively if rules and codes (whether imposed or evolved by government, business or society) exist to ensure free and fair competition.

That is why contributions such as the present one by Galbraith and Stiles are so important today. They infuse flesh and blood into what would otherwise be the sterile bare bones of traditional homo economicus and place him/her in their proper context as part of a complex and dynamic society, which, just like the chapters in this book, makes more sense if taken together as a complete whole. As the authors note, the book is a first step but there is no doubt it will be seen as a much needed and important contribution to this young but growing literature.

Neil Kay
Professor Economics Emeritus,
University of Strathclyde, Glasgow,
Scotland

About the Authors

 **Craig S. Galbraith** holds the Duke Progress Energy/Betty Cameron Distinguished Professorship of Entrepreneurship at the Cameron School of Business, University of North Carolina Wilmington. His Ph.D. in Strategic Management and Mathematical Economics is from Purdue University. He holds an M.Sc. in Molecular Biology from the University of Nebraska, an MBA in Manufacturing Management and B.A. in Economic Philosophy from San Diego State University. Prior to joining UNCW, Galbraith has been on the faculties of the University of California Irvine and Purdue University. He has been the co-founder of several start-up firms in both ocean shipping and biotechnology sectors, and a consultant to many international firms. Galbraith served for many years as a doctorate dissertation supervisor for the Edinburgh Business School, Heriot-Watt University in Scotland. He is also an oblate with St. Meinrad's Archabbey, a Benedictine monastery located in Indiana.

 **Curt H. Stiles** is Professor Emeritus of Strategy and Economic History at the Cameron School of Business, University of North Carolina Wilmington where he teaches strategic management and leadership. He holds an MBA and a Ph.D. in Business Policy from Northwestern University and a B.A. in History. He has been on the faculties of the University of Southern California and Northwestern University. He served in Vietnam as an artillery officer with the U.S. Marine Corps and worked on Wall Street with the New York Society of Security Analysts. He is a Knight Commander of the Holy Sepulcher, a Papal order founded in the First Crusade.

Contents

Introduction: The Problem

Do commercial activity and business, as practiced in modern economies, have the potential of being humane? Can, or have, these activities become fundamentally inhumane? If so, what is it about current practice and behavior in the commercial sphere that could be called inhumane, and can these practices be made more humane in some manner? What is the role of entrepreneurship and small business in this process? Unfortunately, these questions are not routinely asked in a serious manner — not in business schools, not in the popular media, and not in the world of corporate and government bureaucracies.

While there has certainly been a recent increase in the number of publications that claim to discuss topics such as humane capitalism, responsible business, and humane entrepreneurship, they almost always avoid the hard, more fundamental, theoretical and historical questions identified above. In our discussion of "humaneness" in economics, this collection of essays is not meant to be another book on business ethics, sustainable enterprise, or corporate social responsibility. Rather we are taking a deeper look at what it means to be humane in the world of commercial activity at both the institutional and individual levels, and to understand the relationships between humaneness, commercial activity and entrepreneurship. In many of these essays we approach the problems of humaneness in commercial activities in ways that have not been widely discussed.

As a basic premise, we recognize that without addressing these fundamental questions in detail, the notion of simply adding the word humane in front of well-established economic concepts simply creates more buzzwords in the popular vocabulary of business. Does the word "capitalism" sound better to the struggling populations of the world if we call it "humane capitalism?" Do business professors feel better if their lectures and articles are prefaced with the terms "responsible" or "ethical"? Do trainers and consultants get more bookings by labeling their venture management programs "sustainable"? These are serious questions, since concepts of benevolence, charity, sympathy, and ultimately, humaneness are all of interest, at a personal level, and hopefully at a broader institutional level. Yet we all live, work, and exist in a highly competitive world that appears framed by powerful, and seemingly inhumane economic forces.

To properly examine these questions within the context of modern societies, it is critical that we explore important historical, philosophical, ethical, and traditional economic perspectives. We have taken a specific perspective of trying to look honestly at these questions, and not pull punches or fall into the correctness or superficiality that has corrupted much of modern academic questioning. This book is targeted toward "students" of economics, business, and entrepreneurship, whether they are formal students in an undergraduate or graduate college degree program, academic professors and researchers, policy makers, or simply interested readers. The concepts presented in this collection of essays are not hard to understand, but they are nuanced.

On the surface, the purpose of economic activity and business practice is to produce the goods and services needed for human consumption, leading one to argue that few things are more important. People need to eat, wear clothes, and shelter themselves from the elements. People require medical care when sick, books for learning, and modes of transportation. People need trade tools and equipment to create a livelihood. The production and distribution of the products and services for human consumption are simply part of life. Entrepreneurial activity is often recognized as having a special place in this process, particularly as it leads to innovation, economic expansion and societal development. The importance of the work of commerce and entrepreneurial behavior might lead us to accept most business practice without question, to accept practice as we find it without thinking to assess its impact on the natural needs and rhythms of human life.

But is it possible that the acceptance of current business practice might lead to blind acceptance of practices that can be less than fully humane? Is it possible that we might be thoughtless also about the economic output that is created by business practice, output that might be less than fully humane in its impact? Are business school faculty, authors of entrepreneurship books, practicing consultants, government policy-makers, and the managerial elites of the world suffering from a form of "confirmation bias," where seeing that business activity over the past century has led to apparent dramatic wealth creation and broad economic growth, its practices must therefore be considered fundamentally good and proper. But such "confirmation bias" often leads to disasters, particularly when unfamiliar problems, data, trends, and information present themselves to the world.[1] Questions such as these should encourage us to look more closely, and less thoughtlessly, at what it means to be human. It demands a clearer understanding of what it means to practice business humanely, and to live in a humane society, while making full allowance for the practical economic needs of society.

If we argue that few things are more important than economic activity to each individual human and to the society of humans, then how could anything so crucial to the human being be inhumane? And yet throughout human history we are presented with evidence that much of economic activity is indeed inhumane, both in production and distribution. In production, many humans are often forced to labor at tasks they would not choose if left on their own, or forced to labor under inhumane conditions, at inconvenient and inefficient locations, in unnatural or unsafe environments, and separated from their loved ones. For centuries, peasant farming families have been swept off their lands, and thrown into impoverished urban communities.

In distribution, often goods and services of uneven quality and for questionably virtuous purposes, are allocated to humans disproportionately and erratically, with distribution reflecting to a certain extent social class but to a much greater extent reflecting the control of capital assets. Some products have been developed that are downright unsafe. And capital, as it grows, expands, and funds the ever-expanding economies of the world, is increasingly allocated and controlled in a disproportioned and biased manner.

Classical economists, such as Adam Smith and Joseph Schumpeter, not just socialists, are very specific about the power that the controllers of capital have over the distribution of economic wealth. This caution does not apply simply to the satanic mills and sweat shops of early manufacturing but also applies equally to the modern fact that many people must commute long hours in unpleasant traffic, work in sterile modern office environments, and are simply cogs in an organizational hierarchy that subjects them to the petty tyranny of bureaucratic bosses. The modern economic world, regardless of what system it operates under, is changing how people think about each other, not as humans but as a commodity of labor. Not surprisingly, polls show that the majority of people are unhappy, or even "hate" their jobs.

A number of important works, such as Wilhelm Röpke's *A Humane Society*, E.F. Schumacher's *Small is Beautiful: Economics as if People Matter* and Roger Scruton's essay, *The Journey Home*, have appeared that correctly argue that constraints to the market economy for the purposes of a common good, must come from a "bottom-up" perspective, rather than enforced by governmental "top-down" directives. A humane economy must be built upon a decentralist doctrine of smaller economic communities, fueled by entrepreneurship, and guided by the virtues that humankind cherishes. This collection of essays builds upon this notion in detail, but also attempts to explore a deeper understanding of humaneness in an economy. We focus on the very personal level of virtue and humaneness, at the level of the entrepreneur and individual action. In what ways might practices and/or output be inhumane, and why might we be thoughtless about them? Our discussion is built on three major assertions.

First, business and economic activity does indeed tend toward the inhumane. This assertion is not meant as a condemnation but rather a statement of a tendency. This assertion should not be overly surprising. There is ample evidence throughout history that much of human activity, in general, may tend toward inhumaneness. Regional and global warfare, mass genocide, murder and rape, societal destruction, institutional corruption, human slavery, deadly blood sports, and ritualistic cannibalism and human sacrifices, hardly seem to have any humane characteristics, but are still common, if not endemic activities in human history. Why would business be any different, particularly since commercial activities are often intimately tied with, if not profit from, obvious inhumane events.

Perhaps being humane is a quality that is not either-or, either humane or inhumane, but a quality that ranges along a continuum from the absolutely humane, if that is conceivable, to the absolutely inhumane, if that is conceivable. It would be difficult to place any given practice or output precisely on the continuum with any confidence, to smugly label one humane or to fairly label another inhumane, but we can present the humane as an ideal clearly enough to permit questioning. In addition, humaneness may not be a condition, but rather a process of progress and human evolution. And recorded human history spans thousands of years. Hence in making our assertion, we use the phrase "tend toward" the inhumane or humane. The tendency might be found in business practice, entrepreneurial behavior and economic output, affecting all aspects of production, distribution, and consumption. The tendency also implies movement over time, from the humane toward the inhumane. A common theme in these essays is that as businesses age and grow larger, and as business systems become rigid and bureaucratized, they tend to become less humane. This fundamental fact leaves an opening for the role of entrepreneurship, and the actions of the entrepreneur and small business-person to make a difference.

Second, we assert that entrepreneurial activity in pursuit of new ventures is by its nature humane at several different levels. It is the leaven in the mix of business activity that continually moves the economic system toward being more humane. Entrepreneurship is a counter force constantly working to make the business system more humane. Businesses that succeed grow old and large over time and become rigid and less humane. They also tend to become less competitive and to become vulnerable to being replaced by younger businesses that are more humane. Yet throughout history, these large, rigid, and less humane organizations seem to always have a way of protecting their existence by utilizing various institutional and governmental strategies. New ventures, however, continually provide new products and services that break up the older industries and organizational structures and replace them with newer structures that are closer to human beings and to the natural needs and rhythms of human life.

Third, we assert that entrepreneurial activity may also have the potential for humaneness at the individual or personal level. Within this context, we argue that the activity of being entrepreneurial has important philosophical, existential and phenomenological characteristics that may assist the engaged individual to better understand their sense of humanity and experience in life. There may, indeed, be something unique about entrepreneurial action and behaviors that is fundamentally different from other vocations. This is not to suggest that other vocations or careers are inhumane, but rather the nature of entrepreneurial experience opens up a number of philosophical points that need to be understood and discussed. Few, if any, prior literary efforts have approached the issue of humane entrepreneurship from this theoretical perspective.

It may be a timely moment to make these assertions because as mentioned above the generic word "humane" is starting to appear in business school literature, the popular business press, and consulting and training programs. Given this, it is likely to be quickly inserted into the vocabulary of business in general. If initial definitions of humaneness become widespread, it will likely enter the modern university curriculum and will then be hard to dislodge or modify. We have seen this previously in many other popular topics, such as diversity and inclusion, that have critically important implications, but are poorly understood at the theoretical, historical, and foundational level, yet inserted into every corner of organizational life. If the initial definitions are applied in a generic way across disciplines, as we have seen done with the words that have a feel of humaneness, such as "ethics" "social responsibility" and "sustainability," the importance of "humaneness" as a critical concept in economics and business will lose its power. If the initial definitions are self-serving to the literature and curricula as currently practiced, our assertions may be termed irrelevant and possibly ignored.

Humaneness, however, is not a set of skills to be taught. A humane economy reflects a society built on human character and the practice of virtue. It recognizes that people are often driven by a number of moral sentiments, emotions and forces that encourage charity, benevolence, and humaneness. It must incorporate, as Adam Smith recognized, an economic system that accommodates both "self-regarding" and "other-regarding" attitudes.

This book has a particular interest in the role of the entrepreneur. If humaneness is to show itself to be a feature that is attractive enough to help stimulate scholarly demand, then we must try to understand certain things about it before we try to place curricular and pedagogical requirements on it and hold out expectations concerning it. First, what does it mean to be humane, and what would a humane entrepreneur look like? Second, can the work of a humane entrepreneur be expected to have humane outcomes? Is a humane entrepreneur likely to pursue more humane work practices and to produce more humane products? Third, how can humaneness as a virtuous human characteristic be translated into humaneness as a demand generating product characteristic in a business school product called humane entrepreneurship? As a business school product, humane entrepreneurship would have to somehow embody humaneness in the product in a manner that can contribute to its marketing and sale.

We argue that humaneness is a highly relevant characteristic of entrepreneurial action at many different levels. The word humane may be discovered to be more than just a thin dictionary word. It may be a word that introduces us to the entire realm that focuses thought on what it is to be a human being, the purpose of a human life, and the nature of the institutions of human social life including economic institutions. If entrepreneurial behavior can be shown to be truly humane, then the humane component is a strong root that pervades the trunk of the tree of entrepreneurship. But its inclusion, mis-defined and improperly applied, risks turning "humane" into a "weasel word," an adjective that drains the noun of all meaning.

The book is not meant to be an original historical or philosophical thesis, but a highly focused, deeply integrated, and strategic synthesis of other writers' important historical and philosophical insights as they relate to the issue of humane economies and entrepreneurship. In some respects, this may be the most difficult type of analysis and writing. We hope that this fact alone will give our work some appeal to the management reader and that they will find of interest the classic works that we utilize in our analysis.

By design, this book consists of separate essays that are intended to be standalone. As standalone essays, sometimes there are overlaps between the essays in the presentation of concepts, the references and citations from important authors, and the descriptions of historical events. This is on purpose, since to make a topic whole, common foundational concepts sometimes need to be covered. However, each essay in this book has a clear and different focus and purpose. We have organized these chapters into different sections, each covering a broad topic area. The individual essays and sections can be read and understood separately, but perhaps will make more sense if taken together as a complete whole.

Section I, titled "A Humane World" consists of four essays. The first essay in this section, titled, *Humaneness: Definition and Context*, defines the term "humaneness," and examines the development of the concept through history. This essay also lays out the general foundation for examining the concept of humane entrepreneurship. The next essay, *A Race Toward a Humane Economy* examines legendary historical literary examples, such as Plato's *The Republic* and Thomas More's *Utopia*, and how they approach this topic of humaneness within societies. The third essay, *Human Welfare and the Whole Person* looks closely at the aspects of being an individual within an economic system, and the historical conflicts associated with pure profit seeking behavior, and modern culture. The final essay titled, *The Roots of Humanism*, argues that the pursuit of virtue and wisdom involves an ongoing discussion about the nature of the human being, a discussion that is called "humanism." This essay discusses two types of humanism, intellectual humanism and practical humanism.

Section II, titled "Humane and Wise Ventures" offers three essays. The first essay, *Humane Ventures, Natural Liberty, and Undertaking*, looks at a variety of topics, including Natural Liberty and undertaking a venture. The principle of Natural Liberty, as developed by Joseph Schumpeter, represents a condition of both social order and economic growth. This essay then explores the idea of "undertaking," Richard Cantillon's term for "entrepreneurship," as the key to economic growth. This essay concludes by examining the process of combining these concepts into the idea of undertaking a venture. The next essay, *Wise Ventures and Wise Men*, looks at the driving forces behind humane entrepreneurship, such as the meaning of wisdom, time-binding, and entrepreneurial change. These are topics not often discussed in modern entrepreneurship treatises but offer a key to better understanding the nature of entrepreneurial change and humane entrepreneurship. The final essay in this section, *Entrepreneurial Instinct: Keynes vs. Schumpeter*, posits that the desire to be entrepreneurial is always with us, because the role is natural to human beings. Entrepreneurial behavior is a component of the human personality. In this essay we expand our examination of Cantillon's use of the word "undertaker." The essay then concludes with comparison of entrepreneurial instinct between John Maynard Keynes and Joseph Schumpeter.

Section III, titled "Humane Entrepreneurship at the Personal Level," looks at the entrepreneur as a humane "hero" in diverse ways and takes a strong philosophical perspective of entrepreneurial activities. The first essay in this section, *The Entrepreneur as an Existential Being* posits that entrepreneurial activity, in its basic and truest form, is a type of self-managed existential therapy. In this light, entrepreneurial action can become a process of uncovering a deeper understanding of the individual's life as a human, the starting point of humane action. In *Experience as Truth: The Phenomenology of Entrepreneurship*, we continue the philosophical foundation of entrepreneurship at the personal level and explore entrepreneurial behavior from a more phenomenological point of view. In this essay we explore how the upheaval of the industrial revolution gave birth to the "fictitious commodities" of labor and capital in the modern world, concepts that ultimately pushed the modern economic world into a non-humane orientation. The essay titled, *The Meaning of an*

Entrepreneurial Pilgrimage explores the often-referenced idea that the entrepreneurial experience is like a pilgrimage, something deeply meaningful and difficult to complete. What, however, are the implications of this analogy if true? The last essay, *Internalizing Moral Markets: Solving the "Smith Problem"* examines what appears to be differences in Adam Smith's writings, and how entrepreneurial action may resolve some of these apparent conflicts.

Section IV, titled "Non-Random Thoughts on Humaneness," provides a mix of different theoretical ideas to consider. The first essay, *The Power of Wise Leadership* looks at three different, and often dismissed approaches to leadership in a different light — Frederick Winslow Taylor, Lillian and Frank Gilbreth, and the Marine Corp officer training process. In *The Rise and Fall of Responsible Innovation*, we explore the history of innovation, the meaning underlying the relatively new concept of "responsible innovation," particularly as defined by the European Union, and discuss its relevance to humane entrepreneurship. The final essay in this section, *Beauty, Humaneness, and the Object of Economic Behavior* explores the historical development of the concept of beauty, particularly as presented in the various writings of Adam Smith. Within this context, this essay poses an interesting question as to whether the concept of beauty should, in fact, be part of an objective function for a humane economic system.

The last section of the book is titled, "Humane Scale: The Structure of Humane Endeavor." Three essays are presented, all with a focus on scale. The first essay, *Powerful Machines and Humane Growth* takes a life cycle approach, similar to humans. From a humane beginning, almost like a child, corporations grow to be organizations gigantic in size and power, often becoming inhumane in their actions. This essay looks at several case studies. The second essay, *Managerial Capitalism: Statism and Giantism*, examines Edith Penrose's opinions regarding the theory of the firm. Penrose's theory reverses the normal theory of the firm arguments by stating that firms seek to stimulate and generate demand in any shape, place, or time necessary to bring in revenue sufficient to feed the managerial capacity that constitutes the organization. Current demand must be kept high enough to maintain the employment of the current administrative bureaucracy. This creates problems of managerial statism and giantism. The last essay, *A Humane Economy*, starts with understanding the problems of "enmassment," the giantism of virtually all institutions in society, and organizational "disembodiment." The essay then looks specifically at the humane aspects of new ventures, and provides a synthesis of how entrepreneurship, can create a path for a more humane economy.

Endnote

1. Confirmation bias can be defined as a tendency to interpret information, particularly new and novel information, in a way that supports prior results and beliefs. Confirmation bias can be quite dangerous. For example, pilot error in airline crashes is often attributed to confirmation bias, as experienced pilots will sometimes interpret warning signals or odd flight behavior in a way that supports their past experiences, thus not taking the appropriate corrective action.

Section I

A Humane World

Section I, titled "A Humane World" consists of four essays. The first essay in this section, titled, *Humaneness: Definition and Context*, defines the word "humaneness," and examines the development of the concept through history. In this essay we argue that humaneness is a state of being, one that represents a model for humanity, a standard of virtue that constitutes an admirable type of human. Several different references are offered in this essay, including the *Oeconomicus* (c. 400 BC), Charles Dickens' *Bleak House,* works by Shakespeare, and writings by economists F. A. Hayek and Joseph Schumpeter. This essay also lays out the general foundation for examining the concept of humaneness.

The next essay, *A Race Toward a Humane Economy* examines legendary historical literary examples, such as Plato's *The Republic* and Thomas More's *Utopia*, and how they approach this topic of humaneness within societies. This essay also starts an examination of Adam Smith. The essay argues that modern economic thinking has drifted far from the simple humane economy defended by Plato, Thomas More, and Adam Smith. This is apparent when we note that almost all working economies in the modern world are not simple, natural, and personal. Instead, they are mind-boggling in their complexity and intimidating in their conglomeration of central power.

The third essay, *Human Welfare and the Whole Person* looks closely at the aspects of being an individual within an economic system and the historical conflicts associated with pure profit-seeking behavior and modern culture. This essay starts with an analysis of Plato's idea of the "tripartite nature of the soul," and that personal gain-seeking is a part of the tripartite nature of man. This idea is then compared with Adam Smith's perspective as presented in the *Theory of Moral Sentiments* written in 1759. This essay concludes with an argument that to value human variety is to celebrate, not just the obvious dimensions of difference, such as gender, race, ethnicity, language, and geographic location, but most importantly the true nature of humaneness in the world, the broader portfolio of human virtues.

The final essay titled, *The Roots of Humanism*, argues that the pursuit of virtue and wisdom involves an ongoing discussion about the nature of the human being, a discussion that is called "humanism." This essay examines the idea that humanism is ancient and ongoing and that observation of it over the centuries suggests to us that it takes two forms. One we will designate "intellectual humanism," the celebration of the human being in the activity of the mind, and the other we will designate "practical humanism," the celebration of the human being in the work of the world.

1

Humaneness: Definition and Context

That which is humane encompasses, describes, and acclaims that which is natural. To be humane is to value and to embrace and protect what is natural in human nature. The human being is a thing of nature exhibiting all the variety with which nature endows the world. The humane is that which is natural to human beings.

What is "Humane"

The word "humane," a derivation of the word *homo*, "man," comes from the Classical Latin word *humanus*, which was used by Classical Romans to mean "man-like." The meaning of *humanus* was "whatever is characteristic of human beings, proper to man"[1]. In Classical Latin *humanus* had two meanings, "benevolent" and "learned," both of which are characteristics proper to humans. The word *humanus* was used in the Old Testament Book of Wisdom in its translation into Latin in 382 AD from the original Greek. The Book of Wisdom provides a list of the components of wisdom, which in the Latin Vulgate includes "… humanus, benignus, stabilis" … etc., or "… proper to a man (benevolent and learned), benign, steadfast" … etc. Whereas the first characteristic, benevolent, survives today in modern English in the word humane, the second characteristic, learned, was somehow lost in Middle Latin. The Oxford English Dictionary records the first use of the word "humayne" to be c. 1500 with the definition "curtoys & humayn" followed in 1530 by "courtoyse or belongyng to the nature of a man." Other sources say that the first variations of the modern definition begin to be found only in the 1700s.

If the adjective "humane" is to have any enduring impact on our understanding of entrepreneurial behavior, it must be seen to embody much more than the modern definition, of being characterized by "compassion, sympathy, or consideration."[2] These words get their power from the tight connection that they have to the object to which they are directed. One can have compassion, sympathy, or consideration only for a specific, real human being. Compassion, for example, means "suffers along with, and is rooted in the idea of empathy." The subject person who experiences true compassion suffers along with the object person who experiences some misfortune. If the subject does not truly suffer along with the object, then the subject expressing compassion is either deceived or dishonest. If the object of expressed compassion is abstract, ill-defined, diffuse, or distant, the subject expressing compassion can become a person deserving of ridicule, like Mrs. Jellyby in Dicken's *Bleak House* who is driven by compassion for a tribe of people in faraway Africa while being neglectful and cruel to her own children.[3] Unlike the words — compassion, sympathy, consideration — that lose their power when the object is general and diffuse, the word humane has an object that is, by intention, general and diffuse, with the word instead putting its emphasis on the nature and values of the subject person. A subject person directs compassion, sympathy, and consideration to object individuals, but a person is humane in their acceptance of the natural workings of the world. This distinction might be illustrated by looking more closely at Mrs. Jellyby. Dickens might have meant for her to be a clownish villain, and most readers of Dickens's time viewed her that way. Her failure at compassion is extreme, given her cruelty to her children. But if we judge her instead by the standard of the humane, she can be argued to look a little better. In a Victorian England that considered Africans to be near sub-human, her concern for African people looks rather humane. Dickens might even be considered a little inhumane for mocking her efforts and for being blind to the fact that industrial Victorian England might well have been a less humane society than a primitive village in Africa.

Humaneness is a state of being, one that represents a model for humanity, a standard of virtue that constitutes an admirable type of human. Admiration must flow from an understanding of what it means to be truly human, an understanding that can come only through hard-earned wisdom. The pursuit of wisdom, practical wisdom in contrast to divine wisdom, has a long history of human commitment. The word humane comes out of this commitment, and it is our thesis that humane entrepreneurship, if humane is to mean anything more than just that the entrepreneur should try to follow some situational norms, must be rooted in a commitment to virtue and wisdom. A humane state of being can be embodied in human institutions and procedures, making them humane and presenting the challenge of embodying them in entrepreneurship.

Entrepreneurship that is humane would pursue efforts to define and build a healthy community and to make it, like the home, a place of fruitful commitment to the commonweal by all members, a community that the classical Greeks called the *oikos*. Humane entrepreneurship can draw from an ancient literature, most notably focused on the Greek writer Xenophon who was a contemporary of Socrates and Plato. Xenophon can be put forth as a model of the humane man who is motivated by an understanding of a healthy society and the common good and is guided by practical wisdom. In contrast to the more famous Socrates, Plato, and Aristotle, Xenophon was not a specialist scholar but instead was a man who embraced all walks of life. He was a soldier and great leader, most famously taking command of "the ten thousand" Greek soldiers after they had been abandoned and leading them to safety in an epic march across Asia Minor as chronicled in his *Anabasis*. He was a cavalry commander, horse breeder and trainer, writing the earliest surviving training manual entitled *The Art of Horsemanship* that, after 23 centuries, is read and admired by equestrians today.[4] And he also wrote *Oeconomicus* (c. 401 BC), said to be the oldest work in existence on the subject of economics and business.

Usually translated "estate manager," the title *Oeconomicus* has also been translated as "one who knows economics,"[5] but such a one would know an economics with a very different flavor from the body of modern economic and business thought. *Oeconomicus* is not about structure, process, technique, or monetary value but instead is about human character and aspirations. Xenophon's estate manager is a man who seeks to understand the nature of the human being and how a short human life can be made to have purpose. With this understanding, the estate manager seeks to be productive in the fullest sense in order to contribute to total human welfare, of which economic wealth is only a part. He cares little for money and possessions for their own sakes and has virtually nothing in common with profit maximizers and money grubbers. Xenophon's estate manager is said to cut a figure of actual beauty and nobility, a man who embraces the good, the true, and the beautiful, in their true sense.

The estate manager is characterized in classical Greek as *"kalos kagathos,* literally 'beautiful *(kalos)* and *(kai)* good *(agathos)'"*[6] There is no word in English for such a figure, but British classicists in the 18th century "rendered the term as 'gentleman,' a usefully provocative translation which forces readers to compare how men of wealth and station of the ancient world differed from those of other times"[7]

Entrepreneurship as "Beautiful and Good"

We can build on this provocative assertion, the ideal of entrepreneurship as "kalos kagathos," beautiful and good. The ideal of the modern entrepreneur can be thought of as Xenophon's gentleman who seeks to create real wealth to enable himself and others to seek the good life in the most noble sense. No doubt there were money grubbers in classical Greece, but they were not called gentlemen. It took the modern age to defer to oligarchs and to teach young people to admire business hustlers.

Xenophon's gentleman can be argued to characterize Joseph Schumpeter's entrepreneur, who is the catalyst of economic development, because he understands that creative destruction is a positive force of nature, the natural force of birth, decay, and death and thereby the agent of new life and growth. Xenophon's gentleman can also be argued to describe Schumpeter himself, who never sought to parlay his great eminence into prominence, power, and economic wealth by hustling universities and governments, remaining by choice always a professor and a scholar.[8]

This elusive concept, the entrepreneur as gentleman in the manner of Xenophon's *oeconomicus,* one who knows economics, pervades Schumpeter's entire body of work. Schumpeter was an exact contemporary of John Maynard Keynes but, unlike the rest of the Western world, Schumpeter was not an admirer. Keynes became the prototype for the economist as superstar, a model that set the stage for future generations of government economists. Most young economists on the make were ready to apply the Keynesian tools as part of Franklin Roosevelt's "brain trust." John Kenneth Galbraith, a young member of the brain trust, said later that the railroad between Boston and Washington DC was crowded with Harvard economists, all of them eager and proud to increase their power and wealth by helping set economic policy in the expanding New Deal government. Peter Drucker later pointed out that it was all a delusion, that power and control are exerted by politicians and generals, not by booky schoolteachers, but it was, and is, a heady ego trip for the deluded. Schumpeter, although the senior member of the Harvard economics department, would have none of this. He thought such vanity and greed was unseemly and that tempting economists to become government apparatchiks was bad for government and ultimately bad for economics as a discipline.

Schumpeter believed that Keynes and Keynesian economics was not only flawed but also not even interesting, because it addresses a static system whose ideal economy is one in equilibrium, and the policy tools that it provides are for the purpose of helping it arrive at equilibrium. This is not interesting, because no economy is ever in equilibrium and any appearance of being static is an illusion. All economies are constantly changing, and economies of healthy societies are growing. The interesting and important role of economics is to try to understand the causes of change and the directions and rates of growth. Unlike a static economy in an unnatural equilibrium, a Schumpeterian economy exhibits a natural process of birth, growth, maturity, decline, and death. This is a process that would be understood by Xenophon's estate manager, the only thing different today being that rapidly changing technology has the effect of speeding up the process and making the cycles more pronounced.

Schumpeter, like Xenophon, understood that the process of change is humane, i.e., natural to human beings, if it is unobstructed and uncorrupted. A humane economy is one that grows in a natural and fruitful manner, growing evenly across all social classes, all sectors of the economy, and all areas of the country. A humane economy does not lay an undue burden of cost to some classes, sectors, and areas while permitting an undue gain and privilege to others. Obstructions to natural and fruitful growth are the sources of the inhumane, obstructions in the form of monopoly pressures and corruptions both of which are distortions found in what Wilhelm Ropke called the "physics" of economics. "The dehumanization of theoretical economics necessarily includes a human devaluation of the entrepreneur. As against the physics of the economy, we have to underscore its psychology, ethics, intelligence — in short, it's human elements"[9]. The obstructions and corruptions that can work their way into the physics of the economy can lead to four pathologies discussed by Ropke: mass, the enlargement of social and economic structures into giantism and rigidity; concentration, the collection of production into the hands of fewer and fewer corporate producers; centralization, the movement of administration into more and more consolidated control; and proletarianization, the conversion of people into dependent wage-workers that lack capital.

The dehumanization of theoretical economics comes from its tendency to accept, and even justify, the physical elements as necessary to ensure increasing consumption of mass-produced goods and services using mass production techniques. The justification of the physical elements as normal opens society to the obstructions and corruptions that make the economy less humane as products mature and industries become massive, concentrated, and centralized, and that proletarianizes both their producers and consumers. Economies can aspire to the humane if they are given continuing life by the natural process of birth, growth, decay, and death.

Xenophon, Schumpeter, and Ropke all understood that the midwife of new economic life is the estate manager, the "one who knows economics," the "gentleman" — in modern economic language, the entrepreneur. A dehumanized theoretical economics has difficulty finding a place for such a figure, leading economist William Baumol to describe the entrepreneur to be an "elusive ghost" in economic literature,[10] a figure that has no rightful place, but which makes itself at home and won't go away. In his last book, of several, on entrepreneurship, Baumol acknowledged that we still cannot add much to the work of Schumpeter and that we still do not have a real theory of entrepreneurship, although our searches might be bringing us closer.[11]

The Danger of Weasel Words

The acceptance of "ethics and social responsibility" in the business school pedagogical literature has led our search to include the word "humane." If we truly understand the meaning of humane, this word could be a fruitful addition to our understanding of entrepreneurship. But if we misuse and trivialize the word, then it is in danger of becoming just another weasel word. We were alerted to the danger of weasel words by F. A. Hayak, drawing on Shakespeare's *As You Like It*, act II, scene 5:

> It (Jacques's singing) will make you melancholy, monsieur Jacques.
>
> JACQUES: "More, I prithee, more. I can suck melancholy out of a song as a weasel sucks eggs."

Shakespeare here alludes to a folk belief of his day that a weasel can suck the contents of an egg without breaking the shell. Hayak defines a weasel word to be an adjective that "has the power to empty the noun it qualifies of its meaning"[12]. He emphasizes as particularly malignant the weasel word "social," stating that its modern usage originated in the Bismarkian *kulturekampf* of 1880s Germany as an attack on traditional religion and morals. "The confusion that it spreads is due to its describing not only phenomena produced by various modes of cooperation among men, such as in a 'society,' but also the kinds of actions that promote and serve such orders. From this latter usage it has increasingly been turned into an exhortation, a sort of guide word for rationalist morals intended to displace traditional morals, and now increasingly supplants the word 'good' as a designation of what is morally right"[13] To underscore the dangerous spread of the malignant word "social," Hayak performed his own informal research, and generated about 160 examples, all of which he listed, of nouns modified in common usage by the adjective "social", beginning alphabetically with "social accounting" and ending with "social work." Roger Scruton says that a particularly meaningless and politically loaded example is "social justice," a term now so mis-defined but eagerly used as to be treated as a moral standard by a wide variety of business, governmental and religious organizations and institutions. As Scruton notes, "Social justice, as now understood, is no more a form of justice than fools' gold is a form of gold. It is not what justice was for Aristotle and Ulpian — a matter of giving to each his due, taking account of rights, obligations, and deserts. Social justice, as commonly understood, means the reorganization of society, with the state in charge"[14]

Is the word "humane" in danger of becoming a new weasel word? The degree of danger of the word can be highlighted by the dictionary, which has extended the definition of the word to include the welfare of animals, and the word is increasingly appropriated by animal welfare interests. If one looks up organizations with the word "humane" in their title, one is likely to be directed to an animal welfare organization. In these animal welfare organizations, one will encounter, as might be expected, arguments against eating meat and for practicing vegetarianism instead. Interestingly, one will more often encounter arguments against the factory farming of animals. This second emphasis is exceptionally interesting, because it reveals that the biggest concern of animal welfare is the factory method and the factory conditions. The argument is that the factory is inhumane for animals. These are the same factory methods and factory conditions that are accepted as normal in the society of human beings, the same methods and conditions that are argued by Ropke to lead to mass, concentration, centralization, and proletarianization.

Endnotes

1. See V. Giustiniani, "Homo, Humanus, and the Meanings of 'Humanism'," *Journal of the History of Ideas* 46, no. 2 (1985), 167–195 for a detailed discussion of this topic.
2. See various definitions in the Oxford English Dictionary (2021); Merriam Webster on-line (2021); Dictionary.com (2021).
3. This discussion comes from C. Dickens, *Bleak House* (Mineola, NY: Dover Thrift Editions, 2017) Original work published 1855.
4. Xenophon wrote *The Art of Horsemanship* (also known as *On Horsemanship*) in c. 362 BC. A commonly used translation is by M. Morgan in 1893, and more recently published by J. A. Allen in 1962. This discussion follows Xenophon, *The Art of Horsemanship,* transl. M. H. Morgan (Boston, MA: Little, Brown, and Company, 1893) Original work published c. 360 BC.
5. See D. Leshem, "What Did the Ancient Greeks Mean by Oikonomia," *Journal of Economic Perspectives* 30, no. 1 (2016), 225–231.
6. S. Eide and K. Whitaker, "A Philosopher and a Gentleman: Xenophon's Oeconomicus," *Arion: A Journal of Humanities and the Classics* 24, no. 2 (2016), 93–100.
7. *Ibid*, 93.
8. See any biography of Joseph Schumpeter.
9. W. Ropke, *The Humane Economy: The Social Framework of the Free Market* (Washington DC: Regenery Publishing, 1960), 258.
10. Baumol discusses this in detail in W. Baumol, "Entrepreneurship in Economic Theory," *The American Economic Review* 58, no. 2 (1968), 64–71.
11. Baumol expands his discussion of entrepreneurship in a later book; see W. Baumol, *The Microtheory of Innovative Entrepreneurship* (Princeton, NJ: Princeton University Press, 2010).
12. F. Hayak, *The Fatal Conceit* (Chicago, IL: University of Chicago Press, 1988), 116.
13. *Ibid*, 114.
14. See R. Scruton, "The Journey Home: Wilhelm Ropke & The Humane Economy," *The Imaginative Conservative (2020).* https://theimaginative conservative.org/2020/03/journey-home-wilhelm-ropke-humane-economy-roger-scruton-timeless-2020.html. Accessed September 1, 2022. For a more detailed discussion of these issues, see R. Scruton, *The Soul of the World* (Princeton, NJ: Princeton University Press, 2014) and R. Scruton, *On Human Nature* (Princeton, NJ: Princeton University Press, 2017).

2

The Race Toward a Humane Economy

A humane community is one that provides for its members a setting that is most suitable for the human being in the natural world. Nature itself is indifferent to the whims and foibles of the human being, presenting harsh realities and dangerous threats. It also provides humans with the potential to make a bountiful home and satisfying social relationships. A fully humane economy would be one in which humans work with nature's bounty to nourish a healthy and fruitful community that would meet basic human needs, allow for human whims and foibles, invest in building a humane future, and assure the maintenance of the community into the future. To work within nature's bounty is humane behavior, to live in accord with nature's harsh realities is a humane life, and to build and maintain a fruitful community in face of nature's dangerous threats and limitations is to make a humane economy.

A Humane Economy: A Platonic Perspective

Plato gives us in *The Republic*, circa 375 BC an outline, said to be the first, of a humane economy, "So they will live with one another in happiness, guarding against the danger of poverty and war"[1] Plato sketches the parameters of an economy, of small proprietors working according to a powerful division of labor, producing by their own direct efforts the basic goods and services needed for a wholesome and uncluttered life, and exchanging the goods and services in local markets with other local proprietors and consumers. Plato says that a humane economy will nourish a community of happy people, "Leading so peaceful and healthy a life they will naturally attain to a good old age, and at death leave their children to live as they have done." At this point in the dialogue, Glaucon, one of Plato's interlocutors, observes that such a small community and simple economy producing only basic staples would be static and, without the excitements of "modern life," would resemble "a city of pigs."

Plato acknowledges the complaint and responds, "Very well. I understand. We are considering, apparently, the making not of a city merely, but of a luxurious city. And perhaps there is no harm in doing so. From that kind, too, we shall soon learn, if we examine it, how justice and injustice arise in cities. I, for my part, think that the city I have described is the true one, what we may call the city of health. But if you wish, let us also inspect a city which is suffering from inflammation"[2] The inflammation in a city of luxury, the excitability of people and the resulting chaos in society, is caused by a human weakness, the desire for excess, for luxuries, which Plato lists to include such excesses as rich food, fragrant oils and perfumes, ornate clothes and houses, gold and ivory, sweetmeats, and courtesans.

Plato's economy is simple, direct, and personal and, he claims, would support a "city of health." But his economy is not humane, because it is not natural to human beings, our definition of the humane. Glaucon is right, as Plato acknowledges, because, for good or ill, people are naturally creatures of excess and want the luxuries that Plato enumerates. To expect humans to be otherwise is to expect them to be unnatural. To minimize the damage of the inevitable inflammation and to insure adequate productivity, Plato proceeds to lay out the structure of his famous ideal society in *The Republic*, built on three classes of people: "artisans" who will produce the goods and services to meet practical needs, "auxiliaries," police/soldiers who will keep public order and provide safety, and "guardians," philosopher/king rulers who will set policy and make overall governance decisions. The two upper classes control their natural desire for excesses by holding everything in common, famously including unlimited access to communal wives and sharing parentage of children. The excesses of the workers are accepted to be inevitable but are restrained by rules enforced by the elites governing public order and productivity.

Plato's picture of an ideal society has always been controversial. Advocates put it forth as a utopia, a perfect society, orderly, productive, and equitable. Detractors say that instead of providing justice as a natural man would define it, it provides instead a guideline for perfect tyranny.

The method of tyranny lies in the privileged elite classes keeping tight control over the working class, and the motive for tyranny lies in Plato's puritanical standards for human behavior and the belief by the two elite classes that tight control is for the worker's own good. The 20th century Austrian-British philosopher, Karl Popper states that *The Republic* talks about justice but "is not even interested in those problems which men usually call the problems of justice, that is to say, in the impartial weighing of the contesting claims of individuals"[3] or in adjusting the claims of the state to balance the claims of the individual.

The controversy over the ideal society has persisted from the first appearance of *The Republic* to the present. The disagreement seems to be fundamental, on the one hand a society built on a vision of equality in production and distribution among the workers with order enforced by rigid social control by powerful central government to keep the excesses of the people in check, and on the other hand a society built on a vision of minimal social control by limited government that tolerates a certain amount of disorder and inequality as a result of people behaving in accordance with their natural inclinations. Modern critics of Plato's vision argue that it reappears regularly and that various attempts at socialism have never worked because they are unnatural, while modern defenders argue that various forms of Plato's vision would work if done correctly.[4] The fundamental incompatibility and irreconcilable nature of these two visions was captured in the literary classic *Utopia* of 1516.

Humaneness and the "Pig Sty"

Thomas More, the author of *Utopia*, was one of the great English humanist writers of the late renaissance, producing a vast body of work in literature, history, politics, and spirituality, yet his work is read today primarily only by scholars, with the exception being the literary work for which he is known to most of the world, the great satire called *Utopia*. The substance of the *Utopia* satire is a pair of lectures, Book I and Book II, delivered by a boastful, insecure and self-proclaimed world travel named Raphael Hythlodacus trying to ingratiate himself with an important English government official named Morus.[5] The lecture in Book I addresses the wonders Hythlodaeus claims to have seen in his travels, embellishing wonderous tales of fabulous terrain, giant monsters, and societies of freakish people, until Morus reveals that he has no interest is such claims but would be interested in any example that Hythlodaeus might have encountered of a truly well governed society with happy and productive citizens. Hythlodaeus immediately turns from his wonderous tales and assures Morus that he has indeed encountered just such a place, a perfect island society called Utopia and proceeds to contrast its order, equality, and productivity to the disorder, inequality, and economic chaos of England.

The lecture in Book II describes in detail the society of Utopia, presenting a picture of Plato's city of health, but with a difference in its social relationships, through the earthy and sensual eyes of Hythlodaeus. Utopia appears rich, healthy, and peaceful; in fact, Hythlodaeus proclaims it to be the richest, healthiest, and most peaceful society in the history of the world. But in Utopia, unlike Plato's city, wealth is public wealth, health is public health, and peace is public peace. There is no private property, there is no family or private life, and personal disorder is suppressed by violent public repressive mechanisms. In Plato's vision, man's natural inclinations and preferences can deviate from the ideal of the "city of health" but, under the careful leadership and strict guidance of the guardians, the people can be trusted to limit their excesses enough to make the "luxurious city" possible without the need to suppress people's natural desire for family, private life and private property. Not so in the land of Utopia. The people obviously, judging from the long history of places like England that Hythlodaeus denounces in Book I, cannot be trusted to control themselves enough to avoid chaos, injustice, and inadequate productivity. So, Utopia exerts the tightest imaginable social control, enforced by enslavement and capital punishment. Control comes from the top in the person of a ruler for life, selected by a council of 10 magistrates who never change, with the advice of representatives from each of the 54 districts into which the island of Utopia is divided. Any attempt of a person to discuss politics outside of his assigned district is a crime punished by death, and any attempted travel outside of the district is a crime punished by enslavement. All people, except those designated to be farmers, live in one city within each district in cubicles that are identical in every way and with no personal belongings allowed. All people eat in communal dining halls at long tables, with children waiting until adults are finished. Wives are not held in common, evidently that is too much even for Hythlodaeus, but children are raised in common, allowing mothers to work alongside men. The education of children is common, as is continuing education of adults, in practical job skills needed by the jobs to which all people are assigned for life and which they cannot change. Much of the work is done by slaves, whose ranks are continually enlarged by criminals guilty of several lifestyle offenses and by prisoners taken in the numerous wars that Utopia fights on the mainland.

Reading about this horror is made amusing and pleasant by the fact that Hythlodaeus is working so hard to try to ingratiate himself with Morus that he does not realize that he is creating a particularly harsh city of pigs and trying to pass it of as a city of health. He continually remarks on how happy the Utopians are and never misses an opportunity to describe every routine personal interaction as being conducted with joy and in a spirit of generosity and kindness. Even slaves engage in this joyful personal activity, unless they plot to rebel in which case they are summarily executed and any Utopian that did not reveal the plot is made a slave. Morus listens to all of this, evidently as amused as the modern reader.

The Hythlodaeus version of the perfect society has a dark fairytale quality about it, more so than the version of Plato. Assuming a passivity that is a caricature of what is natural to humans, Plato allows people to have a private life, a home, and some responsibility, but Hythlodaeus denies them even that and would probably call Plato a dreamer. Plato is aware of the city of pigs but claims that it can be turned into a city of health by the selfless leadership of the guardians. Hythlodaeus makes no such claim and, in describing the unnatural social structure needed to control the human lack of passivity, inadvertently reveals that Utopia is exactly a city of pigs. In writing *Utopia*, Thomas More used Greek and Latin roots to invent a name for the permanent magistrate that rules Utopia as a ruler-for-life, calling him a "syphogrant." Modern translators disentangle the roots to reveal that syphogrant can mean either "wise ruler" or "ruler of a pigsty." It is, in itself, an interesting evolution of thought that has turned More's worrisome description of Utopia into the modern usage of the word "utopia" as being something beautiful.

If we acknowledge, despite Plato, that humans are by nature not passive and have a desire for excess and luxuries, we might also acknowledge that humans have a desire for the humane community, a desire encouraging both their personal actions and their interactive relations with others to work for the good of the humane community. But there is much that is inhumane in a typical community's economic and social systems, and the inhumaneness tends to persist. The inhumane can persist because of personal shortcomings, if people do not understand how their actions in the moment might degrade the relationships that comprise the systems. But more destructively, the inhumane can persist because it is built into the system itself.[6] Social and economic systems can be, and all too often are, inhumane. Systems are prone to being inhumane because of two tendencies that lie in the nature of a system and hence hard to resist. First, systems tend over time to become ever larger and more complex, and second, systems tend over time to become ever more centralized. Mass, complexity, and centralization are inherently inhumane.[7] The humane lies in the simple and the personal that is natural to humans.

A Division of Labor

The Wealth of Nations became, immediately on its appearance in 1776 and remains today, the foundation of our understanding of modern economics and business.[8] This is so, because it presents us with a humane economy, a model of the simple, the natural, and the personal. It is easy to grasp and is taken to heart by everyone on their first encounter, because it explains the creation of economic wealth to be the results of the personal and simple actions of individuals coming together by their own choice to work together to create a humane economy built on simple exchange relationships. The book opens with simple, but most fundamental, truths. In the opening sentence of the Introduction, the very first sentence of the long book, Smith states the simple truth that all economic wealth comes from the natural act of people working. "The annual labor of every nation is the fund which originally supplies it with all the necessaries and conveniences of life which it annually consumes." A second simple truth comes in the first sentence of Chapter I of the book, "The greatest improvement in the productive powers of labor, and the greater part of the skill, dexterity, and judgment with which it is anywhere directed, or applied, seem to have been the effects of the division of labor." The first truth, called the "labor theory of value," assures us that people love to work and that a humane economy is one that allows them to work most productively in a manner that will allow them to create maximum wealth. Note that Smith's sense of the "labor theory of value" does overlap somewhat with Marx's "labor theory of value," which argues that the value of a product is the cumulative sum of the necessary labor required to produce it. Smith however, also seems to be overlaying an overall natural process of work, and the value associated with this is embedded in labor, rather than simply an accounting device of value as associated with Marxist economic philosophy. This natural element of labor value is often overlooked by many Smith scholars.

The second truth, the division of labor, is so fundamental to human work, it was fully explained by Plato. "No two of us are by nature altogether alike. Our capacities differ. Some are fit for one work, some for another ... more tasks of each kind are accomplished, and the work is better and is done more easily when each man works at the one craft for which nature fits him ... Men will exchange the produce of their labors with one another ... by buying and selling. This will give us a marketplace, and money as a token for the sake of exchange ... and exchange money for goods with those who want to sell, and goods for money with those who want to buy."[9]

Smith and Plato present us with a union of human nature and the physical reality of production, what Wilhelm Ropke calls the "physics" of production. The division of labor is natural to humans, and they will naturally engage in exchange of their special product for the other products that they need. Markets will naturally form, and the resulting exchange economy will increase output, lower costs, and improve quality. A market economy naturally follows. As a result of specializing, "Every workman has a great quantity of his own work to dispose of beyond what he himself has occasion for ... and every other workman being exactly in the same situation."[10]

Markets permit each worker to exchange the fruit of his specialization for the fruits needed of other workers. The division of labor is possible only because markets naturally form, in which a worker "is enabled to exchange a great quantity of his own goods for a great quantity of theirs."

Drifting into the Inhumane

Modern economic thinking has drifted far from the simple humane economy defended by Plato, Thomas More, and Adam Smith. This is apparent when we note that almost all working economies in the modern world are not simple, natural, and personal. Instead, they are mind-boggling in their complexity and intimidating in their conglomeration of central power. Modern economics in universities is taught as an overly complex, mathematically oriented discipline requiring a deep understanding of calculus and differential equations. And modern economic policy often seeks to justify the practice and actively calls for more complexity and more centralized control. For example, the World Bank published a report entitled *The Changing Wealth of Nations 2021* to provide "a new set of tools and analysis to help policy makers guide collective action." It calls for central government to provide universal health coverage, mass "quality" education, and cash transfers.[11] *Oxfam*, the international advocacy organization founded in Britain, concurs with the World Bank policy goals, and takes issue with the World Bank only for not carrying complexity and central control far enough, stating that "a strong and accountable government, rather than markets, is needed" to enable their enactment to create what *Oxfam* calls a "human economy."[12]

Currently popular economics concurs with this call for implementation of more complexity and concentrated government control. French economist Thomas Piketty's *Capital in the Twenty-First Century* became an international best-seller, quite a feat for a 650-page textbook, based on his call for more centralization and complexity. His basic thesis is that wealth accumulation from the growth of capital will inevitably outpace wealth accumulation by labor, leading to serious wealth imbalances across society. His suggested solution is for a more powerful central government to redistribute the wealth, calling this the "democratic control of capital."[13] This bodes ill for entrepreneurship. "The entrepreneur inevitably tends to become a rentier, more and more dominant over those who own nothing but their labor. Once constituted, capital reproduces itself faster than output increases. The past devours the future."

This is far indeed from our ideal of a humane economy, which is exactly the opposite. Such centralized control is inherently inhumane, not natural to human beings. Anything that lessens the power of the division of labor does harm to the humane economy and will become a source of injustice. People must be free to specialize and to exchange "and meddling and interchange among them is the greatest of injuries to the city and might justly be described as the extreme of evil doing."[14]

The entrepreneurial impulse is natural to human beings, the very thing that Piketty fears and disdains. The goal of a humane economy should be decentralized simplicity in which entrepreneurial instinct can flourish. These simple truths lay the foundation for another truth, that self-interest must be acknowledged and allowed to lie at the heart of a humane economy. A humane economy motivates people to work hard at their specialty and to engage in new ventures, because it is in their own self-interest to do so. The power of these truths lies in their natural simplicity, a humane economy in which all people would be free to pursue work and new ventures for their own self-interest and to thereby embrace the commonweal. In so doing a humane economy has the power to create a giant flow of prosperity "like a river, like an overflowing torrent, the wealth of nations."[15]

Endnotes

1. Plato, *The Republic* (New York: Everyman's Library, 1978) (Original work published c. 375 BC), 48.
2. Plato, *The Republic*, 48–49.
3. See K. Popper, *The Open Society and Its Enemies* (London: Routledge and Kegan Paul, 1966).
4. Apologists for the continuous failures of various Marxist and socialist experiments in the 20th century, and the resulting brutality of these societies, whether describing Stalin's Russian communist deadly *gulags*, the National Socialist German Workers Party's (Nazi) concentration camps, or Pol Pot's Khmer Rouge's extermination of millions of Cambodians almost always appear to argue that the Socialist or Marxist ideals in these cases simply weren't implemented the right way. Without thinking through the implications of their arguments, many of these apologists fall back on implementing very Christian notions of charity, humility, humaneness, and other virtues that by definition are at odds with such Marxist economic systems. In fact, monastic communities are probably the only institutions able to combine these ideas successfully over the ages, but they do it within a very spiritual orientation as a starting point and with limited size, like an extended family.
5. T. More, *Utopia,* transl. C. Miller (New Haven, CT: Yale University Press, 2001). Original work published 1516.
6. This is a common concept in much of theological thought. For example, the Catholic Church teaches the reality of "systemic sin."
7. W. Ropke, *The Humane Economy: The Social Framework of the Free Market* (Washington DC: Regenery Publishing, 1960).
8. A. Smith, *The Wealth of Nations* (London: Penguin Books, 1986). Original work published 1776.
9. Plato, *The Republic*. Book II, 370.
10. Smith, *Wealth of Nations*, 115.
11. World Bank, *The Changing Wealth of Nations 2021: Managing Assets for the Future* (Washington DC: World Bank, 2021).

12. R. Dodgson, "Fighting Inequality and Poverty Requires a More Humane View of Economics," *The Conversation* (2017) January 30, 2017. https://theconversation.com/fighting-inequality-and-poverty-requires-a-more-humane-view-of-economics-71600. Accessed August 30, 2022.

13. See T. Piketty, *Capital in the Twenty-First Century* (Cambridge, MA: Belknap Press, 2014), 569–571.

14. Plato, The Republic, Book IV: 434.

15. Isaiah 66: 12.

3

Human Welfare and the Whole Person

Growth and development can lead all too easily to discomforts, inequities and a less humane community if entrepreneurial ventures lose sight of their true purpose, the increase of human welfare in its complete sense, called seeking virtue; to increase the stock of human welfare is to become more humane. Complete human welfare embodies the whole person, in three parts, called the tripartite nature of man, the physical, the mental, and the spiritual. A whole person consists equally of these three parts, coexisting and merging with no clear line between them. Virtuous activity leads to human welfare only if it builds one of these, if not, the effort does not contribute to human welfare. Many activities will even subtract from human welfare. A form of the tripartite nature is found in natural law theology in the form of "Transcendentals," the good, the true, and the beautiful, the connections between nature and man. Beauty, when something is exactly as nature intended, can lead to truth, which in turn leads to goodness.

What is an Economic Person?

A belief in the tripartite nature of man has been held from the earliest times, continuing down to the present day in such forms as of Maslow's popular Hierarchy of Needs, in which the satisfaction of needs progresses upward from physical to mental to spiritual. The belief in the tripartite nature appears to be so true, we may today think that it has always been held to be obvious, but the belief enters human thought in Book IV and

Book IX of *The Republic* (circa 375 BC). Plato introduced the idea as the "tripartite nature of the soul."[1]

In Book IV: 436, Plato writes:

This is a hard question, whether in our actions we always use the same element, or whether there are different ones which are used for different purposes. Do we learn with one and feel anger with another of the elements within us and with a third desire the pleasures of food and drink and propagation, and so on; whenever we have an impulse to action, do we employ the whole soul on each of these different occasions?[2]

And from Book IX:580/581

the soul of each individual is divided into three forms...

Belonging to these three forms there appear to be three pleasures, one special pleasure attaching to each particular form, and so with desires and principles...

first, that by which a man learns; secondly that by which he is angry. The third...we call the desiring form because of the intensity of the desires concerned with food and drink and sex and so on; and we also called it money-loving because such desires are usually satisfied with the help of money...

And if we were further to say that its pleasure and love is in gain ... the money-loving or the gain-loving form...

the spirited element is ever wholly bent on mastery and victory and fame ... the victory-loving and the honor-loving form...

as to the part with which we learn, it is forever straining to know where the truth lies, and cares for money and reputation less than the others... we call it learning-loving and philosophic...

men's hearts are ruled some by this last element, others by one of the other two, as the case may be...

Then it is for these reasons that we say that of men there are three primary classes — the lovers of wisdom, the lovers of victory, and the lovers of gain.

Money-loving and gain-seeking is a part of the tripartite nature of man. In our modern age, "wealth" is often superficially defined to be the possession and consumption of goods and services. If we were to ask the man in the street, "what is wealth," he might reply that it is money or the things that money can buy, Plato's money-loving in clear view. This answer is only partially correct, an answer that is too narrow, because it includes just economic wealth, which is only a part of the totality of an individual's stock of wealth and does not include those things that are not economic goods, such as family and friends, virtue and wisdom. Thoughtless economic growth and development can endanger these things. From the earliest times, wisdom has taught that economic wealth should be sought only in a manner that does not endanger the humane community, an effort called seeking virtue.

Adam Smith never argued that it is a purpose worthy of a human life to make money and consume products. He never intended to teach that the production and consumption of economic goods was worthy of a human life. Economic gain-seeking behavior became an acceptable topic of academic teaching only later, among Smith's disciples, because of the startling increases in economic wealth resulting from the early industrialization in England. Nassau Senior, a Smith disciple, was the first economist ever allowed to teach at Oxford University in its 800-year history. In his inaugural lecture to his fellow professors on December 6, 1826, he argued that: consuming economic products makes people happy, the production of economic products thus makes society function well, therefore, the money-making that comes from production must be virtuous. The professors at Oxford were shocked that young people should be taught the premise that money-making can be virtuous. Many of them got up and walked out of Senior's lecture.[3]

Economic wealth accumulation is not a traditional human value. For virtually all of human history we have been taught that human purpose centered on Plato's tripartite soul, and spiritually related transcendentals, whether from Christian, Islamic, Judaic, or other traditions. As recently as Senior's 1826 lecture, respectable opinion held that business is a rather pedestrian effort, necessary for human existence, but certainly not edifying. Young people should be taught the higher things: love, morality, virtue, and the development of character. The thought that a human life could be spent focused primarily on seeking economic gain was repugnant. Senior's argument that money-making is a virtuous effort was outrageous. Among the Oxford dons who walked out of his lecture was no less a figure than the young John Henry Newman.

The chorus of disapproval encountered at Oxford by the premise that economics is a worthy academic discipline might have been forgotten or relegated to a humorous anecdote were it not for the fact that 28 years after the lecture, Newman immortalized it in his critique in *The Idea of the University*, a monumental treatise on the nature of a true university and its role in maintaining civilization, a role that began with Plato's academy and was argued to be endangered in the increasingly materialist society of the 19th century. Newman and his fellow Oxford dons of 1826 would probably describe the modern university to be more of a trade school than a university, more focused on job skills than on building character and virtue, instilling culture and high learning, and establishing the moral parameters of the interactive behavior required by a humane society. Newman might have stated that the true idea of a university began to decline there at Oxford in 1826, with the unsubstantiated, to his mind, claims made by Senior. "The Professor of Political Economy at Oxford says that his science ranks among the first of the moral sciences ... The Professor states further that no institution is more beneficial than one which increases the power and the wish to accumulate wealth." How did Senior come to make such claims? Newman responds with a direct quote from Senior's lecture. "The Professor has recourse to private judgement and answers for himself. 'The endeavor to accumulate the means of future subsistence and enjoyment is, to the mass of humankind, the great source of moral improvement'"[4] Newman, who is renowned for his restraint and moderation, seems barely able to conceal his annoyance at Senior's pre- sumption in raising Plato's money-loving to the rank of "first among the moral sciences."

Adam Smith, Senior's mentor, personally had no interest in economic wealth, considering himself, and considered by the academic world in which he lived and worked, to be a moral philosopher. As such he was concerned with a much larger theme, the "problem of order"[5]: how does social order come to exist in a natural world of distinctly different indi- viduals each with his own purpose and desires that must be articulated and fought for in competition with all other individuals in a continuous strug- gle that is always in danger of spiraling into dog-eat-dog chaos and vio- lence. All individuals must engage in this social competition, and somehow, all together, they make it work. Society does not degenerate into chaos and violence. How do they make it work? Society works, because all individuals instinctively know and learn that they need to work together in cohesive social entities that we call "organizations." They begin to learn this in nature's most fundamental organization, the family.

An organization is a relationship in which two or more people work together to create something of value to all. Each individual begins to learn the need for organizations in the family, at his mother's breast. The individual needs his mother for something that he cannot do without and cannot do by himself. Each organization exists for a purpose, to create something that does not exist until the organization creates it. There are many types of organizations, small and large, because there are many types of purpose, both intimate and grand. A small and intimate organization is formed when two people come together to create a personal bond, like mother and child, a bond that is important because of the importance of what is created, something that does not exist until mother and child come together to produce it. At the other extreme of large and formal organizations, a giant business is formed of many people working together for a purpose, the production of the product of the business. Both organizations, a mother and child and a business, are important because the purpose of both is to create something that is valuable, sometimes crucially valuable, in the first example, life and happiness, and in the second example, the goods and services that the mother and child need to survive and to prosper. Whatever the thing is that is created, if it is desired by us and is important to us, it constitutes wealth.

Humaneness, Order, and Errors

The problem of order is built on the embracing of the humane. It addresses the question of how order emerges from a group of people who work together in an organization for the common purpose of the organization when each of the individual people have their own separate purpose. Working together in an organization is difficult because the behavior of each individual is by nature motivated by an individual purpose that is valuable to him. But the individual's behavior must be shaped by the requirement to work with others who are motivated by their own individual purpose. It is an exercise in the humane for all the individuals to adjust their personal purpose to the common purpose of the organization.

In *The Theory of Moral Sentiments*, Smith considers the nature of human social interaction in terms of two broad questions. First, how, and why, do individuals rise above their self-absorption and concern with themselves to be concerned with community and with organizations that include concern for the social welfare of others? We are all concerned with ourselves, of necessity. We have our own life that we must manage, and when we die, we die alone. Our own life is central to us, so it is difficult to go beyond our self-absorption to be concerned with public goods, the community, and social welfare, the welfare not only of ourselves but of others. Second, how do individuals develop the beliefs and moral positions that permit them to engage in social interaction, to adapt their personal needs to the personal needs of others in working together to pursue the organization purpose? The personal behavior of each individual must address how a person can engage in the social interaction necessary for organizations to form and prosper.

The desire for economic wealth requires that the individual interact with others. Smith addresses the social psychology of this behavior by positing two premises of human nature: sympathy and the need for social approbation. First, Smith asserts that all humans possess an inborn sense of sympathy. "How selfish soever man may be supposed, there are evidently some principles in his nature, which interest him in the fortunes of others, and render their happiness necessary to him, though he derives nothing from it."[6] Sympathy is our ability to identify with the situation of another, to put ourselves in another's shoes. We can sympathize with others because we are like them, we have been there, so we can understand their desires and behavior. Sympathy gives us the ability to understand our relationships with others because it makes us able to perceive how others judge our actions, able to construct a composite self-image, and able to receive guidance. This makes us capable of learning from our experiences with others. Sympathy therefore makes us amenable to socialization. Being amenable to socialization, because of our inborn sense of sympathy, humans are able to form and be a member of cohesive social entities, organizations in all their many forms and variations.

Smith's second premise is that all humans have a deep need for social approbation, the innermost need of humans. He states social approbation to be "to deserve, to acquire, and to enjoy the respect and admiration of mankind."[7] The need for social approbation is expressed in two aspects of behavior. First is the willingness to submit to social norms, to restrict ourselves and to change and modify ourselves and our behavior to fit within the organization. Submission to social norms establishes and maintains our membership in our chosen organization. Second is relentless status seeking, the effort to establish and maintain our place in the organization. These two behaviors, submitting to organization norms and striving for advantage, generate a tension in social behavior. One must act cooperatively by submitting to social norms to gain admission to an organization. Then one must act competitively in striving for status within the organization. Both behaviors are necessary to the humane community. Cooperative behavior is necessary to make possible the social activities that add to human welfare, and competitive striving for status is the source of leadership and new entrepreneurial ventures.

The human being is a child of nature, exhibiting all the variety with which nature endows humanity: the good, the true, and the beautiful along with the not so good, true, and beautiful. To truly value human variety is to celebrate not just the obvious dimensions of difference, such as gender, race, ethnicity, language, and geographic location. These are measurable and might be called structural elements because they are fixed descriptors of human existence and are thus relatively easy to address. Long human history suggests that the structural elements play little or no role in human flourishing.

It is a challenge to address the variety honestly and all too easy to address it dishonestly. It is morally dishonest to stir up discontent followed by dissension and animosity and then to call it humane. The dishonesty can embody two errors: first, for a society to proclaim that its welfare choices and resulting methods are superior and are appropriate to and preferred by all humanity and, second, for the society to then think that it is being humane in its actions to inflict those welfare choices and methods on all humanity. These errors can lead to rigidity and blindness. We suggest that a lengthy period of dominance of any culture throughout history can lead societies to commit these errors.

Aleksandr Solzhenitsyn sees this for the cultural sin that it is and warns that the wages of this sin may be greater than we now realize. He states, for example, that the industrial West has attempted to recreate the pre-industrial world in the West's image "with contempt for any possible values in the conquered peoples' approach to life."[8] Now the tables may be turning with the rise of China, India, and other non-Western tradition countries. Solzhenitsyn notes, "It is difficult yet to estimate the size of the bill which former colonial countries will present to the West, and it is difficult to predict whether the surrender not only of its last colonies, but of everything it owns, will be sufficient for the West to clear this account."[9] For saying this at the height of his celebrity in 1978,

Solzhenitsyn ceased to exist in the US media and literary world.[10] This was called being "disappeared" in the Soviet Union and is called being "cancelled" in modern social terminology.

It would be incorrect to conclude that the West is alone in its propensity to inflict its definition of the humane on the world "with contempt for any possible values" in other approaches to life. Every dominant culture throughout history, such as the early Persian empire, the ancient Romans, the Ming dynasty of China, the medieval Islamic powers of the Middle East, and the Aztecs of Mexico, suffered from the same cultural propensity to define humaneness for its own purpose of maintaining and expanding power. The ability to inflict one's conception of humaneness on others is the result of economic and political power and the dominance that comes from power. The possession of dominance, even though wisdom and knowledge of history should teach us that dominance is always temporary, always seems to make us think that our virtues are superior, universal, and permanent. This is particularly unfortunate, because the temporary possession of dominance by a culture pushes to the fore not the actual virtues of the society but rather the social conventions that came to the surface in the wake of the power. What is put forth to the world is a display of those social conventions and not even the true cultural traits of the dominant society but rather a caricature, often a gross caricature.

We argue, however, that societies can change with deep self-reflection, particularly when confronted with increasing competition from other societies. China, India and other developing countries, combined with Russia's realignment away from the West due to the longstanding Ukraine-Russia conflict, presents a serious challenge to the West's modern evolution toward a materialist and more non-humane secular society that embraces the economics of mass consumption and concentrated production. To change, however, a culture must have the foundational political, educational, spiritual, and personal elements to initiate honest self-reflection. One important component would be to develop and teach humane economics on a human scale.

Endnotes

1. Plato, *The Republic* (New York: Everyman's Library, 1978). Original work published c. 375 BC. The numbers in the Everyman edition refer to the page numbers of the H. Stephanus edition of 1578.
2. Plato, *The Republic*, 136.

3. P. Oslington, "Nassau Senior, John Henry Newman and the Separation of Political Economy from Theology in the Nineteenth Century," *History of Political Economy* 33, no. 4 (2001), 825–842.
4. J. Newman, *The Idea of the University* (Chicago: Loyola University Press, 1927), 88. Original work written 1854.
5. See D. Wrong, *The Problem of Order: What Unites and Divides Society* (New York, NY: The Free Press, 1994) and M. Hector and C. Horne, *Theories of Social Order: A Reader* (Redwood City, CA: Stanford University Press, 2002).
6. A. Smith, *The Theory of Moral Sentiments* (Washington, DC: Regnery Publishing, 1997). Original work written 1759. Smith actually produced six editions of *The Theory of Moral Sentiments*, some with more significant revisions such as the 2nd edition in 1761 and the 6th edition published in 1790 some fifteen years after the publication of the *Wealth of Nations*. His 6th edition had the most significant revision, including a new section related to, in Smith's words, a "practical system of morality". The 2nd edition in 1761 added a little more discussion of "sympathy."
7. Smith, *Moral Sentiments*.
8. A. Solzhenitsyn, *A World Split Apart: Commencement Address Delivered to Harvard University, June 8, 1978* (New York: Harper & Row, 1978), 5.
9. Solzhenitsyn, *A World Split Apart,* 7.
10. See A. Solzhenitsyn, *Solzhenitsyn at Harvard.* (Washington DC: Ethics and Policy Center, 1980).

4

The Roots of Humanism

The pursuit of virtue and wisdom involves an ongoing discussion about the nature of the human being, a discussion that is called "humanism." The discussion must seek to design the institutions and social arrangements that are most suitable to the human person and must then agree on the behaviors required of the human being to fit within and make optimal use of the institutions and social arrangements. The discussion must center on a debate about the definition of what it means to be a human being and the place of the human being in the created order, an order that reflects some form of natural wisdom. Humanism is ancient and ongoing, and observation of it over the centuries suggests to us that it takes two forms. One we will designate intellectual humanism, the celebration of the human being in the activity of the mind, and the other we will designate practical humanism, the celebration of the human being in the work of the world.

The Roots of Intellectual Humanism

Intellectual humanism has been the occasion for contentious dispute, as is appropriate for anything so central to human character. It has a large literature found across many cultures, including Confucius and the Chinese tradition, the Upanishads and the Indian tradition, and Averroes and the Muslim tradition. In Western culture, intellectual humanism's deepest and most extensive roots lie with the classical Greeks: Protagoras, Epicurus, Socrates, Plato, and particularly Aristotle. Aristotle was a devout man, consumed by a yearning for the practical and divine wisdom. It was left to the Scholastics, such as Thomas Aquinas to refine the work of Aristotle to accommodate it to Western Civilization. For the first 1,800 years of Western Civilization the human person was defined as being a spiritual being who must fit his institutions and behavior to God's natural law. The debate was over what He expects of us, the demands made by His natural law, and how our human institutions could accommodate themselves to natural law and could best allow for human shortcomings and enhance human aspirations and abilities.

The seeds of contentious dispute appeared when Renaissance scholars broadened the definition of humanism to be "a system of thought or action that is concerned with human interests as against divine."[1] Serious disagreement was not at first apparent, because the primary interest in the Renaissance was not so much religious doctrine as it was pure scholarship. R.W. Chambers, a major biographer of Thomas More, states that the sole concern of the Renaissance scholars in northern Europe, a group that included More and Erasmus, was not the human–divine distinction but rather the study of the classical Greek language and the translation of ancient documents, in order to permit scholars direct access to the body of classical Greek writings without being limited to those works, primarily Aristotle, that had been translated into Latin. This scholarship, today called Northern Humanism, was not even called humanist at the time, instead being called the "New Learning," and much of it was quite practical. Chambers tells the tale of Thomas Linacre, the father of English medicine, who focused exclusively on his scientific studies, but was a priest/scholar, friend of More and Erasmus and a prominent member of the group of Northern Humanist scholars. A warning of what was to come lay in the fact that the New Learning invited ambiguity and controversy by critiquing divine natural law using human reason.[2]

With the advent of the European Enlightenment, man was progressively redefined to be a material object driven by reason. Under the Enlightenment, the rule of reason took its highest perceived form in defining philosophy, social mores, and institutions — even the Church. Even the natural law that evolved from earlier times had to be discounted and made subject to human reason.[3] The word "humanism" made a later appearance resulting from these modifications, with the first use of the word not recorded until 1836,[4] much later than the word "humane." With the Enlightenment, intellectual humanism came to be associated with rationality and attacks on the established Church, leading to the phrase "secular humanism," to distinguish it from the "Christian humanism" reflected by the writings of people such as Thomas More and Erasmus, that seeks to maintain the ancient concern with the human being within Christian culture.[5]

The emphasis of secular humanism against orthodoxy is emphatic and pervades the writings of secular humanists in prominent and widely read literature. For example, Bertrand Russell in his survey of Western philosophy[6] provides no introduction to humanism and makes no reference to it until he turns to examination of Renaissance Italy. He then describes humanism to be a prominent characteristic of Renaissance scholarship and accuses the Catholic popes of the era of being secular humanists, without providing much explanation of what he means by humanism and of what he is accusing the popes, except for over-concern with classical learning.[7] He states that "Italians were in earnest about culture, but not about morals and religion," and that "Nicholas V, the first humanist pope, gave papal offices to scholars ... encouraging humanism rather than piety or orthodoxy."[8] Russell reveals that secular humanism gravitates toward materialism and extreme rationalism and attempts to purge secular humanism of the spiritual. Despite possible disagreement with other modern secular humanists, Russell accepts the divide between the material and the spiritual and acknowledges the lessened spirituality of the secular.

Russell also illustrates the difficulties that arise from this split. He approves of the role of humanism in the weakening of traditional orthodoxy, and its traditional moral ideals, and goes on to make a bold assertion, one for which he offers rather weak support: the assertion that the weakening of orthodoxy freed up human thought and led to creative human development. But then, rather inconsistently for a logician, he laments that the emancipation from orthodoxy had two bad effects, the first being "not to make men think rationally but to open their minds to every kind of nonsense," and the second being to open the traditions of statecraft to "treachery and ruthless cruelty".[9] The emancipation from orthodoxy provided social conditions that "favored individual development, but were unstable; the instability and the individualism were closely connected ... A stable social system is necessary, but every stable system hitherto devised has hampered the development of exceptional intellectual merit. How much anarchy are we prepared to endure for the sake of great achievements?"[10] Russell's alternatives, great achievements vs. stability, would seem to be a false dichotomy, surprising for so renowned a rationalist. The history of practical humanism suggests that Russell, and others like Russell, may have it backwards; stability may be necessary for great achievements.

The Roots of Practical Humanism

Practical humanism is ancient, but the relatively modern word humanism is not typically applied to it. Its roots lie in all efforts to define and build a healthy community and to make it, like the home, a place of fruitful commitment to the common weal by all members, a community that the classical Greeks called the *oikos*. Practical humanism has a literature that is also ancient, one of the earliest (c. 400 BC) and most notable contributions being Xenophon's *Oeconomicus*. It is said to be the oldest work in existence on the subject of economics and presents a portrait of what we can today call an entrepreneur, a life-giving figure working for the general welfare.[11]

To see entrepreneurship as falling within the world of practical humanism transcends contentious arguments that can characterize intellectual humanism and places emphasis on the display of human nature by real, life-giving institutions. To be truly life-giving, such institutions must cohere around the creation of wealth in all its forms. One form of wealth is of course economic; the human must be fed, clothed, and housed. Another form of wealth is the human need for community; so a humane institution must also address the practical need for community to nurture and protect the human being.

One of the most ancient, and still viable, humane institutions is the Order of Saint Benedict of the Roman Catholic Church. Rather than debate the nature of human beings and the purpose of a human life, Benedictine monks established the parameters of such a life and proceeded to create the communities that made such a life possible. Not only did the Benedictines demonstrate that such a life was possible, but they also built communities that embodied economies that changed the Western world and that have continued to flourish for 16 centuries.

The Benedictines, with an official founding date of 529 AD, were not the first monks and their order is not the oldest order of monks in the Catholic Church, but it is the oldest order to have survived unchanged. From earlier times men and women had chosen to seek virtue by living disciplined lives of focused spirituality. Some of them practiced their discipline in isolation and some in communities. Some of the discipline was extremely severe and some of it was lax. The Benedictines responded by firmly establishing two lasting principles. First, community is necessary for human happiness and productivity and therefore spirituality and virtue must be sought within a stable community. Second, discipline, to be productive, must be in exactly the right balance, not too severe and not too lax, and for the right purpose, to enhance human ability to embrace the humane ideal of living fruitfully. They codified these principles into a Rule written by Saint Benedict in 540 AD that stimulated the founding of numerous Benedictine communities, numbering in the thousands, and was then adopted by other later orders of monks.

Over the ensuing 1,000 years Benedictine and related monastic communities were established over all of Europe and the Middle East, numbering approximately 20,000, and proved themselves to be so productive that by the early-16th century, the Benedictines also grew to be the largest landowners in Europe, competing with the established aristocracy.[12] As productive landowners (vs. the generally less productive aristocracy), the Benedictines constituted a large portion of various countries' capital base until their property was confiscated and ownership of the capital base was secularized and given into the hands of oligarchs, beginning with King Henry VIII and reaching a peak in the revolutionary upheaval and its attempts at land reform, that began with the French Revolution. Karl Marx argues that this violent wealth transfer provided the capital base for the birth and rapid growth of capitalism.[13]

The Benedictines live their principles, then and now, in an inhumane world. In Saint Benedict's day[14], the decadence and collapse of Roman order took Roman culture along with it, with tribes of primitive peoples rushing to fill the vacuum left behind. Society withdrew to isolated and backward villages that administered erratic and often unjust law and were able to support little learning, art, or charity, and were desperately poor. "The tribal confederations which filled the vacuum of Roman power in the West were subsistence societies... To succeed among them, the Church had to be a carrier of superior economic techniques."[15] The historic success of the Benedictine Order was based upon its economic success. The Order brought to Europe in the period 550–1000 AD effective institutions of education, art and culture, and charity, but this was all made possible by the prosperity that resulted from its remarkable economic accomplishments. Large parts of Europe had reverted to foliage, much of it useless and unhealthy marshes and swamps, which the great warlords that constituted the government were happy to pass off to any party that promised to be a loyal and productive subject. Benedictine monks pushed out into barren inhospitable terrain far from any habitations and, over the ensuing centuries felled the timber, drained the swamps, and transformed useless areas into the strikingly fertile farmland that came to characterize Europe.

In the process, they established free-hold land tenure law that protected not only their titles but also the land titles of the secular landowners around them. Farming became less vulnerable to raiding and confiscation by powerful interests and more suitable for long term capital improvements. This alone is said to have laid the foundation for the revolution in agricultural productivity.[16] On the great Benedictine agricultural estates, capital improvements came to include advances in industrialization. Benedictine technological improvements and capital accumulation over the centuries grew into what Jean Gimpel calls the medieval industrial revolution and "the medieval machine."[17] Benedictine, and the Benedictine inspired Cistercian monasteries, were often large and innovative manufacturing establishments, very advanced for the age. During medieval times, not only did the Benedictines found a system of local charity, education, hospitals, manufacturing, and orphanages that did not otherwise exist, but they also advanced the science of wine making, brewing, and liquor making. Benedictines keep Greek/Roman literature and legal/philosophical writings intact during the dark ages through their libraries and scribes, and they created the modern system of road-side hospitality, allowing trade to flourish.

Benedictine effort has always reflected economic and entrepreneurial life at its most humane. John Henry Newman argues that the foundation of modern life is rooted in the community, whose legitimacy flows from a sense of the common membership of people with inherent worth and whose efforts are for the common good of all. From such a foundation, social and economic development was freed from the constraints of the legalistic and inhuman imperial system that preceded the Benedictine effort and was enabled to explore new methods and to embrace new development, while maintaining a humane community based in the original natural condition of man. A humane world will maintain a humane base with a "discriminatory badge" in the poetical, balanced by efforts to enlarge and improve the humane base by continuous venturing into growth and development with its discriminatory badge, the scientific. The poetic reflects the imagination in humankind, and the scientific reflects reason. "Poetry is the antagonist of science. As science makes progress in any subject matter, poetry recedes from it. Science results in system [forcing complexity into a common frame]. Poetry delights in the simple [seeing unity in diversity]."[18] The work of the Benedictines (and their oblates) was [and is] to build a civilization that is humane, into which men and women are drawn, not forced, and which they are convinced, not compelled, to contribute their maximum fruitfulness. Such a humane civilization will embody charity, but a practical charity drawing on a pool of riches that can result only from healthy growth and development of productivity.[19]

Continuous effort to perceive and defend the humane is needed as an antidote to the discomforts and inequities that can result from growth and development. Newman argues that nature may be trusted to ultimately "set right the evil, if left to itself, but she requires time; science comes in to shorten the process, and is violent that it may be certain …They whose duty lies in what may be called *undertakings*, in science and system … have a noble and meritorious mission but not so poetical a one."[20] Newman's use of the word *undertakings* (his italics) is, interestingly, the very word that is used by economists in early works on entrepreneurship. The undertakings of the entrepreneur have a noble mission, even though the immediate aftermath of economic change can often be discomforting. Working for humaneness stands as a defense against the harshness and potential inhumaneness that might accrue, however inadvertently, to the science and system of economic development.

Endnotes

1. R. Chambers, *Thomas More* (Ann Arbor, MI: Ann Arbor Paperbacks, 1958), 83–85. Original work published 1935.
2. *Ibid*, 84.
3. O. Chadwick, *The Secularization of the European Mind in the 19th Century* (Cambridge, UK: Cambridge University Press, 1993).
4. According to Merriam Webster, 2021.
5. See S. Law, *Humanism: A Very Short Introduction* (Oxford University Press, 2011) for a further discussion of this issue.
6. See B. Russell, *History of Western Philosophy (And Its Connection with Political and Social Circumstances from the Earliest Times to the Present Day)* (London: The Folio Society, 2004), Original work published 1945.
7. Which came to be called "the humanities."
8. Russell, *History of Western Philosophy*, 477–478.
9. *Ibid*, 481.

10. *Ibid*, 482.
11. D. Leshem, "What Did the Ancient Greeks Mean by Oikonomia?" *Journal of Economic Perspectives* 30, no.1 (2016), 225–231.
12. P. Johnson, *A History of Christianity* (New York, NY: Atheneum, 1977).
13. This is discussed by Marx in various sections of *Capital* (also known by various titles depending on county of publication, such as *Das Kapital,* or by its English title, *Capital: Critique of Political Economy*). See K. Marx, *Capital* (London: Penguin Classics, 1990). Original work published 1867.
14. St. Benedict, also known as Benedict of Nursia (480–547), wrote his Rule of Benedict in 540 for the monks in his community. The monastery at Subiaco in Italy was founded c. 529.
15. Johnson, *History of Christianity*, 138.
16. *Ibid*, 139.
17. See J. Gimpel, *The Medieval Machine: The Industrial Revolution of the Middle Ages* (New York, NY: Penguin, 1976) for a discussion of the Benedictine contributions to economic develop in the 11th–14th centuries. See C. Galbraith and O. Galbraith, *The Benedictine Rule of Leadership* (Avon, MA: Adams Media, 2004), for a discussion regarding the contribution of the Benedictines to modern leadership theory.
18. J. Newman, *The Mission of the Benedictine Order*. (London: John Long, 1908), 40.
19. *Ibid*, 54–62.
20. *Ibid*, 67.

Section II

Humane and Wise Ventures

Section II, titled "Humane and Wise Ventures" offers three essays. The first essay, *Humane Ventures, Natural Liberty, and Undertaking*, looks at a variety of topics, including natural liberty and undertaking a venture. The principle of Natural Liberty represents a condition of both social order and economic growth. Social order is necessary to prevent a Hobbesian war of all against all and to permit the human coordination necessary for growth. The social arrangements used to maintain order must also provide the opportunity and the motivation for people to work most productively. The two works, *The Republic* and *Utopia*, appear to present a dilemma: does the need for social order require either a fanciful hope in the passive world of Plato or an acceptance of the necessity for brutal control in the rambunctious world of More's *Utopia*? Adam Smith demonstrates that neither alternative is necessary. Order can be made available by means of the humane principle of Natural Liberty. As Natural Liberty offers society a solution to the need for order, capital investment offers society a solution to the need for economic growth.

This essay then explores the idea of "undertaking," Richard Cantillon's term for the modern vision of "entrepreneurship." Undertakers, to

Cantillon, are those who, not being wage earners, must initiate ventures. Undertakers may have access to capital that makes possible the use of extensive resources and large-scale action. This essay concludes by combining these concepts with the idea of undertaking a venture. It is the nature to risk much, if not all, for an end not fully understood and demanding the pledge, "We are able." The undertaker thereby enters a new world of possibilities, a hearty entry into a world that would not otherwise exist and that might entail truths not expected or yet understood.

The next essay *Wise Ventures and Wise Men*, looks at the driving forces behind humane entrepreneurship, such as the meaning of wisdom, time-binding, and entrepreneurial change. Wisdom is defined, since ancient times, to be spiritual wholeness, the enlargement of mind to embrace completeness, comprehension of the entire course and meaning of existence and of life within that existence, life as a whole and the life of each individual person. It is knowledge, not of things but of the mutual relations between things across all parts. "Time-binding" is a term not often heard in modern discussions. The idea of time-binding is associated with Polish-American scholar Alfred Korzybski's development of "General Semantics." Korzybski's work has had an impact on a number of fields including academic disciplines of philosophy and literary works of science fiction. The unique thing about human beings is the capability to transcend time, to live in the past, the present, and the future. According to Korzybski, the nature of man is that he is a time-binder, able to move across time. The ability to transcend time flows from the human being's unique organic chemistry. If guided by wisdom, entrepreneurship can provide an opportunity for human betterment by means of a continuing process of change that is life-getting and humane.

The final essay in this section, *Entrepreneurial Instinct: Keynes vs. Schumpeter* argues that the desire to be entrepreneurial is always with us, because the role is natural to human beings. Entrepreneurial behavior is a component of the human personality. The essay concludes with comparison of entrepreneurial instinct between John Maynard Keynes and Joseph Schumpeter.

5

Humane Ventures, Natural Liberty, and Undertaking

A humane economy requires that there be social order and economic growth. Adam Smith describes an economy in which order and growth are assured by what Joseph Schumpeter calls "the principle of Natural Liberty." Social order is necessary to prevent a Hobbesian war of all against all and to permit the human coordination necessary for growth. The social arrangements used to maintain order must also provide the opportunity and the motivation for people to work most productively. Smith's *The Wealth of Nations* presents the elements of a humane economy, built on a Natural Liberty that both maintains order and creates conditions to encourage optimal growth. Both Plato's city of health and Thomas More's land of Utopia seek order by means of central control, the two societies differing only in the power of the control needed to ensure personal restraint.

Natural Liberty

Plato assumes that it is natural for people to be capable of a degree of self-control, thus a central control that is benign is adequate to permit the reasonable luxuries that are natural to humans while keeping within limits the excesses that endanger a city of health. This is Plato's idea of a humane economy. More, in contrast, suggests that it is natural for people to be brutish in their tastes and self-indulgent of their animal passions and that maintenance of order therefore requires a central control that is total, malignant, and violent. In the satire of *Utopia*, the narrator, Hythlodaeus, presents himself to his audience, Morus, as the voice of the natural man and then presents numerous censorious examples of primitive and savage societies that are subject to complete disorder and contrasts them with his approval of the absolute order in Utopia. Instead of accepting the natural inclinations of humans and examining how a humane economy can be built upon them, Hythlodaeus provides a warning of where central control might go if natural human inclinations cannot be kept moderate and under control in any other way.

Smith, in contrast, provides another way. *The Wealth of Nations* outlines how a humane economy can function in a society in which order is based on the principle of Natural Liberty. By this principle he meant "the analytic proposition that free interaction of individuals produces not chaos but an orderly pattern that is logically determined." The principle of Natural Liberty led Smith to propose as a "canon of policy — the removal of all restraints except those imposed by justice."[1] Humans can be trusted to moderate their behavior, practice self-restraint, and limit their excesses, without unnecessary restraints, if an economy is structured in such a way as to make it in their self-interest. This is Adam Smith's idea of a humane economy.

Schumpeter states that Smith is the most important of all economists and that *The Wealth of Nations* is "the most successful not only of all books on economics but also, with the possible exception of Darwin's *Origin of Species*, of all scientific books that have appeared to this day."[2] Likewise, Frank Taussig likens *The Wealth of Nations* to the *Bible* and states that it provides "a text appropriate for an economist's homily." Taussig held the senior chair in economics at Harvard from 1885 until 1935, when the chair was filled by Schumpeter and held until his death in 1950.

After Schumpeter's ringing endorsement of *The Wealth of Nations*, he then states that there is little in Smith's book that is entirely new. This is not as devasting a criticism as it might sound, because Schumpeter knew that many of the ideas in *The Wealth of Nations* are found in their germinal form in Plato. *The Republic* (375 BC) gave us, among other fundamental ideas, the labor theory of value, the division of labor, exchange, markets, pricing, and the three-fold factors of production.

The principle of Natural Liberty does, however, add something truly new, contra Schumpeter, to our understanding of a humane economy. Plato with his puritanical view of the world might have thought his city of health to be humane, leading him to approve of a static economy with few luxuries, to assume that benign guardians of central control could restrain people's excess from corrupting the city of health into a city of luxury and to assume away the likelihood of his guardians being incipient tyrants.[3] Thomas More was famous for his sense of humor, and it shows in *Utopia* with the clownish Hythlodaeus, "speaker of nonsense" in classical Greek, painting a picture of a hellish world of deadening austerity and oppression, apparently thinking such a world to be humane, no doubt to the amusement of Morus and the reader. More's gentle satirical humor contributes to the popularity of *Utopia* and provides an enduring warning of the ever-present danger of public tolerance of any degree of tyranny, because many readers seem to agree with Hythlodaeus that Utopia is a humane society, as evidenced by the modern use, contra More, of the word Utopia to mean an impossibly ideal society. The two works, *The Republic* and *Utopia*, appear to present a dilemma: does the need for order require either a fanciful hope in the passive world of Plato or an acceptance of the necessity for brutal control in the rambunctious world of More's *Utopia*. Smith demonstrates that neither alternative is necessary. Order can be made available by means of the humane principle of Natural Liberty.

The Wealth of Nations is a long work, about 1,500 pages, divided into five books, but the economic theory that we have today is taken almost entirely from the first two books, about 40% of the entire work, Book I on labor and Book II on capital. Book I is an introduction to the economic realities of production and distribution, of how goods and services are produced using human labor and how the goods and services are then distributed among the populace. It points out that labor can increase its productivity only when it can make use of tools, i.e., capital, which Smith calls "stock," the more capital that is used, the more output can be produced. Book II presents the theory of capital, saving, and investment, which "however much transformed by development and criticism, remained the basis of practically all later work"[4] until quite recently.

Book III is a historical study of the "natural progress of opulence" and examines the economic growth and development of societies "as distorted — hampered or propelled — by the policies sponsored by various interests." Smith warns of the danger of accretions of special interests that can obstruct and distort an economy, an elaboration of Plato's warning that these dangers are the greatest evil. Book IV critiques the mercantile system of the day, criticizes colonialism, and denounces government backed monopolies, all of which Smith echoes Plato in believing is evil. Book V provides recommendations concerning public finance which, according to Schumpeter, remained a useful treatise on the subject until modern governments intruded with the "social" viewpoint, that taxation is a legitimate instrument of social reform.

It might not be too much of an oversimplification to say that the first two books of *The Wealth of Nations* explain how an economy must work if it is to be humane, and the last three books explain how easy and typical it is to deviate from the humane economy, how easily a city of health can morph into a city of luxury subject to "inflammation" or can be weighed down by special interests that can stymie growth. Smith emphasizes that a humane economy must maintain a healthy growth rate, both to encourage family formation and expansion of the population and to permit a continual improvement in people's lives.

The Meaning of "Undertaking"

As Natural Liberty offers society a solution to the need for order, capital investment offers society a solution to the need for economic growth. The economies of Plato and More are static, with production and distribution basically fixed over time. Production methods are traditional, and no effort is made to develop new methods, distribution is locked into standard and fixed proportions of output distributed to the workers and to the rulers, and there is no social mobility and no movement between classes. In Smith's economy built on Natural Liberty and with workers motivated by self-interest, there will be a high degree of social mobility. There is every opportunity and reason for workers to embrace change in an effort to seek to improve their position and to rise in prosperity and social status. Smith even tells how to do it: work hard, save a part of the income, and invest the savings in new capital equipment and new techniques. In the simple economy of Plato's city of health there is a hint of capital investment, although it plays no significant role, and in More's Utopian economy there is not even a hint. Smith gives capital investment a central role and makes it the catalyst and cornerstone of growth. According to Smith, growth in economic output results from the application of capital to labor.

Capital accumulation results from minimization of consumption by some people and the addition of the unconsumed wealth to savings; "Parsimony is the immediate cause of the increase of capital." Those who save become capitalists, called "money-owners" by Richard Cantillon and "owners of stock" by Adam Smith until Karl Marx coined the word "capitalist." Capital accumulation permits an increase in capital investment which makes people more industrious, less idle, giving up leisure for labor, and more motivated to work hard. Economic growth is then induced by the decision by someone with access to the new capital to use it to undertake a new venture, to hire additional "industrious people" for the purpose of producing additional output.

> As soon as stock [capital] has accumulated in the hands of particular persons, some of them will naturally employ it in setting to work industrious people, whom they will supply with materials and subsistence, in order to make a profit by the sale of their work, or by what their labor adds to the value of the materials. In exchanging the complete manufacture for money, over and above what may be sufficient to pay the price of the materials, and the wages of the workmen, something must be given for the profits of the undertaker of the work, who hazards his stock in this adventure... He could have no interest to employ them, unless he expected from the sale of their work something more than what was sufficient to replace his stock to him; and he could have no interest to employ a great stock rather than a small one, unless his profits were to bear some proportion to the extent of his stock.[5]

The spark that ignites economic growth is the go or no-go decision by the undertaker to initiate a new venture in hopes that it will succeed.

The undertaker is thus the key figure in economic growth and development. He is not just an ordinary capitalist, those into whose hands capital has accumulated. Note that Smith says that only "some of them," the capitalists, will make the decision to employ the capital, to pursue a perceived economic opportunity, to make the decision to undertake the work. This key decision maker will later be embellished and much considered under the name "entrepreneur," but Smith calls him an "undertaker." Although this one quote from Book I Chapter VI does not tell us much about entrepreneurship and is the only attention given to it by Smith, it is clearly a central concern of his, as central as it would come to be for later economists, led by the work of Joseph Schumpeter. The undertaker/entrepreneur must first decide whether or not to initiate the work, whether to go or no-go. If the decision is no-go, then nothing will happen. If the decision is a go, then the decision maker has chosen to "undertake" it, and then must decide where and on what to use the capital. The initiative deserves a rich reward, "something must be given for the profits of the undertaker of the work who hazards his stock in this adventure," because the adventure is ill-defined and uncertain.

The important function of the undertaker and the justification for his reward was first articulated by Richard Cantillon. Adam Smith knew Cantillon's work and considered it to be important enough to warrant a mention of Cantillon by name in Smith's book, something quite special because Smith is notorious for never citing the names of any authors however much they influenced him. Cantillon must have cast a big shadow in Smith's day, and his book of 1730, *An Essay on Economy Theory*, the earliest work that is accepted to be a serious treatment, puts forth the undertaker as an early version of the entrepreneur.[6] Cantillon used the word undertaker, and Smith dutifully followed suit 46 years later, before the word was embellished and muddied a bit and given an exotic flavor by an errant translation into French in 1755 by an unknown translator without Cantillon's involvement. Cantillon's definition and description of the function of the undertaker is not a bit muddy and instead is quite precise.

Cantillon was a financial speculator who made an immense fortune by the time he was 20, being a principal in a massive banking and securities scam, later called the Mississippi Bubble because its promoter, John Law, was given a charter by the government of France to set up a bank for the purpose of selling shares in the profits generated from settlement of Louisiana on the Mississippi River soon after the arrival of the first French settlers. The heavily promoted securities were rapidly bid up in price to the reckless heights of a classic bubble, and when the bank collapsed in 1721, it took the French economy with it, but Cantillon got out early with a huge fortune and escaped prosecution. He did not, however, escape controversy and was subsequently murdered at the age of 37.

In *An Essay on Economic Theory*, Cantillon divided people into two classes, independent and dependent. The independent class is divided into three: the prince, landowners, and "money owners." These are the only independent people in society; everyone else is dependent. The dependent class is divided into two: hired workers and "undertakers." Hired workers are dependent on wages. Some wage earners are well paid and others are not, and, likewise, some wage earners have security, and some do not, but they are all dependent. Those wage earners with security are assured of their payments and are often prominent and well-paid, e.g., "the general who has his pay and the courtier [bureaucrat] his pension." Wage earning is not necessarily associated with poverty and low status, but it is always dependent. All members of the dependent class other than wage earners are undertakers.

Undertakers are those who, not being wage earners, must initiate ventures. The livelihood of an undertaker depends upon initiating some form of economic activity that must make use of some resources, must take some action, and must then receive some form of reward for the action. Cantillon provides a specific definition of an undertaker: anyone who must buy at a fixed price to pursue their venture and must then sell at an uncertain price to receive their reward. To an undertaker, costs are certain and revenues are uncertain.

Undertakers may have access to capital that makes possible the use of extensive resources and large-scale action. If so, they stand to receive substantial reward or to take significant losses on their venture, but the outcome is uncertain. Undertakers with little or no access to capital must pursue their ventures on a much smaller scale but are also exposed to the same uncertain outcome. Cantillon points out that even "the beggars and the robbers" are undertakers. They must buy their inputs (food and clothing if nothing else) at prices fixed by the market, but their hope for a return on their expenditure is completely uncertain.

Cantillon's insight that robbers are undertakers, an insight that perhaps came to him from his own experience, leads him to then state that "It may perhaps be urged that undertakers seek to snatch all they can in their calling and to get the better of their customers, but this is outside my subject." Such honest detachment and objectivity should seal his legitimacy in the minds of his scholarly readers; he acknowledges that he personally is a snatcher and an exploiter of his customers, if not an actual crook, but that is beside the point; his concept of the undertaker is valid, and his definition is clear and precise. Cantillon's precision contrasts with the muddle of so much of the subsequent discussion of the concept as it evolved from the undertaker to the entrepreneur, much of which muddle comes from the lack of precision in using the word entrepreneur. John Maynard Keynes built his policy recommendations on his own definition of the word, and Joseph Schumpeter rebutted Keynes using Schumpeter's own very different definition. Modern writers may participate in the muddle by their tendency to seek originality by adding nuance to the word. There was little nuance or subtilty in Cantillon, but then he did not use the word entrepreneur, instead using the word undertaker. An invitation to muddled nuance may lie in the exotic word itself.

The exotic sounding word "entrepreneur" adds a hint of excitement and adventure to such a clear and simple idea, and the invitation to excitability might lend itself to a pattern of thought that is not so clear and simple. Schumpeter and Baumol, later, examined the muddle that tends to shelter under the exotic word. But any blame does not lie with Cantillon; he used the word undertaker, as did Adam Smith after him, with a precise meaning: anyone who is willing and able to endure costs that are real and certain while embracing a hope for revenue that is anything but real and certain. Only later was the word undertaker relegated in English, but not in German, to mean a mortician, while the French word entrepreneur came to mean in English a person who performs a special role in economic development activity, with debate about what that role includes. The exotic word entrepreneur in English has an origin that lies in its curious translation history.

Cantillon's treatise was translated into French in 1755 by a still unknown translator without, obviously, any participation by Cantillon, and the English original was subsequently lost, apparently forever. The translator gave the work the title *Essai sur la Nature du Commerce en General* and chose to translate Cantillon's known use of the English word undertaker into French as entreprendre. The translator is said to have created the word entreprendre from the Old French words entre meaning "enter," which in modern French means "between," and prendre meaning "to take." It is amusing and revealing to examine relevant words using a modern machine translator. Going from French to English, Google Translate translates entrepreneur as "contractor" and entreprendre as "undertake." Going from English to French, Google translates entrepreneur as "chef d'enterprise," contractor as "prestataire," and undertaker as "pompes funebres."

Cantillon's treatise was not translated back into English until 1931, and the translator, Henry Higgs, kept the original French translator's title, *Essay on the Nature of Commerce in General* but put the word entreprendre back into the original word undertaker. There was not another translation until 2010, when the translators, Chantal Saucier and Mark Thornton, changed the title to *An Essay on Economic Theory*. They changed

Cantillon's word undertaker, kept by Higgs, into the word entrepreneur, accepting that the exotic French word had by then become standard usage in English, but curiously they kept some of Cantillon's archaic words. They left his word "courtier," which in Cantillon's day meant an attendant to the royal court but today should be understood to mean "bureaucrat," and they left his quaint phrase "money owner" which today should be "capitalist."

German literature may have kept a clearer view of the role of the entrepreneur as an "undertaker" by the avoidance of a foreign word "entrepreneur" that has no clear definition in English or German except by way of the very thing trying to be defined. Instead of the word entrepreneur, the German language uses the word "unterneher," literally "under" (*unter*) and "taker" (*neher*), or "undertaker." This provides German with the original clarity of Cantillon and encourages variations on the idea, permitting scholars in the German language to make finer distinctions. An important distinction is between *unterneherlohn*, the "wage of the entrepreneur" and *unternehergerwinn*, "the profit of the entrepreneur." This captures in two German words two questions that are central to our subject: Is the entrepreneur paid a wage for his expertise, innovative vision, risk-bearing, and courage? Or does the entrepreneur have a claim on a portion, often large, of the economic value created by the venture?

Cantillon's definition of the undertaker is precise but narrow, addressing only the uncertainty of the venture and not its value to economic growth. Jean-Baptiste Say (1803) gave more importance to Cantillon's undertaker by adding weight to the value of the venture.[7] Since an undertaker must buy at a fixed price and sell at an uncertain price and therefore may or may not gain from an economic venture, he may, with good reason, choose to forego the venture, unless the potential value is significant. Say underscores, more than Cantillon, the fact that the undertaker is the individual that makes the go or no-go decision, the person who makes the actual decision whether to proceed with the venture. Without the undertaker, there will be no new venture. He can choose to proceed and expose himself to personal loss, or he can choose to not proceed and leave the economy static. An undertaker becomes important if the venture is important if it contributes to fruitful economic growth.

Schumpeter says that this insight strengthens a long prevailing weakness in our understanding of the role of entrepreneurial ventures in economic development. Economists going back to St. Antonine of

Florence (1389–1459) and the medieval Scholastics had been aware that those who engage in business had the sole responsibility for executing some special function; in discussing the function, economists tended to talk about some form of "combining the factors of production into a producing organism." But they "failed to realize that the phrase 'combining factors,' when applied to a going concern, denotes little more than routine management; and that the combining of factors becomes a distinctive one only when applied not to the current administration of a going concern but to the organization of a new one." The undertaker/entrepreneur is "the pivot on which everything turns."[8]

Undertaking a Venture

Schumpeter's statement highlights the uniqueness of entrepreneurship by emphasizing that the pivot on which everything turns is a decision to undertake a venture that is entirely new, not just the organization of any new concern. For it to be a pivot, the undertaking must be a venture that is a new concern that addresses a product or method that is unique and important. This unique importance of a venture is not given much attention by the modern dictionary. A "venture" according to the dictionary is "an undertaking involving chance, risk, or danger." The word is close in meaning to the word "adventure," whose dictionary definition is the same, "an undertaking usually involving danger and unknown risks;" the word venture is an aphetic (a word formed by dropping an unaccented syllable of a similar word) of the word "adventure." The definition of the modern word adventure, and its aphetic, goes back to the Middle English meaning "fortune, chance, risk" derived from a Latin root meaning "to arrive at, reach, arise, develop." These definitions are rather thin and encourage shallow thinking about ventures. Cantillon and Say offer an understanding of a venture that is more robust in that they make clear that the cost of pursuing a venture is certain and real, often substantially so, therefore the potential reward must be valuable and important enough to make the go or no-go decision a true pivot. The significance of a venture as a pivot lies more in its potential value than in its uncertainty.

Calling something a venture when it only offers a reward that is relatively trivial can, unless we are careful, lure our conventional modern talk into being largely about hustle and hype. Modern society appears to be awash in ventures. Our economy is chaotic with a seemingly unending stream of ventures, each venture hoping to succeed with new gadgetry of little significance and adding to an endless stream of variations on current gadgetry. Much of this frenetic activity about new ventures is just noise — sound and fury signifying very little — that adds little to the general welfare and to our hopes for a humane economy. This frenetic activity can also be destructive. Pointless ventures not only can waste resources and divert economic attention and energy but also can distort fruitful development and whip up unwise enthusiasms that do lasting damage to society. In 1516, Thomas More wrote *Utopia*, a short gentle satire, to warn about social destruction and tyranny that might await a society that is overwhelmed by unwise enthusiasms.[9] By 1528, More found his society to be much further down the road to repression and stagnation and wrote a lengthy theological and philosophical treatise that addressed the danger already threatening his society and the visible damage already inflicted on the general welfare and public order by the disruption of traditional ways. In his *Dialogue Concerning Heresies*, said by scholars to be possibly the best Platonic dialog in English, More passionately tries to teach moderation and restraint to a world whose institutions are under violent assault, assaults that in More's traditional world came to be called heresies but today less loaded words might be more precise, such as "acts of sedition."[10]

It is revealing, and maybe sinister, that the modern English-speaking world has chosen to use the word "business" to mean "economic activity." The word may retain a lingering warning of the danger to social stability of feverish excess production and excess consumption of gadgetry. The word "business" is a modern derivative of the word "busynes" which in More's day did not mean economic activity as it does today but instead meant out-of-control and destructive activity of any type. To More, busynes was a characteristic of a world trying to flee from God. Busynes was the work of "the noonday devil," meaningless hyperactivity in the full light of day, leading to the sin of acedia — the pointless pursuit of frenetic activity, a "restlessness of mind" called *evagatio mentis* — and eventually leading to indifference to salvation. This caution comes from Psalm 90: 5–6. In the Latin Vulgate, Psalm 90:5–6 reads:

> non timebis a timore nocturno; a sagitta volante in die, a negotio perambulante in tenebris, ab incursu, et daemonio meridiano.

The Douet Rheims 1610 English translation of Psalm 90:5-6 reads:

> thou shalt not be afraid of the terror of the night. Of the arrow that flieth in the day, of the business that walketh about in the dark: of invasion, or of the noonday devil.

The Latin phrase "a negotio perambulante in tenebris" is translated "of the business that walketh about in the dark." The King James 1615 translation of the same phrase is: "for the pestilence that walketh in darkness." Virtually all other versions, old and new, translate the word "negotio" — "business" — as "pestilence."

In Thomas More's day busynes was also considered to be politically dangerous because it could unsettle conventional practice and descend into lawlessness. In rendering More's pre-Shakespearian English in *Dialog Concerning Heresies* into modern English, the translator used such words as "trouble" and "feverish activity" where More used "busynes" and "busynesse." For example, here is the way one of More's sentiments is translated:

> More, 1528: "For well you wote that heresys be false byleyfe and faccyous ways full of busynes. And suche as geue theym selfe therto be stourdy and studyouse about the furtheranunce of theyr sedycyouse sect."

> More, 2006: "For well you know that heresies are false beliefs and factious ways full of feverish activity. And such as give themselves thereto are staunch and studious about the furtherance of their seditious sect."

A humane economy built on Natural Liberty will not be vulnerable to false beliefs and factious ways and will not be full of feverish activity and seditious actions that endanger public order.

According to Baumol, factious ways and feverish activity abound in the modern economy. Cantillon's humorous observation that beggars and robbers and their ilk can be said to be undertaker/entrepreneurs was examined by Baumol in 1990. In a paper provocatively entitled "Entrepreneurship: Productive, Unproductive, and Destructive," he observed that, if we use Cantillon's definition of an undertaker and allow the social value imputed to the product of the venture to be determined by the busynes of our modern world, then we may want to add lawyers, investors, bankers, politicians, physicians, college professors, and other respectable personages to Cantillon's cast of beggars and robbers. "If entrepreneurs are defined simply to be persons who are ingenious and creative in finding ways that add to their own wealth, power, and prestige, then it is to be expected that not all of them will be overly concerned with whether an activity that achieves these goals adds much or little to the social product or, for that matter, even whether it is an actual impediment to production."[11] Baumol argues that, by this criterium, much in popular parlance that passes for entrepreneurship can actually be unproductive or even destructive. Many ventures accepted and praised in our modern world of busynes, could be argued to not even be entrepreneurship and hardly deserve the name.

If the modern conception of business ventures appears to be driven more by the feverish activity of speed to market, scalability and quick personal enriching "exits," than by fundamental and lasting additions to human value, it could be because we have lost a full appreciation of the place of the individual in our conception of true economic value and the commonweal. A better appreciation of the nature of a venture that is humane might be better reflected in the related word "advent," meaning the yearning for and anticipated coming of something precious to the individual. The feverish activity of modern economic life may obscure the search for meaning that each individual faces, a search that is bounded and magnified by the uncertainty inherent in life, with its fragility and implacable death. A humane economy can only be built on concern for the welfare of each individual, a concern better addressed by philosophers and theologians than by economists. An essay by John Henry Newman entitled "The Ventures of Faith" teaches that we all must venture, we have no choice, if we would have a life of worth. If we would embrace a venture to gain something much coveted, we must embrace not an assurance of the gain but instead a willingness to endure the cost.

> Here then a great lesson is impressed upon us, that our duty lies in this, in making ventures for life without the absolute certainty of success... No one among us knows for certain that he himself will persevere; yet everyone among us, to give himself even a chance of success at all, must make a venture. As regards individuals, then, it is quite true, that all of us must for certain make ventures, yet without the certainty of success through them. This, indeed, is the very meaning of the word 'venture;'

for that is a strange venture which has nothing in it of fear, risk, danger, anxiety, uncertainty. So it certainly is, and in this consists the excellence and nobleness of action; that we have the heart to make a venture...It follows that our duty lies in risking what we have, for what we have not; and doing so in a noble, generous way, not indeed rashly or lightly, still without knowing accurately what we are doing, not knowing either what we give up nor again what we shall gain; uncertain about our reward, uncertain about our sacrifice...It is in its very essence the making present of what is unseen; the acting upon the mere prospect of it, as if it really were possessed; the venturing upon it, the staking present ease, happiness, or other good upon the chance of the future.[12]

This is the nature of a true venture, to risk much, if not all, for an end not fully understood and demanding the pledge, "We are able." The undertaker thereby enters a new world of possibilities, a hearty entry into a world that would not otherwise exist and that might entail truths not expected or yet understood. "They pledge themselves as if unawares, and are caught, and, as it were, craftily made captive. But, in truth, their unsuspicious pledge was, after all, heartedly made, though they knew not what they promised".

A true entrepreneurial venture addresses something that is only dimly understood but that holds out the possibility of attaining that which we covet. If what we covet is wise, we can lay the groundwork for a humane economy and society. The undertaker makes a pivotal decision to embark on an adventure that may lead us there. The undertaker commits to an "unsuspicious pledge, heartily made." and thereby takes on the leadership role of a humane entrepreneur.

Endnotes

1. J. Schumpeter, *History of Economic Analysis* (New York: Oxford University Press, 1954), 185.
2. *Ibid*, 181.
3. Plato, *The Republic* (New York: Everyman's Library, 1978). Original work written c. 375 BC.
4. Schumpeter, *History of Economic Analysis*.
5. A. Smith, *The Wealth of Nations* (London: Penguin Books, 1986), 151. Original work published 1776.

6. R. Cantillon, *An Essay on Economic Theory*, transl. C. Saucier and M. Thornton (Auburn, AL: Ludwig von Mises Institute, 2010). Original work published 1730.
7. J. Say, *A Treatise on Political Economy: Or the Production, Distribution, and Consumption of Wealth*, transl. C. Prinsep (Franklin Classics, 2018). Original work published 1803.
8. J. Schumpeter, *History of Economic Analysis*, 554–555.
9. T. More, *Utopia* (New Haven, CT: Yale University Press, 2001). Original work published 1516.
10. More didn't use the word "heresy" in his long original title, instead using the phrase "divers matters." The modern title stems from 1557, when More's title was shortened and changed to *Dialogue of Heresies*. See T. More, *Dialogue Concerning Heresies* (New York: Scepter Publishers, 2006). Original work published 1528.
11. W. Baumol, "Entrepreneurship: Productive, Unproductive, and Destructive," *Journal of Political Economy* 95, no. 5, pt. 1 (1990), 893–921.
12. J. Newman, "The Ventures of Faith," *Parochial and Plain Sermons* 4, no. 20 (Kerry, Ireland: CrossReach Publications, 2018), 90–92. Original work published 1842.

6

Wise Ventures and Wise Men

Entrepreneurship provides an opportunity for human betterment, by means of a process of continuing change. If the change is wise and humane, then entrepreneurship becomes the tool — humane entrepreneurship — that contributes a step toward building an economy that is humane. In the vast pool of human needs and desires that constitutes aggregate demand, economic change is a powerful process. If the process is to make sense to human aspirations, we must give thought to what it means for change to make a person truly better off. If we define economic change to be only about the frivolous addition of more gadgetry to the surfeit of a consumerist society, our understanding of the power of change is weakened, and we miss an understanding of the central importance of the humane entrepreneur. Change, guided by wisdom, can be seen to offer instead the pathway to a humane economy, to fruitful happy lives and to the growth in human virtue.

Wisdom

Wisdom is an ancient topic, with a long tradition of weighing its meaning and its importance to human thought and to the human spirit. It has an old literature, much discussed in the classical Greek and Roman era, but with an earlier origin among the ancient Hebrews, where seven books of the *Old Testament* are called the Wisdom Books, including the well-known books Psalms and Proverbs, and a lesser-known book named Wisdom.[1] Modern discussion of wisdom seems to be mostly found in the psychology literature, which even has a subfield called "psychological wisdom" that uses all the phrases to be expected of such a literature: "contextual factors, integrating and synthesizing concepts, cross-disciplinary approaches, conceptualizing placidity, ego-decentering cognitive mindsets," etc., phrases that have no meaning except to those within the community of like-minded enthusiasts. It confines its attention within its ranks, hardly ever even alluding to ancient literature, and it vigorously cites its works back and forth, giving it a circular and in-bred feeling. And it never seems to actually define wisdom; wisdom is simply to think wisely.[2]

This kind of modern work could be said to be an example of busynes, the work of the noon-day devil on full display. The classical Roman philosopher Seneca might respond with:[3]

> Is there any more benefit in knowing this than to know countless other items besides that are either crammed with lies or improbable? For even if you grant that people say all these things in good faith, and even if they guarantee the truthfulness of their writing, whose mistakes will such items of information make fewer? Whose passions will they hold in check? Whom will they make braver, or more just, or more generous of spirit? We wonder whether it is better to apply oneself to no researches at all than to be embroiled in these.

Modern writings on wisdom are not of much help in understanding the humane economy, and modern writings in business and economics are often little better. In the face of this busynes, wisdom sounds simple and pure: braver, more just, more generous of spirit, with passions held in check; to lead people to these virtues might be said to be the wisdom of the humane entrepreneur.

Wisdom is defined, since ancient times, to be spiritual wholeness, the enlargement of mind to embrace completeness, comprehension of the entire course and meaning of existence and of life within that existence, life as a whole and the life of each individual person. It is knowledge, not of things but of the mutual relations between things across all parts, it "implies a connected view of the old with the new; an insight into the bearing and influence of each part upon every other; without which there is no whole and could be no centre. It is the knowledge, not only of things, but of their mutual relations."[4] Such wisdom knowledge seeks to grasp that life exists within and across time and space and seeks a connected view of the old with the new and the near with the far. To an individual, wisdom is clear, calm, accurate vision, and comprehension of the whole course. To the ancients, it was Divine Wisdom, Hagia Sophia, grace, a gift from God:

> For it is He who gave me unerring knowledge of what exists,
> to know the structure of the world and the activity of the elements;
> the beginning and the end and middle of times,
> the alternations of the solstices and the changes of the seasons,
> the cycles of the year and the constellations of the stars,
> the natures of animals and the tempers of wild beasts,
> the powers of spirits and the reasonings of men,
> the varieties of plants, and the virtues of roots;
> I learned both what is secret and what is manifest,
> for wisdom, the fashioner of all things, taught me.[5]

The pursuit of wisdom requires more than mere effort. It requires the devoted pursuit of virtue. In fact, wisdom and virtue are cousins, if not identical twins. Discipline is one of the virtues required by wisdom, with literature treating wisdom and discipline to be found together. Seneca's call to be braver, more just, more generous of spirit, with passions held in check requires discipline. Wisdom and discipline are instilled by teaching the formation of character, the seeking of the virtuous path to follow.

Wisdom is the understanding of what constitutes the good life and the knowledge of how to pursue it. In seeking wisdom, how to deal with reality is an art the learning of which begins in the home and continues under the strong institutions of society, one of which is formal education. Learning wisdom comes from observations and experiences that challenge and from admonition based on virtuous tradition. To grow in wisdom requires a belief in objective truth and acceptance of virtuous codes of conduct.

The wholeness of wisdom is oneness across both space and time, with every existing thing in its place and in its temporal order: "the structure of the world, the activity of the elements, and the beginning, the middle, and the end of all times" says *The Book of Wisdom*. And all of this is subject to "alternations and changes." The most subtle and difficult thing to comprehend is the relationship between the old and the new, that which currently *is* and that which does not yet exist.

The oneness of time is a truth of which all humans should be aware. Some people are virtually obsessed with memory, both good and bad, both haunted and made happy by what has happened, and with expectations good and bad, both stressed and made excited by thoughts of what may be coming. This human truth can be found expressed in literature, two examples being seen in William Faulkner and in Charles Dickens. Faulkner's work is haunted by the past and a sense that the past is always present. The past endures in every moment of every life. We are what we are and where we are because the past has made us so and brought us hither. In *Requiem for a Nun*, a character, in confessing failures and corruptions of the past and revealing a forlorn hope that there can ever be recompense, proclaims, "The past is never dead. It's not even past."[6] Dickens echoes the same truth in *A Christmas Carol* in some of the most famous lines in literature when Scrooge vows: "I will live in the Past, the Present, and the Future. The spirits of all three shall strive within me."[7] The past endures in every moment of our lives, in every fleeting moment that we think of as the present, as the present continually recedes and becomes part of the past. The present has no meaning alone but only within "the whole past on which it depends, and which keeps overtaking the present second by second."[8]

Alfred Korzybski, a prominent and influential Polish-American scholar, provides a clear and precise analysis of how humans uniquely transcend time and can thereby embrace wisdom. Korzybski developed his basic principles as a form of "general semantics,"[9] presented in his 1933 book, *Science and Sanity*. Korzybski founded the Institute of General Semantics in Chicago and had a wide range of influence with both philosophers, such as Alan Watts, and science fiction writers, such as Robert Heinlein and A. E. van Vogt.

Korzybski argues that humans, as does all creation, exist under the laws of nature which makes possible all human behavior but also strictly limits what behaviors will be fruitful and humane. We must learn what Man is, how he fits into the laws of nature, and therefore what human acts of behavior are in accordance with nature. "A true conception of man as man will transform our views of human society and the world, affect our human conduct and will give us a growing body of wisdom regarding the welfare of mankind, including all posterity."[10] The requirement that virtue and wisdom places on people, particularly those suited to lead, is the acceptance that man is a natural creature, subject in every way to the laws of nature. "The power of human beings to determine their own destinies is limited by natural law, nature's law. It is the council of wisdom to discover the laws of nature, including the laws of human nature, and then to live in accordance with them. The opposite is folly."[11] What then is the unique nature of man? "Man is a being naturally endowed with-time binding capacity; a human being is a time-binder. Men, women, and children constitute the time binding class of life."[12]

When talking about what it means to be humane it is easy for the talk to go unto "ethics," but such talk is not useful if we wander from a clear grasp of the nature of man. "In discovering the characteristic nature of man, we come to the secret and the source of ethics. Ethics is the obligation which the essential nature of man imposes upon human beings. It will be seen that to live righteously, to live ethically, and to live in accordance with the laws of human nature, and when it is clearly seen that man is a natural being, a part of nature literally, then it will be seen that the laws of human nature are the only possible rules of ethical conduct."[13]

Time-Binding

The unique thing about human beings is the capability to transcend time, to live in the past, the present, and the future. The nature of man is that he is a time-binder, able to move across time. According to Korzybski, the ability to transcend time flows from the human being's unique organic chemistry. Inorganic chemistry addresses the realm of minerals in which the concept of life has no place. Life finds its place when organic chemistry expands the realm of existence to include the "new and unique energetic phenomena of 'life,' the phenomenon of the 'mind' and of the 'mind' in general." Life takes three different forms — plants, animals, and humans — with their strikingly different natures making each a different class of life: the Chemistry-Binding class, the Space-Binding class, and the Time-Binding class.

Chemistry-Binding: Plants are a Chemistry-Binding class of life that provide the origin of life by combining the minerals of inorganic chemistry with sunlight to transform solar energy into organic chemistry. It appropriates one kind of energy, sunlight, and converts it into another kind of energy, life, and nutrition. It also stores energy over time in the form of fossil fuels, oil and coal, and serves as a kind of storage battery for solar energy.

Space-Binding: Animals are the Space-Binding class of life, building on the Chemistry-Binding class by using plants as food. Where plants are frozen in place, animals add to life the amazing quality of movement through space. Animals transform stationary plants into the ability to move about, adding kinetic energy to the chemical energy of plants. Animals have the ability to transcend space by means of the freedom and faculty of movement, thus conquering space.

Time-Binding: Humans uniquely constitute the Time-Binding class of life, combining Chemistry-Binding with Space-Binding to create the ability to reason across time. The ability to think gives humans the astounding ability to capture time — to literally bind time — to move across it, backward into the past, pausing in the present, and casting forward into the future. Time-Binding gives humans the capacity to:

(1) summarize, digest, and appropriate the labors and experiences of the past
(2) use the fruits of past labors and experiences as intellectual or spiritual capital for development in the present
(3) employ as instruments of increasing power the accumulated achievement of the all-previous lives of the past generations spent in trial and error, trial and success
(4) possess virtue of which man is at once the heritor of the by-gone ages and the trustee of posterity
(5) exhibit a natural agency by which the past lives in the present and the present lives in the future
(6) conduct their lives in the ever-increasing light of inherited wisdom.[14]

Time-Binding is a unique, capability of humans. It makes it possible for humans to pursue wisdom. Korzybski echoes the ancients in stating that wisdom is the understanding of the oneness of time — past, present, and future — and working within that understanding. The opposite of being wise is not being unintelligent or unlearned but rather is being a fool, one who is buffeted by circumstances without awareness, comprehension, or resistance.

Korzybski identifies three types of fools, "ways in which one may be a fool," each of which most of us can identify with from personal experience: drifting fools, static fools, and dynamic fools. *Drifting fools*, probably the most common, are those who ignore the past like animals, who give little thought to the past and just drift along thinking that things will always remain the same. *Static fools* are those who misunderstand the relation of past, present, and future. Some worship the past, idealize it, and view it in a manner that is almost idolatrous. Idolatrous fools must live with a sense of frustration, but more seriously, they lessen their ability to prepare for the inevitable change. Others worship the present, in a manner that is smug and self-satisfied, almost always those who profit from present circumstances. They seem to ignore the fact that the past offers proof that present circumstances will not remain the same. Still others are fearful of the future, even cowardly in their reaction to the unknown. *Dynamic fools* are those who scorn the past and hate the present, angry fools who not only are deceived but also are dangerous. Scorning the past and hating the present is the definition of Jacobinism. Any form of Jacobinism that gains political power offers a sure road to hellish worlds, in literature Thomas More's *Utopia* and in reality the French Jacobins with their Reign of Terror, the National Socialists' concentration camps, and Russian Communists with their gulags.

"In striking contrast to the three-fold division of Folly, the counsel of Wisdom is one, and it is one with the sober counsel of common sense. What is that counsel? What is the united counsel of Wisdom and common sense respecting the past? ... The counsel is this: Do not ignore the past but study it — study it diligently as being the mightiest factor among the great factors of our human world; endeavor to view the past justly, to contemplate it as it was and is, to see it whole..."

"Such I take to be the counsel of Wisdom — the simple wisdom of sober common sense. To ascertain the salient facts of our immense human past and then to explain in terms of their causes and conditions ... Past, Present, Future — these cannot be understood singly and separately — they are welded together indissolubly together as *one*."[15]

Entrepreneurial Change

Difficulty in coping with change occurs when we are not adequately rooted in the past, in tradition. Roman philosopher Seneca warns us that the difficulty lies in the fact that the "greatest impediment to living is expectancy, which relies on tomorrow and wastes today. You map out what is in fortune's hand but let slip what is in your own hand." We waste the current moment by thinking that we have plenty of time and by thinking that we can follow a path that is disconnected from the path that brought us to the current moment. We risk losing control of change if we fail to understand that there really is no Present, fail to understand that the Present is merely the point, with no substance, at which the Past has arrived. Seneca says "Life is divided into three parts: past, present, and future. Of these, the present is brief, the future doubtful, the past certain. For this last is the category over which Fortune no longer has control and which cannot be brought back under anyone's power. Preoccupied people lose this part, for they have no leisure to look back at the past." Preoccupied people are those who are burdened by acedia, the noon-day devil. Humane entrepreneurship requires a leader who is "not constricted by the same limit that confines others. He alone is released from the limitations of the human race ... Some time has passed? He holds it in recollection. Time is upon us? He uses it. Time is to come? This he anticipates. The combining of all times into one makes life long. But for those who forget the past, disregard the present and fear for the future, life is very troubled."[16]

If guided by wisdom, entrepreneurship can provide an opportunity for human betterment by means of a continuing process of change that is life-getting and humane. Humane entrepreneurs hold the power of a change process that can lead to more virtuous and fruitful lives and to human growth and wisdom. Humane ventures are in fact wellsprings of happy and healthy people and a healthy society with an understanding of what constitutes the good life and the knowledge of how to pursue it. And to pursue is to venture. All life, both personal and organizational, consists of one venture after another. A well spent life is a life in which ventures are pursued with the intent of an understanding of what is meant by the good life. If guided by wisdom, a humane venture can deliver change that draws on a deeper knowledge of the good life as revealed in traditional ways, to turn consumers away from the noon-day devil and toward an understanding of a happier life and a healthier society.

Endnotes

1. The seven Wisdom Books include: Psalms, Proverbs, Wisdom, Job, Ecclesiastes, Sirach, and the Song of Songs.
2. For an example of this literature see U. Staudinger and J. Gluck, "Psychological Wisdom Research: Commonalities and Differences in a Growing Field," *Annual Review of Psychology*, 62 (2011), 215–241.

3. Seneca, Lucius Annaeus, *De Brevitate Vitae* (On the Shortness of Life), 49 AD.
4. J. Newman, "Wisdom, As Contrasted with Faith and Bigotry." in *A Reason for the Hope Within: Sermons of the Theory of Religious Belief.* (Denville, NJ: Dimension Books, 1985), 285. Original work published 1841.
5. *Old Testament, Wisdom* 7: 17–22
6. W. Faulkner, *Requiem for a Nun* (New York: Vintage Books, 1975). Original work published 1951.
7. C. Dickens, *A Christmas Carol* (New York: Grosset and Dunlap, 1989). Original work published 1843.
8. Faulkner, *Requiem for a Nun.*
9. It should be noted that Korzybski's "general semantics" is different from the discipline of "semantics". See A. Korzybski, *Science and Sanity: An Introduction to Non-Aristotelian Systems and General Semantics* (Lakeville, CT: The International Non-Aristotelian Publications, 1958). Original work published 1933.
10. A. Korzybski, *Manhood of Humanity* (Jefferson Publication, 2016), 6. Original work published 1921.
11. *Ibid.*
12. *Ibid.*
13. *Ibid.*
14. Korzybski, *Science and Sanity,* 58–59.
15. *Ibid., * 59.
16. Seneca, 49 AD.

7

Entrepreneurial Instinct: Keynes vs. Schumpeter

The entrepreneur is always with us because the role is natural to human beings. Entrepreneurial behavior is a component of the human personality. Every person is an entrepreneur at heart, even though not all people are equally active and aggressive at it. Some people may feel more comfortable with the risks, and some people are more successful at it, their efforts bearing more fruit than the efforts of others. The acts of the entrepreneur are common to all people. Entrepreneurship, the acts of the entrepreneur, is natural to human society and therefore an ever-present component of human society. In addressing the entrepreneur as a person and entrepreneurship as interpersonal behavior, the emphasis is placed on the word *natural*.

Being natural to humans and human social behavior, entrepreneurs and entrepreneurship have been on display throughout human history. All the ventures that constitute human history could be described as acts of entrepreneurship. All the adventurers, some virtuous and some not so virtuous, that fill the pages of history could be called entrepreneurs. Until the early economics literature settled upon the word entrepreneur to label those who attempt to execute bold business ventures such people were, in fact, called merchant adventurers. The word entrepreneur is a latecomer, post-dating Adam Smith. Both the *Wealth of Nations* published in 1776 and the *Essay on the History of Civil Society*, published in 1767 by Smith's Scottish contemporary Adam Ferguson used the word "undertaker" having taken it from the work of Richard Cantillon.[1]

Entrepreneurial Instinct

Two questions concern the core of an ongoing debate that addresses the very nature of entrepreneurship and the question of the role of the entrepreneur. First, is the entrepreneur a manager who facilitates a process of societal change that is driven by causal factors in the environment? If so, then the entrepreneur will be rewarded in the form of a wage, possibly a very high wage, because entrepreneurship requires skills and talents that are rare, but a wage, nonetheless. Second, is the entrepreneur a change agent, a mover and shaker, who causes the societal change by changing the actual mechanism of causation at work in the environment? If so, then the entrepreneur is, in a sense, an owner of what has changed in society, typically societal enterprises, and thereby lays claim to a portion not only of the additional wealth created but also of any loss incurred. The two sides of the debate were taken by, arguably, the two most important economists of the modern era, John Maynard Keynes and Joseph Schumpeter.

In considering the principals in the two sides of the debate, we should note the fact that the early theorists of entrepreneurship did not come from universities. Richard Cantillon (1697–1734) was a banker, international financier, speculator, and promoter who made a vast fortune before age 30. Jean-Baptiste Say (1767–1832) was a major industrialist and a pioneer in the textile industry. David Ricardo (1772–1823) was a banker and securities trader in the City of London who retired in his 40s to become a large landowner. Their writings anchor entrepreneurship firmly in the world of business practice and investment. Adam Smith did come from a university but was not a professor of economics but instead of moral philosophy. He lived and worked in a world confined entirely to books and scholarship, as far from the rough and tumble of entrepreneurship as one can get. He was an Enlightenment rationalist and sought simplicity, balance, and harmony in social relations. He alludes only once in passing to entrepreneurs in all the *Wealth of Nations*, and calls them undertakers.

Schumpeter argues that the virtual absence of entrepreneurship in the development of economic theory in England is explained by the fact that English university scholars worked under the long shadow of Adam Smith. The first major university appointment of an economist was not until 1826 with Nassau Senior at Oxford, and Senior's appointment was probably due to his being an expert devotee of Smith; Smith's work having become by then widely read and followed. English universities proceeded to open their ranks to economists, many of whom became the architects of modern economics in English, such as Alfred Marshall at Cambridge and Francis Edgeworth at Oxford, among others. According to Schumpeter, these economists were solidly grounded in the tradition inspired by Smith and built their economics around the movement toward equilibrium in a static economy, leaving little room for the chaos of change and the work of the change agent, the entrepreneur. Economic scholarship in English was placed in a straitjacket by the obsession with equilibrium bequeathed by Marshall and Edgeworth, an obsession that was cemented into place by Keynes. His world of equilibrium works to minimize the importance of, if not eliminate entirely, the role of the entrepreneur.

John Maynard Keynes

John Maynard Keynes gives us, in *The General Theory of Employment, Interest and Money*, a methodology for analyzing movement toward full employment in a static economy. Presented in formal propositions and mathematics, it is an impressive methodology, well suited for codification in university textbooks and teaching in university classrooms. The textbooks were soon written, and most college economics departments came to teach his methodology, and "Keynesian economics" came to dominate economic thinking. In addition, Keynes offered government policy recommendations which led to a virtual cottage industry of university economics professors being employed by government, particularly the Federal government, to offer economic policy advice. Under the New Deal of Franklin Roosevelt, the cottage industry became a growth industry that continues to the present time.

Keynes was obsessed with the impact of market inefficiencies and the importance of government to mediate these inefficiencies in order to obtain full employment. He openly admits to advocating for socialism, but he says that it will be a mild form of socialism that will involve state control of only three elements of an economy: the propensity to consume, the interest rate, and the rate of capital investment.[2]

> The State will have to exercise a guiding influence on the propensity to consume partly through its scheme of taxation, partly by fixing the rate of interest, and partly, perhaps, in other ways. Furthermore, it seems unlikely that the influence of banking policy on the rate of interest

will be sufficient by itself to determine an optimum rate of investment. I conceive, therefore, that a somewhat comprehensive socialization of investment will prove the only means of securing an approximation to full employment ... But beyond this no obvious case is made out for a system of State Socialism which would embrace most of the economic life of the community. It is not the ownership of the instruments [factors] of production which is important for the state to assume. If the state is able to determine the aggregate amount of resources devoted to augmenting the [factors] and the basic rate of reward to those who own them, it will have accomplished all that is necessary.[3]

Keynesian state control of the economy need be limited only to the amount and allocation of capital investment, "the resources devoted to augmenting the [factors of production]" and to the payments to the factors, "the rate of reward to those who own them." The primary target of government control in Keynes's brand of socialism is the "functionless investor," an idle and useless person whose only contribution is his money, Cantillon's "money-owner," who charges for the use of his money just as the idle landowner charges for the use of his land. Keynes calls the functionless investor a "rentier," a person who lives off their ownership of money or land and is a burden to society by charging high scarcity rents. Rentier is a pejorative word that the dictionary says was first used in Revolutionary France in 1798 to describe the landowners that the Jacobins sent to the guillotine.

> This state of affairs ... would mean the euthanasia of the rentier. And consequently, the euthanasia of the cumulative oppressive power of the capitalist to exploit the scarcity value of capital. Interest today rewards no genuine sacrifice anymore than does the rent of land.[4]

Keynes does not just downplay the role of the entrepreneur; he clearly states that the entrepreneur's involvement with the "functionless investor" must be eliminated if the ideal of full employment is to be realized. Keynes views the entrepreneur to be essentially a manager, albeit one of high and greatly valued expertise, the one who directs the factors of production and determines the wage bargains with labor: "the real wages of Labor depend on the wage bargains which labor makes with the entrepreneurs."[5] The problem, as Keynes sees it, is that the entrepreneur facilitates the use of investment funds obtained from the functionless investor and then takes a large portion of any economic gain that results.

I see, therefore, the rentier aspect of capitalism as a transitional phase which will disappear when it has done its work ... Thus we might aim in practice at an increase in the volume of capital until it ceases to be scarce, so that the functionless investor will no longer receive a bonus; and add a scheme of direct taxation which allows the intelligence and determination and executive skill of the financier, the entrepreneur et hoc genus omne (who are certainly so fond of their craft that their labor could be obtained much cheaper than at present), to be harnessed to the service of the community on reasonable terms of reward.[6]

The aim of Keynes is to make capital so common that it no longer can claim a scarcity rent. The entrepreneur will then be able to make no claim on the value created by a new venture, and the expertise of the entrepreneur can then be obtained at a reasonable wage and can be "harnessed to the service of the community on reasonable terms of reward."

Joseph Schumpeter

Joseph Schumpeter was the exception to all the excitement of the Keynesian revolution. He opposed socialism in all forms: the national socialism of Germany, the international socialism of Russia, and the "socialization of investment" of Keynes in Great Britain. He disapproved of Keynesian economics and flat out refused to have anything to do with the Federal government. Schumpeter believed that Keynesian economics is wrong and not even very interesting. Wrong, because an economy cannot be managed, "Individuals seeking to optimize their self-interest and guided by their perception of reality will always find a way to beat the system." Not interesting, because Keynesian economics is built on the false assertion that the healthy society/economy is an economy that is in, or is moving toward, a state of equilibrium and full employment. Not only is this wrong, but also it is not even interesting, because anything that can be in equilibrium is something that is static, and the world is never static. The world is always changing, and thus the only interesting phenomenon is change.

To Schumpeter entrepreneurship is the phenomenon that drives economic growth and development. He taught that "The central problem of economics is not equilibrium but structural change," and the entrepreneur is the agent and manager of change. Schumpeter's defining statement is that when we talk correctly about the nature of entrepreneurship, we are talking about the nature of change. This means change in its universal sense, transcending current practice and current interests, transcending particular cultures and value systems, and transcending the world of business and economics. To examine change, he urged deeper study of history and deeper awareness of arts, politics, and culture. He made a fundamental statement in 1947, late in his life that ended in 1950, in his paper, "The Creative Response in Economic History," a statement that can be argued to be a summation of his lifelong effort to study economic change.[7] Schumpeter's concept of the "creative destruction" wrought by change is so widely accepted as to have become almost a cliché. He argued that the study of change is the central issue of economics because it is the study of both growth and decline. He first addressed change in his 1911 book entitled, *The Theory of Economic Development*,[8] and continued it in his later work, most importantly *Capitalism, Socialism, and Democracy* in 1942.[9] The statement in the 1947 article is particularly important, because it also addresses creativity, something not often addressed in detail in economic literature.

We must enter Schumpeter's realm of creativity to understand productive action in the face of change that is radical. Most people believe uncritically "that all that is needed to explain a given development is to indicate causal factors."

If (causal factors) **then** (a given development)

But, in many cases, knowledge of causal factors is insufficient to explain the outcome of change. "No factor acts in a uniquely determined way and, whenever it does not, the necessity arises of going into the details of its *modus operandi*, into the mechanisms through which it acts." Schumpeter uses as an example changes in population. In the static world of equilibrium economics, it was commonly believed:

If (increase in population) **then** (decrease in per capita income)

Sometimes this is true, usually for specifically defined units with constraints on their resources (such as families or small communities) and over limited periods of time. But often the opposite is true:

If (increase in population) **then** (increase in per capita income)

Population increase may have an energizing effect that changes the causal mechanism in an unexpected way and may actually lead to a rise in per capita real income. Growth in India and China can be cited as an example of this. In Schumpeter's day, it was conventional economic wisdom to state that only severe population control could prevent mass starvation in India and China, and today we know that personal income is rising rapidly in India and China despite (and Schumpeter might suggest because of) a continued rise in population. The only way to explain such a spectacular error in economic judgement is the failure to understand the difference between adaptive and creative response to change.

Schumpeter explains the difference between adaption and creativity this way: "Whenever a society adapts itself to a change in its data in the way that traditional theory describes, whenever, that is, it reacts within its existing practice, we may speak of the development as *adaptive response.*" On the other hand, "Whenever a society does something else, something that is outside of the range of existing practice, we may speak of *creative response*" [italics Schumpeter]. Creative response has three essential characteristics: First, the creative response and its outcome cannot be understood beforehand; it cannot be forecasted. Second, the creative response changes everything, and there is no way back to what prevailed before or to the path of development that might have prevailed in its absence; it changes the causal mechanisms of the economy, and there can be nothing deterministic in the historical process. Third, the creative response depends upon the characteristics of the people involved, their qualities and virtues; the virtues of the people enable them to respond to the leadership of the entrepreneurs in their midst. Therefore, says Schumpeter, "a study of creative response in business becomes coterminous with a study of entrepreneurship. The mechanisms of economic change in capitalist society pivot on entrepreneurial activity."

Schumpeter claims that the obsession with equilibrium of the English economists left the field open to German and Austrian economists, from whence Schumpeter came and who taught him, and to American economists, to whom Schumpeter was attracted and who welcomed his greatest work. German inspired scholarship has been more open-minded and has produced much more valuable work in entrepreneurship, although interestingly American society appears much more entrepreneurial in practice. While not as widely read as his later works, the benchmark work on entrepreneurship and economic growth came from Schumpeter's *The Theory of Economic Development*. He wrote this work in German when he was a young professor in Austria where he had been taught, and it was not translated into English until 1931. Even if it had circulated rapidly and been embraced widely, it was too late to make an adequately deep impression before the English-speaking economics world was swamped by the Keynesian tsunami.

Fifty-seven years after Schumpeter's benchmark work, in 1968, Baumol in "Entrepreneurship in Economic Theory," lamented that the entrepreneur "has virtually disappeared from the theoretical literature."[10] He stated that the entrepreneur is the apex of the forces that determine the behavior of the business firm and bears responsibility for the vitality of the free enterprise society, and yet only Schumpeter has "succeeded in infusing him with life and assigning to him an area of activity." Baumol says that the traditional economic theorist is focused on model building, and it is difficult to model that which is distinctive about the entrepreneur: strategy choices, attitudes toward risk, sources of ideas, opportunity recognition, and most of all, the question of why anyone would want to be an entrepreneur. Baumol asked the same question again, 42 years later in 2010, in one of his last statements, *The Microtheory of Innovative Entrepreneurship*, where he argued that the entrepreneurial process can be viewed as a "lottery that offers just a few mega-prizes," and therefore, like a lottery, entrepreneurial activity is intrinsically unfair.[11] On average, the entrepreneur does not get any premium in comparison to a wage worker of similar circumstances. And yet entrepreneurs keep playing the lottery. Why? The answer to that question may lie in the fact that entrepreneurship is by its nature humane, i.e., natural to the human being. There is, arguably, an entrepreneurial impulse in human nature.

The first sentence in Smith's *The Wealth of Nations* states that, "The greatest improvement in the productive powers of labor ... seem to have been the effects of the division of labor." Economic growth, all increases in productivity, come from the division of labor. Schumpeter states that "nobody, either before or after A. Smith, ever thought of putting such a burden upon division of labor." He finds it remarkable that Smith puts so much weight on the division of labor *alone* [italics Schumpeter's]. More remarkable still might be the fact that Smith attributes the division of labor to a single thing, the human "propensity to truck, barter, and exchange," a propensity that Smith says is found in all human beings and in no other living being. He says that all the advantages that flow from the division of labor *alone* come from this propensity *alone*. He says that all the benefits of the division of labor, all its utility, come from this "propensity in human nature which has in view no such extensive utility," in other words, all human productivity comes from blind human instinct. Smith says, "Whether this propensity be one of those original principles in human nature, of which no further account can be given; or whether, as seems more probable, it be the necessary consequence of the faculties of reason and speech, it belongs not to our present subject to inquire."[12]

An alternative to the inhuman economics of static equilibrium, Schumpeter has bequeathed to us the very human economics of change and growth in the person of the entrepreneur, the *unterneher/*undertaker, the person who commits to new ventures into the unknown. Schumpeter's benchmark treatise of 1911 was greeted in 1915 by a treatise by Frank Taussig, the senior economics professor at Harvard who was instrumental in bringing Schumpeter from the University of Bonn in Germany in 1932 to replace Tausig in the senior chair at Harvard, where Schumpeter remained until his death in 1950. In his 1915 book, *Inventors and Money-Makers*, Tausig expresses disbelief at Adam Smith's remarkable assertion, that all human productivity emanates from a single primitive animal instinct in humans.[13] Tausig says, "It has long been a matter of wonder for me that this passage received so little attention — indeed, so far as I am aware, no attention at all — from Adam Smith's successors." Tausig goes on to propose that instead human productivity emanates from "an instinct of contrivance," an innate human urge to contrive, to build, to create. To support his proposition, Tausig draws on the work of Thorstein Veblen who asserted that humans are driven by an "instinct for workmanship."

This we also assert. Entrepreneurship is natural to human beings, and therefore humane, because it is motivated by Tausig's instinct of contrivance and Veblen's instinct for workmanship. Schumpeter's thesis draws on these instincts to focus entrepreneurship on technology; the entrepreneur acts as the agent of change by moving resources from old technologies to the new. Our thesis draws on these instincts to focus on scale; the entrepreneur acts as the agent of change by continually launching new ventures that work to scale down the giantism common to enterprises in the modern economy to a more humane size.

Endnotes

1. The example of Pin Factory in the first pages of the *Wealth of Nations* to illustrate the concept of division of labor is often considered one of Smith's most important contributions. However, it can be argued that Adam Ferguson developed the same idea some 10 years prior in his *Essay on the History of*

Civil Society, published in 1767. In fact, Smith and Ferguson actively discussed their ideas with each other during their lifetime. To quote from the *Essay*, (which also illustrates the use of the word undertaker), "Every undertaker in manufacture finds, that the more he can subdivide the tasks of his workmen, and the more hands he can employ on separate articles, the more are his expenses diminished, and his profits increased." The *Essay* also has a chapter (Section VI) on "Moral Sentiment" in business. See *A. Ferguson, Essay on the History of Civil Society* (Cambridge: Cambridge University Press, 1996). Original work published 1767.

2. A strong form of socialism is government involvement in all market functions, including setting pricing, demand, and supply conditions — arguably for the betterment of society and full employment (thus the term socialism). For example, The National Socialist German Workers' Party (Nazi Party) advocated a strong form of socialism in pre-WWII Germany and did achieve full "official" employment by 1938. Socialism, whether weak or strong, still allows for elements of capitalism, — individuals can still own capital (property), they can individually invest this capital, and they can benefit from the investment of capital. It should be noted that socialism is not communism, which requires the elimination of various private property rights, replacing it with state "communal" ownership. Full employment is still also a stated objective in most communist systems. The terms socialism and communism are often confused in the popular literature and in many college classrooms.

3. J. Keynes, *The General Theory of Employment, Interest, and Money* (New York: Harcourt Brace, 1964), 378. Original work published 1936.

4. *Ibid.*, 375–376.

5. *Ibid.*, 10.

6. *Ibid.*, 378.

7. J. Schumpeter, "The Creative Response in Economic History," *The Journal of Economic History* 7, no.2, 149–159.

8. J. Schumpeter, *Theory of Economic Development*, transl. R. Opie. (Boston, MA: Harvard Economic Studies, 1934). Original work published 1911.

9. J. Schumpeter, *Capitalism, Socialism and Democracy* (New York, NY: Harper & Row, 1942).

10. W. Baumol, "Entrepreneurship in Economic Theory," *The American Economic Review* 58, no. 2 (1968), 64–78.

11. W. Baumol, *The Microtheory of Innovative Entrepreneurship* (Princeton, NJ: Princeton University Press, 2010).

12. This is a remarkable statement and if true there is no room for entrepreneurship in the economics of static equilibrium that Smith bequeathed to us.

13. F. Taussig, *Inventors and Money-Makers* (New York, NY: The Macmillan Company, 1915).

Section III

Humane Entrepreneurship at the Personal Level

Entrepreneurship textbooks are filled with discussions about how entrepreneurs are different from other careers and professions at the personal level. Entrepreneurs have different personality characteristics, they take risks, they show greater self-efficacy, and they often come from different social, economic, family, and cultural backgrounds than non-entrepreneurs. While interesting, and perhaps true, these lists of differences do little to capture the true uniqueness of entrepreneurial activity from a more basic point of view, particularly as it relates to the notion of their relationship to a humane economy. This is a critical issue, since any deep discussion of humane entrepreneurship must be built upon a set of characteristics that also make entrepreneurs humane at a more personal level.

Much of this book focuses on important, macro-oriented institutional and economic elements that provide a foundational understanding of what constitutes a humane economy, and how entrepreneurial activity represents a potentially more humane path within the larger, complex, and impersonal system of modern, post-industrial age capitalism. This more macro-perspective is important for a foundational understanding of how humaneness and entrepreneurship are deeply connected. But entrepreneurial behavior also exhibits important personal characteristics. In the next four essays we argue that true entrepreneurial behavior, both present and past, has the potential for humaneness at the individual level and that entrepreneurial activity has special meaning from a subjective, more philosophical perspective.

In the first essay, *The Entrepreneur as an Existential Being*, we posit that entrepreneurial activity, in its basic and truest form, is a form of self-directed or self-managed existential therapy. In this light, entrepreneurial action can become a process of uncovering a deeper understanding of the individual's life as a human. Realizing one's human nature is the starting point for understanding humaneness. In this essay, we draw heavily upon the philosophical tradition of existentialism, particularly Danish theologian and philosopher Søren Kierkegaard.

In the second essay titled, *Experience as Truth: The Phenomenology of Entrepreneurship*, we continue the philosophical foundation of entrepreneurship at the personal level and explore entrepreneurial behavior from a more phenomenological point of view. In this essay we examine the historical and very human symbiotic relationships between work and property. We then explore how the upheaval of the industrial revolution gave birth to the "fictitious commodities" of labor and capital in the modern world that ultimately pushed the modern economic world into a non-humane orientation. We suggest that entrepreneurial thinking, however, offers a natural mechanism to potentially resolve some of the inherent conflicts of world experiences related to "fictitious commodities." In this essay we therefore draw upon the theoretical and historical relationships between work and property/labor and capital and how this has impacted world perceptions within the framework of phenomenology.

In the third essay, *The Meaning of an Entrepreneurial Pilgrimage*, we explore the idea that the entrepreneurial experience is like a pilgrimage, something deeply meaningful and difficult to complete. But the notion of a pilgrimage is fundamentally different from a vocation or other life experiences. The analogy of entrepreneurship as a pilgrimage appears more than simply poetic license. Throughout recorded times, humans have undertaken pilgrimages. And just like entrepreneurial action, pilgrimages are uniquely a human action that involve continuous and difficult experiences of decisions, emptions, and meaning. And when successful, they ultimately offer a sense of satisfaction of completion. Similar to entrepreneurial action, the majority of people have never undertaken a true pilgrimage while others have tried and given up. And like a serial entrepreneur a few hardy souls have made multiple pilgrimages in their life. This essay explores the underlying theory, philosophy, and psychology of pilgrimages, and how it might relate to the true entrepreneurial experience and ultimately contribute to a deeper orientation of humaneness.

While the other essays in this section examine important existential, phenomenological, and social/psychological benefits of the entrepreneurial experience, benefits that all point to a more humane way of thinking, the fourth essay titled, *Internalizing Moral Markets: Solving the "Smith Problem"* focuses more on the implementation or "action" associated with humane thinking, beneficence, charity, and human virtue. This essay examines this behavior within the context of Adam Smith's writings, and in particular the underlying nature of what has been called the "Smith Problem." Adam Smith appears to present two different, and apparently conflicting perspectives of humaneness, charity, and efficient economic behavior between his two major treatises, *The Theory of Moral Sentiments*, published in 1759, and his later, more well-known and cited work, the *Wealth of Nations* published in 1776. The essay examines the "Smith Problem" from different perspectives and suggests that entrepreneurship helps resolve the "Smith Problem" in a very practical manner.

8

The Entrepreneur as an Existential Being

Individuals, regardless of their professional pursuits, are existent persons. Individuals live, work, play, and ultimately die as humans. In this fact alone, the act of being human, people need to take their role in life with all the seriousness, dedication, understanding, respect, and opportunity it deserves. But it takes individual courage and persistence to look at one's existence deeply and honestly. It is a fundamental role of philosophy, and for many, theology, to explain this important process of self-reflection.

Historians of philosophical thought often suggest that there are essentially two basic philosophical forces throughout history.[1] The first force, represented by Greek philosophers such as Aristotle (384–322 BC), the medieval Scholastic philosophers such as St. Thomas Aquinas (1225–1274) and John Duns Scotus (1266–1308), the 17th and 18th century Rationalism philosophical movements represented by Gottfriend Wilhelm Leibniz (1646–1716) and more recently, Alfred North Whitehead (1861–1947), attempt to understand the broader world about us through complex discussions of metaphysics, logic, and natural philosophy.

In fact, the vast majority of professional and academic philosophers in the modern world tend to focus on grand systems of philosophical thought. One driving force behind this focus on philosophical "systems" is the world of academic publishing and the nature of university professional advancement. Like any academic profession, it is far easier to publish complex analysis about detailed and specialized systems in academic outlets than to focus in a simpler manner on what is most important.

While important within a grand perspective, these overarching philosophical approaches generally address the problems of individuals and their existence only in an indirect and sometimes superficial manner.

The second philosophical force, and the one most relevant to our discussion in this essay, are those thinkers that directly address individual existence, and how the individual navigates the perils of living. These are the philosophies of individual human transformation. Many early mystical writers, such as John van Ruysbroeck (1294–1381), Catherine of Siena (1347–1380), and Richard Roll (1300–1349) focused on the individual person, the importance of human transformation, and the process of attaining a greater life. Mystical writers, while presenting a powerful and very personal perspective of life always view this human transformation as a unification process with higher Being.

More fundamental to our discussion, however, is the rise in the 19th century of what is now known as existentialism. Existentialism, by definition, also addresses human existence at the individual level, but from a different perspective. This approach includes a wide range of foundational authors, such as Søren Kierkegaard (1813–1855), Albert Camus (1913–1960), Friedrich Nietzsche (1844–1900), Martin Heidegger (1889–1976), and Jean-Paul Sartre (1905–1980). Existentialism, as a school of thought, continues to the present day and includes a diverse collection of writers from around the world such as Israeli philosopher Martin Buber (1878–1965), German-American theologian Paul Tillich (1885–1965), American existentialist John Daniel Wild (1931–1972), and Czech novelist Franz Kafka (1883–1924).[2] These writers, and many other existentialist thinkers, all explore, sometimes with almost frightening detail, the fears, difficulties, and personal perils of human existence. They ultimately present the problem of human transformation through the personal mechanism of understanding the realities of human existence.

Not surprisingly, the individual search for life's meaning and other existential topics have become common themes in visual art (e.g., Munch's *The Scream* and Cezanne's *The Card Players* series), theater and plays (e.g., Sartre's *No Exit* and Beckett's *Waiting for Godot*) and novels (e.g., Dostoevesky's *The Gambler*, Kobo Abe's *The Box Man* and Seidlinger's *The Face of Any Other*). Existential themes are particularly popular in the media of popular film, such as Martin Scorsese's *The Taxi Driver* (1976), Federico Fellini's *La Dolce Vita* (1960), David Lynch's *Mulholland Drive* (2001), Ingmar Bergman's *The Seventh Seal* (1957), Stanley Kubrick's *2001: A Space Odyssey* (1968), and Terrence Malick's

The Tree of Life (2011). While powerfully presented, modern literary explorations of existential themes generally focus on the "sickening" realization, often when a person is near death or under the stress of a personal crises, of the "meaningless" of life. Only occasionally do these literary efforts explore the existential seeds of humanity, how conscious individuals understand their humanity, or the solutions for navigating life in a meaningful manner.

It is within this framework that we explore the idea that entrepreneurial action, by its very nature, encourages existential thinking, and ultimately a humanistic orientation. We argue that the true entrepreneur is almost by definition, an existential being, or at least more oriented toward an existential understanding of life. From a philosophical point of view, this makes entrepreneurship unique among the business and administrative professions. It is this existential aspect of entrepreneurship that allows for a discussion of human transformation, and ultimately a humanistic orientation that is fundamentally and significantly different than simply overlaying broad notions of corporate social responsibility and business ethics onto a class of economically active individuals now called entrepreneurs.

The Frustration of Modern Society

Søren Kierkegaard, considered by many to be the founder of modern existential thought, was born into a successful family in Copenhagen in the early 19th century, a time when Copenhagen was rapidly expanding both economically and artistically after a decade of devastating battles with England. Copenhagen was also becoming an important port city, a center of trade in the Baltic Sea region. His family clearly expected the young Kierkegaard to join the rising bourgeois class, to become an influential businessman, pastor, or civic leader. But by his early 20s, like many young people of the modern era, Kierkegaard started to rebel. He became increasingly distressed by what he saw about him, not so much in the notion of success, but rather by the world perspective of those living the life of bourgeois success. As Kierkegaard famously notes in *Either/Or, Part 1*,

> Of all the ridiculous things, it seems to me the most ridiculous is to be a busy man of affairs, prompt to meals and prompt to work. Hence when I see a fly settle down in a crucial moment on the nose of a businessman

... then I laugh heartily. And who could not help laughing. What do they accomplish these hustlers.[3]

Kierkegaard clearly saw the ridiculousness nature of the orchestrated, mundane life of "men of affairs," bourgeois characters of apparent busyness and importance; but he also saw the ridiculousness of the "hustle," the wheeling and dealing of these people within the growing port city. As a young man, a disenchanted Kierkegaard soon associated with other young liberal radicals of the "Young German Movement," poets, writers, and journalists inspired by the German poet, Heinrich Hiene (1797–1856).

Kierkegaard ultimately rejected this approach, and other dominant Hegelian thought of the times. Hegel (1770–1831) was a post-Kantian idealist who developed a complex and detailed philosophical system that argued that society is full of divisions, classes, and contradictions that ultimately will need to be resolved into a more harmonious system. Kierkegaard, however, believed that Hegelianism simply codified bureaucratic ideals. Kierkegaard recognized that Hegelian thought, whether oriented toward the system of bourgeois virtues and its pursuit of affluence and organized business/politics, or the later derivative Marxist system of proletariat drones dominated by a self-appointed bureaucracy, is still a grand system where the individual is relegated to the background. Kierkegaard rejected the whole idea of social systems as the solution. He saw the need to focus on the individual's existence, and thus modern existentialism was born.

Life Meaning and the "Person"

Before we discuss the humanistic nature of entrepreneurs, it is important to understand the nature of "a person" from a philosophical perspective, and how entrepreneurial activity fits in to this discussion. Early and late Scholastic philosophers combined notions of substance, with certain characteristics that distinguished what a "person" was, such as rationality, completeness, separation from others, and subsistence. By the 15th and 16th centuries, with the rise of scientific rationality, increasing transoceanic exploration and international trade, and the impending social disruptions of the industrial revolution, new philosophical approaches were coming to the forefront. English political philosopher Thomas Hobbes (1588–1679), for example, saw a person as a semi-mechanical, natural being where a person's actions and behavior are ultimately guided by the various laws of physics, mechanics, chemistry, and biology. Kierkegaard, however, saw "man as spirit," that is, a spirited synthesis of conflicting and opposite tendencies.

But unlike Hegel, who would argue that there is a natural trend toward harmony in this conflict, Kierkegaard viewed a person as continuously in conflict, buffeted by powerful and conflicting emotions, feelings, and tendencies until death. And the problem of personal conflict may be getting worse over time. Existential philosopher and social critic Gabriel Marcel, for example, argues that as civilization evolves into the modern world, it becomes even more broken due to the "misplacement of the idea of function"[4]. To Marcel, in the modern world, increasingly fewer individuals really seek out a true understanding of their existence, preferring rather to live in a world of existential denial and consumerism, blinded by technological colored lens, government promises of life-long security, and a willful denial taught in our schools and universities of what it really means to be human.

In most existential thinking, a synthesis can occur only by "human will." But individuals need to understand that human will is always incapable of fully eliminating these conflicts. It is only through a process of "positive synthesis" that a person can understand, and tenuously hold together their life — this is human will in its basic form. But this requires conscious choices, and a continuous process of individual either/or decisions. Thus, unlike animals and plants, an individual human is fundamentally a non-settled being, an entity of conflicts. And when conscious of this conflicted existence, it ultimately becomes the source of Kierkegaard's "fear and trembling" grounded in the anxiety of human decisions. Anxiety, within this context of understanding a person's humaneness, is therefore completely natural, and should not be confused with "pathological anxiety" or depression.

The anxiety that Kierkegaard discusses is a deep and natural emotion that stems from the realization of existence, and what this existence entails — actionable decisions given conflicting tendencies and positions. Marcel uses similar terminology and discusses the inevitable personal despair of living in the modern world. Sartre provides an even more vivid, and less positive imagery, calling it "nausea." It should be noted, however that for Kierkegaard and other more "positive" existentialists, the idea of "anxiety" derives more from the existential realization of the inevitable conflicts and decisions of humaneness, while the "nausea" of Sartre stems primarily from the realization of life's meaninglessness.

Understanding and managing existential anxiety through "positive synthesis" is what creates true human development at the individual level. Thus, anxiety is a necessary condition of being human, or as Kierkegaard notes, "Flee from anxiety he cannot, for he loves it; really love it he cannot, for he flees from it."[5]

While different existential philosophers offer different solutions and perspectives, they tend to all share the foundational position that true humaneness comes from this realization of conflicted existence, the resulting powerful emotions of anxiety, fear and despair, and the need of an individual to work within these conflicts. But almost all existential philosophers, from Kierkegaard to Marcel to Heidegger to Sartre, recognize that the vast majority of humanity either by choice or ignorance, do not ever realize this conflicted nature of human existence — they "flee from it." This ignorance ultimately results in the false virtue of bureaucracy, an institutional arrangement that organizes the lemminglike behaviors of the "busy men of affairs."

Jean-Paul Sartre was particularly interested in people's effort to consistently overlook this fundamental responsibility of existence. For example, in discussing authenticity, individuality, and self-realization he emphasizes that ignoring the existential crises of even small decisions, is almost always the easiest path. In his classic 1943 treatise, *Being and Nothingness*, Sartre provides a classic analogy of the problem.

> Take the example of a woman who has consented to go out with a particular man for the first time. She knows very well the intentions which the man who is speaking to her cherishes regarding her. She knows also that it will be necessary sooner or later for her to make a decision. But she does not want to realize the urgency ... But then suppose he takes her hand. This act of her companion risks changing the situation by calling for an immediate decision. To leave the hand there is to consent in herself to flirt, to engage herself. To withdraw it is to break the troubled and unstable harmony which gives the hour its charm. The aim is to postpone the moment of decision as long as possible. We know what happens next: the young woman leaves her hand there, but she *does not notice* that she is leaving it. She does not notice because it happens by chance that she is at this moment all intellect. She draws her companion up to the most lofty regions of sentimental speculation; she speaks of Life, of her life, she shows herself in her essential aspect — a personality, a consciousness. And during this time the divorce of the body from

the soul is accomplished; the hand rests inert between the warm hands of her companion — neither consenting nor resisting — a thing.

We shall say that this woman is in bad faith. But we see immediately that she uses various procedures in order to maintain herself in this bad faith.[6]

In this quote, "bad faith" becomes the means to escape responsibility, and ultimately the freedom that is inherent in each individual's life. To Sartre, bad faith is a form of lying, and is the opposite of human freedom. Individuals acting in bad faith not only take the easiest path of non-decisions, of postponing hard decisions by lying to themselves, but they also start to believe that these lies are true. While not examining the philosophical implications, researchers in behavioral economics have also recognized the same phenomena of taking the easiest path in decision making. This is often called "default choice," resulting in a human tendency toward a long-run "default-bias" of taking the easiest path in life's decisions. In existential thinking, bad faith, the conscious or even unconscious effort, or inability to understand the deep context of decisions, is the opposite of human freedom. But this is the path for the vast majority of people in the world.

The Entrepreneur as an Existential Being

The argument in this essay is that the entrepreneur, by the very actions of being entrepreneurial, is forced into a world of decisions and anxiety, and thus becomes intimately aware of him/herself as an "existential being." An entrepreneur consciously accepts inordinate risk, an entrepreneur regularly self-reflects, and most importantly, recognizes the need to constantly "pivot," or to use Kierkegaard's phraseology, "move from the spot." Unlike the employed clerk or "busy man of affairs" who commutes, then labors 8 am to 5 pm in a world of a well-defined set of responsibilities only to return the next day under the same regimen, the independent tradesman and entrepreneur is constantly being reminded they are human, that their life is a series of small and large choices that take on a real sense of importance and cannot be avoided like Sartre's hand-holding analogy. These decisions have true impacts on their lives. Entrepreneurs can certainly make poor decisions, but simply by making decisions, they avoid the bad faith process of doing nothing. One might argue that at least for economic issues, entrepreneurs are constantly forced out of a bad-faith dilemma because they are dealing with a continuous flow of decision points; the entrepreneur can't escape into the world of default-bias.

Almost by definition, the entrepreneur realizes this particular focus of existence, a professional life built upon choices. Thus, the entrepreneur is acutely aware of the existential predicament in life, and Kierkegaard's phrase, "I exist, therefore I think" makes perfect sense. This represents a free being more in control of one's life, of deciding who they want to be on an almost constant basis — the root of a person's humaneness from a phenomenological point of view.[7]

Existential thinking underlines the idea that human life is a process of conflicts, made up of decisions and solutions that often appear incompatible. Within this context, an existential approach to understanding entrepreneurial humaneness is possible. The entrepreneur, particularly in early stages of the ventures, has the potential to become a true existential being. Kierkegaard noted that humans, in consciously realizing the choices they constantly make, have the ability to live a fully human life rooted in the personal search for values. The human act of committing oneself to creation imbeds humaneness in a new venture. Entrepreneurs cannot hide from making decisions.

It is this apparent contradiction that drives many entrepreneurs. How often are entrepreneurs asked by their non-entrepreneurial friends, "Why do you do this, why suffer the risk, and work so hard — why not get a salaried job — or better yet, work in a safe government job?" Contradiction of all forms, in their social, family, and economic life, is inherent in the entrepreneur's world. But we argue that entrepreneurship, in its raw form, is in fact, a human's personal journey toward freedom. This idea echoes both Martin Heidegger (1889–1976) and Karl Jaspers (1883–1969) in their views of the human condition, the will to find meaning in life. This does not, of course, imply that non-entrepreneurs cannot find humaneness in an existential manner, but rather that entrepreneurs, minute by minute, during their daily processes of economic and personal life are closer to realizing the existential life, that basic foundation of true humaneness.

One legitimate question is whether existentially inclined individuals are more likely to seek out an entrepreneurial life, or does the life of an entrepreneur, filled with intimate points of conflict push individuals into a more existential perspective. This in itself is an interesting question, and somewhat similar in nature to the debate as to whether entrepreneurs are born or created. The major difference, however, is that existential thinking is not inherited, but rather a process of insight, reflection, and discipline.

Entrepreneurship as a Form of Existential Therapy

If we develop the second perspective, that entrepreneurial activity pushes the individual into a more existential oriented existence, then entrepreneurial behavior becomes a form of self-directed "existential therapy" as developed by Rollo May (1909–1994) and Viktor Frankl (1905–1997). It recognizes the inherent conflict of entrepreneurial actions while holistically applauding its aspirations, and consciously recognizing its obvious limitations and dangers. Entrepreneurship, by the actions of being entrepreneurial in the classic sense, thus becomes a process of "healing through meaning."

Viktor Frankl (1905–1997) is a particularly important figure in understanding this perspective. Frankl was Jewish, born and raised in pre-World War II Germany. Like all psychology students of the time, he studied Sigmund Freud's approach to therapy. But Frankl ultimately saw the limits of the Freudian perspective. He started a promising career as a psychoanalyst, receiving his M.D. and Ph.D. from the University of Vienna. In 1942 Frankl, along with his family, was arrested by the Nazis. For three years he was confined to the worst of the concentration camps, Auschwitz and Dachau, where his pregnant wife, brother, and parents all perished. This experience forever changed Frankl's perspective on human development. After his liberation he published the seminal work, *Man's Search for Meaning* in 1946.[8]

His experiences in the concentration camps confirmed Frankl's idea that the true meaning life should be viewed under the lens of existentialism. Frankl, along with Rollo May, are considered the founding fathers, and driving forces behind "existential psychiatry."[9] To Frankl, most humans live in an existential vacuum, an "inner void" of lost life meanings which has been increasing in all societies into the modern world. He notes that, boredom and apathy are the main manifestations of existential vacuum, and argues that education, which used to provide a sense of meaning to life and has now become simply a reductionist process that leads to increasing feelings of "emptiness and meaninglessness."[10] To Frankl, the meaning in life cannot be discovered in simply the perspective of "being in the world," a common perspective of pop culture and liberal mentality, but rather ultimately discovered by a difficult and conscious combination of (a) doing deeds/creating works (being productive), (b) experiencing something important, and (c) the attitude one takes toward unavoidable suffering that this involves. This three-step process is also clearly echoed in Aleksandr Solzhenitsyn's writings of surviving the Soviet gulags.[11]

It is this combination of purposeful action that results in a form of healing through meaning. Humans cannot always avoid suffering, but the key is how we deal with it. In combination, this path to finding existential meaning, and thus humaneness, appears both naturally and regularly to self-aware entrepreneurs in their normal work activities of founding and managing new ventures.

In this respect, the sequence of large and small decisions an entrepreneur must consciously progress through — building the business model, raising funds, creating an organization, managing suppliers, commercializing the product or service, combined with the anxieties of constantly being reminded of rejections and failures, the stress of meeting payrolls and bills, the need to continuously "pivot" given competitive changes, all at the same time balancing family and social obligations — provides a clear platform for existential thinking. And the entrepreneur does all this, with a constant self-analysis at the end of the day of "why," but then ultimately pushes ahead to the next day. This entrepreneurial development model fits nicely within Frankl's general model of logotherapy, of developing a series of creations/deeds and experiencing something important, while maintaining an overall positive life view of the conflicts inherent in the entrepreneurial experience.

The first two stages of Frankl's existential therapy, doing deeds/creating works and experiencing something important, are generally part of any true entrepreneurial experience. The third stage — the attitude we take toward unavoidable suffering — needs further analysis. As Frankl points out, "Facts are not fate. What matters is the stand we take toward them"[12] For the existential *nihilist*, the ability to personally manage the existential crises is somewhat limited — a conclusion that led Nietzsche, Heidegger, and others to appeal to the notion of exuberant will power, and ultimately to the idea of super leaders — an orientation that can lead to dictatorships such as Hitler and Stalin. While never able to clearly define how to manage these conflicts, Sartre did recognize that action, in the form of being "fully committed and willing to take risks" appears to help.[13]

However, other existentialists, such as Frankl, Kierkegaard, Tilloch and Marcel offer a more positive approach that fits better with the entrepreneurial experience. Kierkegaard, for example, discusses the notion of positive synthesis as the behavioral and intellectual component to manage personal existential conflicts. Positive synthesis involves several components. The first component can be described as the "positing of self," or the clear recognition of the existential issues involved in being human.[14]

The second component involves the notion of "earnestness." Kierkegaard calls this process "inwardness," or the idea of attentive care deeply focused on the inner self — the wanting to do something. Earnestness is also part of "passion," and to Kierkegaard the power of "passion" is critical. As Earle notes, "the problem of man is not to think about existence, rather, *thinkingly, to exist*, and we do not exist insofar as we reflect but rather insofar as we live passionately"[15] Navigating life in a person's subjective existence is rooted in the notion of "passion."

And third component, is the "determination of the will," the constant attention to the problem. This determination of will moves a person into the "ethical" realm. As Gupta writes, truth is action oriented, "truth in something to be attained, actualized, lived."[16] Likewise, Marcel discusses the importance of "hope" as a mechanism for overcoming existential despair. To Marcel, however, "hope" is not passive or occasional, but rather an active process of continuous assertion that ultimately stems from humility.[17]

Frankl, as a psychotherapist, put the personal management problem into a more practical setting. Drawing from his experience of surviving the horrors of the Nazi concentration camps, Frankl argues that while people need to recognize the deeply conflicted nature of living, the key lies in the action of creating something important combined with positive adaption to suffering. This adaptation must come from seeing a meaning in life. But to Frankl, like any existentialist, this is not a "pop" solution. He notes, "life itself means being questioned ... life no longer appears to us as a given, but as something that is given over to us; it is a task in every moment. This therefore means that it can only become more meaningful, the more difficult it is."[18]

This is the unique advantage of the entrepreneur. Not only is entrepreneurial life conflicted at many different levels, but for most true entrepreneurs, it is a difficult life, and thus, as Frankl argues, a more meaningful life. It is Kierkegaard's earnestness and determination of the will, combined with Frankl's increasing difficulty, that creates meaning in this life of conflicts, despair, and anxiety.

As mentioned above, the notion of passion is a concept key to "positive synthesis." In his 1843 book, *Fear and Trembling*, Kierkegaard writes that passion is "the genuinely human quality."[19] Passion is not an emotion, but a deep actionable desire, that combines earnestness and understanding. It drives the notion of "inwardness" and allows a positive synthesis of human existence. In fact, in developing his concept of "passion," Kierkegaard was influenced by Plato's discussion of Eros in the *Symposium* — it is, thus, a powerful desire. Passion becomes that desire that allows us to overcome the despair, anxiety and conflicts that stem from an existential understanding of life. It is the actionable desire that binds the individual to life itself. It is perhaps no coincidence that in the entrepreneurship literature there is much discussion about the notion of "entrepreneurial passion" as a driving force behind successful entrepreneurs. Entrepreneurial passion is more than simply will power to accomplish tasks, but something deeper. Entrepreneurial passion represents the "positive feelings and attitudes for activities that are crucial to the self-identity of the individual."[20] It therefore speaks to the same desire that Kierkegaard discusses — the desire to overcome difficulties and push forward, but with a sense of life-meaning embedded into this desire.[21]

Frankl often uses analogies, such as a rock climber who, while keenly aware of the increasing danger, continues with earnestness and determination. Such is the true entrepreneur. But in this respect, we are talking about entrepreneurship in the classic Schumpeterian sense, that is, individuals who are the dynamic agents of change; those individuals who take risks, show ingenuity, and exhibit incredible perseverance and diligence to periodically disrupt the conventional ways of doing business, even on a small scale.[22] For these types of individuals, their entrepreneurial activities seem not only productive in nature, but also truly existential in character in comparison to the "busy men of affairs" who diligently go about their mundane, predictable lives. Unfortunately, entrepreneurship has also been associated with the hustlers, and those driven by the quick exit — for these individuals, there is nothing truly existential in character; and one cannot find life-meanings in its activities. But it is a fine line of distinction. Canadian philosopher Charles Taylor, for example, argues that a focus on individual subjectivism, whether in business, politics, relationships, and social life, has also led to the modern "culture of narcissism."[23] It is certainly this culture of narcissism which perhaps best defines the hustlers, wheeler-dealers, exit kings, and fast buck artists (and the educators that promote this behavior), that often work around the coattails of true entrepreneurship.

While we have so far argued that by its very nature, true entrepreneurial activity offers the individual great potential for becoming an existential being in its most classical definition, there still is the question of humanism. To what extent does existential thinking lead to humanistic thinking? That question is the focus of the next section.

The Existential Path to Humane Entrepreneurship

Existentialism, by its very nature is a "subjectivist" philosophy, it focuses on the individual, the nature of personal existence, and how to address the despair, fear, and anxiety that arises from this realization. But most philosophical systems, and resulting political/social institutions, throughout history, whether Socratic, Aristotelian, Hegelian, or Marxist, are objectivist in nature. Systems thinking, in fact, demands this objectivist perspective, even when applied to people, communities, and societies. In the objectivist tradition, when everything thing has an objective value, and humans are purely mechanical entities and biological cogs in the system, the relationship of the individuals to society is a rather obvious process — the community is simply larger and more important that the individual. The group, therefore, ultimately determines the individual. In this context, individual humanism is simply doing what is best for the larger community — the worker bee and the hive. Within this objectivist perspective, humanism is the overlaying of moral laws and behaviors onto the individuals, that individuals need to always behave in a way that betters the community. The problem becomes then, what are the right moral laws? Not surprisingly, throughout history, objectivist thinking has often led to arguments that appear repulsive in hindsight — development of slavery to support economic growth, infanticide when environmental carrying capacity is reached, the death squads of Pol Pot's Khmer Rouge regime in Cambodia, the communist run gulags for political dissenters, and the concentration/work camps for Jews, Christians, and ethnic groups who were fundamentally at odds with the Nazi "national socialism" objectivist perspectives.

In the objectivist perspective, similar to a beehive in its most extreme form, the community good is always more important than the individual good, so the debate will always be about the appropriate natural laws and moral imperatives that individuals and institutions must live under.[24] In the business literature, this perspective has resulted in the idea that corporate social responsibility (CSR) and utilitarian ethical concepts are simply overlaid as a moral imperative on entrepreneurs and relabeled as "humane entrepreneurship." In fact, with only a few exceptions, all published "humane entrepreneurship" papers have assumed this objectivist approach with its overarching CSR perspective. But as we have discussed above, this objectivist perspective ultimately strips away the human existence part of humanity and makes it hard to argue there is anything unique about entrepreneurs, or that humane entrepreneurship has any special meaning.

On the surface one might argue that existentialism, by definition, focuses on the individual while humanism has a broader orientation. But existentialism, particularly as presented by the more positive approaches of Kierkegaard, Marcel, Tilloch, Frankl and others, is actually a philosophy of human development, and ultimately one of humanistic tendencies. We can explore the humanistic nature of entrepreneurial action under the lens of existentialism in several ways.

First is the sense of the subjective individual as part of a broader community. As John Wild argues, "If human existence is no longer conceived as being contained within objective substances but dynamically understood as being stretched out into a field of action, the whole question of the relation of the individual to the group appears in a new light."[25] An individual that deeply understands the conflicting nature of his or her existence, and has successfully, through earnest passion, addressed the consequences of the natural anxiety that stems from this realization, has ultimately developed as a human. This developed individual has, in fact, achieved a "meaning in life" and freedom that uniquely separates them from the drone-like behavior of "busy men of affairs."

Second, as we have argued, true entrepreneurial action is actually a form of self-directed existential therapy, a self-induced Frankl-like "logotherapy" with its roots in the world of difficult and conflicting personal economic decisions. Entrepreneurial action creates the conditions for human realization in the most classic existential sense. In this sense, the entrepreneur has moved toward the side of existential "freedom." But freedom involves enlightened choices, choices to assist and help those about, that are, in fact, part of community — but for the existential being, these choices stem from enlightened freedom of truly understanding the nature of humanity. This is the fundamental difference of subjectivist entrepreneurial humanism versus the persistent overlaying of moral rules (as generally defined by the community bureaucracy, ruling dictator, or Royal governor) of objectivist humanism. According to our argument, the humanistic entrepreneur is fundamentally different from the "busy men of affairs," who as part of their mundane life of bourgeois rules and feel they must contribute to charity because somebody says they should. Rather the existentially oriented entrepreneur's humanism is deeply grounded in the notion of freedom, and a clear understanding of the human condition — this is what leads to humanistic action.

In his *Sickness Unto Death*, Kierkegaard noted that a physician typically has a clearer view of sickness that is different from that of the patient, "Because the physician has a definite and developed conception of what it is to be healthy and ascertains a person's condition accordingly."[26] Arnold Come, in his 1995 book, *Kierkegaard as Humanist* emphasizes this point — that understanding the self is ultimately an act of humanism.[27] This is a key issue for our argument about the unique nature of entrepreneurs, and their relationship to humanistic orientation.

Because existentialist philosophers take a subjectivist perspective, with a focus on the individuals, they are not generally considered "moral philosophers," since moral philosophy requires a more objectivist perspective of community systems, and the ultimate overlaying to systemic rules of behaviors. But not considering existentialists as moral philosophers is a mistaken point of view. As several Kierkegaard scholars have noted,[28] to the existentialist such as Kierkegaard, a moral perspective stems from individual freedom and a true understanding of what being human is all about — this results in a better understanding of both individual action in a community, and a relational point of view of the community. Thus, a person who understanding the existential nature of being does not ignore moral rules and standards, but rather the objectivist set of moral philosophies, and their resulting moral codes of behavior, whether secular or religious, is understood from a position of true individual human freedom. It is this sense that can provide a balance against the evilness of bureaucracies, hustlers, and dictators. And in this sense, the entrepreneur has the capability of becoming a truly humane player within the modern, impersonal economy.

Concluding Thoughts

This essay argues that entrepreneurs are, indeed, unique — not because of any personality, social or economic differences that are discussed in modern entrepreneurship textbooks and academic articles, but rather from a much deeper philosophical perspective. Entrepreneurial action, by its very nature, becomes a form of self-directed "existential therapy;" it forces the individual to understand that human activity is, in fact, a life of conflicts and decisions. It is a life sometimes filled with dread, anxiety, and despair. It is a life of business, financial and family decisions, it is a life of constantly "pivoting" one's perspective, and it ultimately is a life of interior reflection. But successful entrepreneurs can navigate this realization of the human condition, through Kierkegaardian-like passion, earnestness, and positive synthesis. This is the path of existential understanding, the path to better understanding life's meaning, and ultimately to personal freedom.

It is this character that makes the entrepreneur unique, versus the world of "busy men of affairs." This is what pushes entrepreneurs toward the path of existential being. This is also what makes entrepreneurs humanistic. One cannot be humanistic, or talk about entrepreneurial humanism, without first understanding the human condition from a sub-jectivist, existential point of view. To the true entrepreneur, humanism stems from freedom, a freedom of truly understanding what it is to be human, and a freedom to then understand true human relationships.

This essay is not meant to suggest that non-entrepreneurs are excluded from an existential understanding of their humanness. Nor does it imply that all entrepreneurs have found a true "meaning in life" from an existential perspective. What is does argue, however, is that unlike other professions, the very nature of true entrepreneurial activity lends itself to the conditions that many existential philosophers, such as Søren Kierkegaard, Martin Heidegger, Gabriel Marcel, John Wild, and Paul Tilloch argue are necessary to human understanding. Entrepreneurial activity is, we argue, a form of existential therapy to use Viktor Frankl's perspective — it helps.

Finally, we certainly recognize that the writings in existential philosophy are deep and immensely complicated. We also recognize that all existentially oriented philosophers have their own perspective, often in conflict with each other. What we have tried to do in this essay is simply suggest the basic foundation of existential thinking and apply these basic concepts to the problem of entrepreneurship and humanism.

Endnotes

1. While this dichotomy is often debated, in general the distinctions between objectivism and subjectivism approaches to philosophy still exists. See for example, J. Dewey, "The Objectivism-Subjectivism of Modern Philosophy," *The Journal of Philosophy* 38, no. 20 (1941), 533–542 and J. Wild, "Existentialism as a Philosophy," *The Journal of Philosophy* 57, no 2 (1960), 45–62.
2. Almost all existential philosophers and writers come from either a Christian/Jewish perspective, or a non-theistic orientation. There are a few Arab writers (e.g., Abdur Rahman Badawi, 1917–2002) that could be considered existential

in nature, but very few from other religious backgrounds. A discussion of the reasons behind this is beyond this essay, but in general the differences tend to focus on the nature of "will" that is required to overcome the existential realization of humanity and create a sense of "meaning in one's life."

3. S. Kierkegaard, *Either/Or, Part I,* transl. E. Hong and H. Hong (Princeton, NJ: Princeton University Press, 1992), 24. Original work published 1843.
4. See G. Marcel, *The Mystery of Being,* Vol. 2, *Faith and Reality.* transl. R. Hague (London: The Harvill Press, 1951), 36–37. Original lectures given in 1949 and 1950.
5. S. Kierkegaard, *The Concept of Anxiety,* transl. A. Hannay (New York, NY: Liveright, 2014). Original work published 1844.
6. J, Sartre, *Being and Nothingness: A Phenomenological Essay on Ontology* (London: Taylor & Francis, 1956). Part One, Ch. Two, 55–56. Original work published 1943.
7. For a more phenomenological perspective of Kierkegaard writings see J. Mullen, *Kierkegaard's Philosophy: Self-Deception and Cowardice in the Present Age* (New York, NY: Times Mirror, 1981).
8. V. Frankl, *Yes to Life: In Spite of Everything* (Boston, MA: Beacon Press Books, 2020). Original work published 1946.
9. Frankl originally titled his approach to psychotherapy "logotherapy". As an alternate name, in the 1930s Frankl offered an alternate title of *Existenzanalyse,* which later authors translated to "existential analysis" in English. Frankl clearly preferred the term, "logotherapy."
10. V. Frankl, *The Will to Meaning* (New York, NY: World Publishing Company, 1969), 61–63.
11. In his personal memories of surviving the Soviet Communist forced labor camps, or gulags, Solzhenitsyn describes an emotional process similar to that suggested by Frankl. See A. Solzhenitsyn, *The Gulag Archipelago* (New York, NY: Harper & Row, 1973) and other writings by Solzhenitsyn.
12. Frankl *The Will to Meaning,* 105.
13. For a further discussion of this point, see H. Fisher, "Jean Paul Sartre's Existentialism as Answer to Existential Crises," *Πoιειν Kαι Πpαττειν — Create and Do.* http://poieinkaiprattein.org/philosophy/jean-paul-sartres-existentialism-as-answer-to-existential-crisis-by-hatto-fischer/. Accessed August 30, 2022.
14. As a devout Christian, Kierkegaard certainly saw the relationship between God and the individuals as part of the positive synthesis process. Likewise, Frankl also articulated the role of spirituality in managing these existential conflicts.
15. See W. Earle, "Phenomenology and Existentialism," *The Journal of Philosophy* 57, no. 2 (1960), 75–84.
16. A. Gupta, *Kierkegaard's Romantic Legacy: Two Theories of the Self* (Ottawa, Canada: University of Ottawa Press, 2005), Ch. 5.2, 19.

17. See G. Marcel, *The Philosophy of Existentialism,* transl. M. Harari (Citadel: New York, 1995), 27–32.
18. Frankl, *The Will to Meaning,* 49.
19. S. Kierkegaard, *Fear and Trembling,* transl. E. Hong and H. Hong (Princeton, NJ: Princeton University Press, 1983). Original work published 1843.
20. For this definition that links entrepreneurial passion to a self-identity see A. Huyghe, A., M. Knockaert, and M. Obschonka, "Unraveling the 'Passion Orchestra' in Academia," *Journal of Business Venturing* 31 (2016), 344–364.
21. To Kierkegaard the notion of "passion" is closely linked to Christian faith and love. Frankl, Tilloch, and many others also see this notion of willpower and passion linked to spiritual belief. However, for this essay we consider the actionable desire with a sense of life's meaning to be the key issue that ties this concept to entrepreneurship.
22. This relationship is discussed in J. Schumpeter, *Capitalism, Socialism and Democracy* (New York, NY: Harper & Row, 1942).
23. Charles Taylor writes extensively about the issues of" modernity". See C. Taylor, *The Explanation of Behaviour* (London: Routledge Kegan Paul, 1964) and C. Taylor, *The Malaise of Modernity* (Concord, Ontario: House of Anansi Press, 1991).
24. John Wild discusses in detail the contrast between the more common objectivist thinking in Western philosophical traditions and the more subjectivist thinking of existentialism, and how these overlaps with both modern phenomenological thinking and new methods of behavioral analysis. For example, "utilitarian" approaches to understanding ethics tends to be an objectivist perspective. It is interesting to note, that most of what is promoted in business ethics and corporate social responsibility (CSR) discussions tend to be grounded in an objectivist, "utilitarian" approach. This essay takes a completely different perspective. See J. Wild, "Existentialism as a Philosophy," *The Journal of Philosophy* 57, no. 2 (1960), 45–62.
25. *Ibid,* 57.
26. S. Kierkegaard, *The Sickness Unto Death,* transl. A. Hannay (New York, NY: Penguin Random House, 1989), 159. Original work published 1849.
27. See A. Come, *Kierkegaard as Humanist: Discovering Myself* (Montreal, Canada: McGill-Queen's University Press, 1995).
28. See R. Roberts, "Kierkegaard and Ethical Theory," in *Ethics, Love, and Faith in Kierkegaard: Philosophical Engagements,* ed E. Mooney, (Bloomington, IN: Indiana University Press, 2008), 91–92 and specifically A. John, "Kierkegaard and Ethics," *Cetana: The Journal of Philosophy* I, no. I, 18–35.

9

Experience as Truth: The Phenomenology of Entrepreneurship

It can be argued that entrepreneurial activity, by its very nature, acts as a type of self-directed existential therapy. Simply by being entrepreneurial in the classic sense, an individual has the advantage of becoming more "existentially aware" of their "humanness" than individuals following other professions. There is, indeed, a certain uniqueness about the trials, tribulations, and anxieties embedded in true entrepreneurial decision making that makes it different from most professions, those of the "busy men of affairs" to use Kierkegaard's phrase. We suggest that there are other personal characteristics that are somewhat unique to entrepreneurs. These characteristics, while not directly existential in nature, are still important from a more phenomenological point of view since they fundamentally impact the manner in which an individual perceives the surrounding world.

The Natural Communion of Work and Property

For eons prior to the modern industrial age, in the natural order of society human work and human property were intertwined with each other, and almost synonymous with nature.[1] While intertwined, however, the notion of work and the notion of property had different composite and theoretical roots.

The 2nd and 3rd centuries pioneered a notion of property rights that was fundamentally new in the world, and not really evident in the prior Egyptian, Persian, Greek, or Roman periods. It is sometimes, albeit incorrectly, suggested that early Christian leaders and theologians were only interested in the moral aspects of humans and did not consider important economic issues of the time. Most economic historians, including even Joseph Schumpeter, tend to focus on the development of modern economic theory as starting in the 15th and 16th centuries, with the Catholic universities at Salamanca and Alcalá de Henares in Spain. Schumpeter, for example, in his 1954 *History of Economic Analysis* provided only a limited, single page analysis of the early medieval philosophers and theologians on this issue, noting almost casually that, "the Christian Church did not aim at social reform in any sense other than that of moral reform of individual behavior ... The How and Why of economic mechanisms were then of no interest either to its leaders or to its writers."[2]

But this argument appears to be in error.[3] In reality, the philosophers and theologians of the early Middle Ages were starting to develop a very new theoretical perspective of property rights, a perspective that would last almost 1,500 years. Early theologians and Church Fathers, such as Tertullian (c.155–c.240), Ambrose of Milan (c.340–c.397), John Chrysostom (347–407) and Augustine of Hippo (354–430) all discuss important and subtle issues related to both property and property rights. Much of these early discussions of property revolved around the concept of charity, and the obvious differences between the wealthy classes and poor, since early Christian communities had a radically different perspectives of assisting the poor and needy than the existent Imperial Roman culture. As Tertullian observed in *Ad Nationes* and other writings, Christian communities, from their foundational beginning, provided charitable assistance to their surrounding communities, and aggressively distributed funds to the poor and needy. Tertullian also notes that it was this charitable behavior that often incurred the wrath of the Roman elites. The reduction of poverty, the support of the poor, and the uniting of different economic classes became a central and well-established part of ethical thought and moral behavior by the 3rd and 4th centuries. To these writers, this idea of charitable activity between the wealthy and poor clearly had spiritual and moral overtones, at both the individual and institutional levels. However, charity, by definition, requires a transfer of property — one cannot give away or donate something that they do not rightfully own — thus the fundamental nature of property, and the issue of property rights, needed to be addressed.

But individual and institutional property rights to these early Church Fathers came with important individual and institutional responsibilities. In an often-referenced statement, Augustine of Hippo argues, "certainly what is lawfully possessed is not another's property, but 'lawfully' means justly and justly means rightfully. He who uses his wealth badly possess it wrongfully, and wrongful possession means that it is another's property." Most early medieval historians have argued that Hippo of Augustine, and other early medieval theologians and philosophers, saw private property and wealth differences as an inevitable function of a Fallen state, as a "non-natural, remedial institution" that can be corrected.[4] Within this context, the ownership of private property comes with a clear, active, and moral responsibility of proper use, whether in distributing property to the poor, or personally holding property as in a "trust" in order to perform dutiful, fulfilling and proper work for the ultimate benefit of society. Thus, property becomes a form of natural governance; and the proper use of property becomes synonymous with the right of property ownership.

Likewise, the importance of productive work, particularly physical work, was also starting to evolve significantly from the earlier Roman and Greek eras. In Roman and Greek cultures, occupations requiring physical labor, or employment in the trades, or work generally unbecoming a "gentleman" were considered "vulgar" to use Roman statesman Marcus Cicero's (105 BC–46 BC) terminology.[5] Cicero writes, "and all mechanics are engaged in vulgar trades; for no workshop can have anything liberal about it. Least respectable of all are those trades which cater for sensual pleasures, fishmongers, butchers, cooks, and poulters, and fishermen." The common notion of work, as articulated by Cicero and other Roman thinkers of the time, was that "commerce, trade, and manufacturing were deemed inferior" to diplomacy, administration, and the ownership of large, slave holding agricultural estates.[6]

But this philosophical notion of work started to change dramatically as the early Christian era established a foothold. Productive work, physical labor, and the trades began to take on a moral and even spiritual tone. For example, in the 4th century, Ambrose of Milan (339–397), writes, "Reward is not obtained by ease or by sleep. The sleeper does no work, ease brings no profit, but rather loss. Esau by taking his ease lost the blessing of the first-born, for he preferred to have food given to him rather than to seek it. Industrious Jacob found favour with each parent."[7] Koehler (2017) clearly shows that Schumpeter, and other economic historians are in error in this respect regarding the history of economic thought. By the early 6th century, Benedict of Nursia's (480–548) famous dictum, *ora et labora* ("*pray and work*") had firmly established the spiritual nature of work into the community-based way of life.

Herbert Applebaum, in his comprehensive review of Ancient and Medieval concepts of work, concludes that "a survey of attitudes toward work among Christians reveals some important changes, as compared with ancient Greeks and Romans ... The Greeks saw manual work as fit for those would could not afford the leisure for a good life, the Romans shared this view ... Christianity had a different view. Masters and slaves were both regarded as brothers, Idleness was considered an evil. Lowborn Christians attained high positions in the early Church, while highborn Christians did manual labor in the lowest occupations."[8]

This type of work activity requires using property, the instruments of production. Farmers, butchers, shoemakers, carpenters, stone masons, bakers, and cooks all require tools of the trade. Farmers needed their land, and tradesmen needed their shops of commerce. Thus, the two concepts of work and property had to be tied together in a natural union.

Later thinkers, such as St. Bonaventure (1221–1274), Roland of Cremona (1178–1259), and Thomas Aquinas Thomas Aquinas (1225–1274), refined this notion, and examined the characteristics of property ownership and work within the broader context of nature and natural law. The idea of property rights within a broad institutional framework, however, finally became codified by Pope John XXII (1244–1334) during a dispute involving the Franciscan Order founded by St. Francis of Assisi in 1209. The Franciscans strongly believed in extreme poverty, and the forsaking of all property ownership as a spiritual directive.[9] Not surprisingly, this position created important philosophical debates that needed to be resolved. Pope John XXII issued a number of Papal Bulls between 1322 and 1329, ostensibly in response to the Franciscan Order's' aversion to property ownership, whether by individuals or institutions. These Papal rulings clearly established property rights for all.[10] The broad arguments were primarily constructed upon the notion of natural law, that property is a natural and enduring component of humanity, and that property rights applied equally to rich and poor, to aristocracy and low-born — and civil law needed to respect this.

This underlying argument regarding natural law and property appears well founded. German philosopher Gabriel Biel (1420–1495), the "Humanism" writers of the 15th and 16th centuries, such as

Thomas More (1478–1535) and Erasmus (1466–1536), the Spanish thinkers of the 16th century's "School of Salamanca", such as Francisco de
Vitoria (1483–1546) and Francisco Suárez (1548–1617), and even writers
of the later "Age of Enlightenment", such as John Locke (1632–1704)
affirmed the moral stance that property ownership, property rights and
their relationship to productive work were part of "natural law."[11] While
European philosophy was certainly the most developed in understanding
natural law and its relationship to the idea of property, other cultures also
understood this important connection. For example, the concepts of
Istislah in Islam and *Dharma* in Hinduism probably comes closest to the
more Western natural law tradition.

Property within this context was viewed as something more than simply a social contract confirmed by civil authorities; rather it was an important component of the natural process of humanity. Property, in its right
use and governance, and applied appropriately to productive work,
become something naturally, deeply, and spiritually tied to individuals. It
is a right that is supported in both philosophical thought and civil law.
This relationship between work and property become to be seen as an
important part of what is most human, and what most clearly separates us
from animals, more so even than the ability to organize and work in
concert.

This union between work and individual property ownership can be
seen in the professions in medieval Europe. Early census records and
government documents, such as the *Liber Divisionis* of 1371 and the
English *Domesday Book* of 1086 indicated large percentages of the
working-class population in the trades.[12] Most commonly, these trades
were identified as garment/shoe making, merchants, preparation of food,
innkeeping, construction, barbers and outside the major urban areas, in
various agricultural activities. For the most part, the individuals in these
trades worked as small, family-owned businesses or work units. Given
there were no modern concept of property/casualty insurance or external
financing/private equity markets for small enterprises, these tradesmen
and merchants essentially internalized all market risks and financial
obligations. They needed to personally own the property, tools, and
instruments of their specialized trades.

While there was certainly hired employment in both urban and rural
environments during early and late medieval times, a large percentage
of employed "laborers" also owned their trade tools.[13] For example, agricultural "laborers" are often identified in census records as owning a "cart

and ox" Farm laborers owned their grain flails, axes, scythes, and shovels.[14] Even peasants, serfs and sharecroppers in medieval times still generally personally owned the trade tools, farm implements, and "beasts of burden" used in daily work even though they might actually live and work on the landlord's estate. In many cases throughout feudal Europe, the higher classes of agricultural serfs might even own small plots of land under various legal contracts with the feudal Lord.[15]

This understanding of the synergistic nature between work and property does not mean that medieval laborers were always a happy lot — many of the working and tradecraft populations survived at a bare subsistence level, and there were certainly instances of abuses by the aristocracy and feudal lords. But the philosophical relationship between work and property was still viewed as a natural relationship.

The modern analogy of this relationship might be carpenters and auto mechanics, who although they might work for a large building contractor or auto repair shop respectively, still own their own tools, take pride in the quality and care of these tools, and personally bring these tools to their work environment. Not surprisingly, these modern trade occupations are often paid as independent contractors for this reason. They are, in many respects, the modern version of "tradesmen" discussed in early economic treatises.

In this line of thought, humans are natural beings, and both property and productive work are natural processes of being human. Eternal law, natural law and civil law are not in conflict. Laborers have their trade tools; farmers have their land, beasts of burden, and farm instruments; artists have their clay, brushes, and paints; shoemakers have their leather working equipment, and the man and wife have their home and garden. Tied together in this way, work and property together becomes a primary form of natural human expression and growth. Property and work were viewed within the context of man's stewardship, as part of life itself. Based on these characteristics, economic historians have often called the medieval European economy a "natural economy" defined by the natural combination of work and property, local self-sufficiency, small markets, reliance on barter, and little money in the hands of the vast majority of the population.

But urbanization was starting to alter these relationships. In addition to the working classes, by the 1500s there was a substantial, and increasing percentage of the population, particularly in the rapidly expanding cities and trade centers, that were made-up of aristocracy, bureaucrats, clergy, educators, administrators, and courtiers. But many humanist writers of the time viewed these occupations suspiciously. For example, the character Hytholdaus in Thomas More's *Utopia* identifies these classes as unproductive professions and warns that a properly run system needs to aggressively limit the number of the unproductive occupations of bureaucracy, and that any necessary bureaucrats should regularly rotate to manual work.[16] Similarly, Erasmus saw private enterprise properly applied under Christian stewardship as productive, a natural combination of work and property — the problem was the corruption of the closed political and economic systems, with its inherent human greed and conflicts. As Mansfield notes, "In the *Institutio* and elsewhere [Erasmus] pictured cities built up and enriched by the enterprise and labors of private and productive citizens but then despoiled by rulers and their henchman".[17]

Fictitious Commodities and the Preeminence of Labor and Capital

These changes reached a milestone by the end of the 16th century. In their analyses of early European economic history, several historians note that although capitalism had been emerging in many industry sectors over the centuries, the process accelerated into the 16th century.[18] Gilbert, for example, identifies the industries of shipbuilding, international trade, printing, mining, agriculture, heavy manufacturing, textiles, and finance as essentially capitalist industries by the 16th century.[19] Throughout Europe, people were leaving the agricultural regions to seek work in the increasingly urbanized cities.

This process was accelerated, particularly in 17th and 18th century England and Scotland, and to a lesser extent in Germany, Spain, Italy, and France, by the agrarian reforms and "enclosure movements" designed to adapt the Feudal system to the onrushing wave of capitalism.[20] Countless thousands of farming families who had worked small plots of land as their own for centuries were dispossessed of their property, becoming simple laborers for the farming and herding enterprises of the landowners, or relocated to the larger population centers thereby expanding the pool of wage labor. The development of commercially efficient steam engines by Thomas Savery in 1698, Thomas Newcomen in 1712, and finally by James Watt, whose design was released commercially in 1774, sealed the transition of productive small-scale, family job-shop activities to large, urban factories — the Industrial Revolution had arrived in full force.

When economic life changes from a foundational "human" oriented endeavor to a system based on measured output, then the old order will ultimately break up and the new order of "capitalism" is born. As Schumpeter stated, "When the stream of productive revolutions sweeps away this world, and when man forgets the Holy Grail [i.e. the ideal of a human life as a pilgrimage from birth to death] and bethinks himself of his property, then this order breaks up like a corpse."[21] When measured output becomes the standard of value, then it is inevitable that the effort to increase output will look to the factors of production with the intent to measure them, to increase their quantity, and ultimately to increase their impact on output. Human productive work and human property are thus redefined as factor inputs, the capitalist commodities of labor and capital. Karl Marx says that this process of separation of humans from their work and the transformation of work into a commodity is the key step in the creation of a capitalist system, "What the capitalist system demanded was the transformation of the mass of the people into servile mercenaries, and the transformation of their means of labor into capital."[22] Schumpeter called this the "break up of community,"[23] and Marx called it an "epoch making revolution" where the masses were "torn from their means of subsistence."[24]

Capitalism in its basic form embodies the understanding that economic wealth is created by the productive application of capital to labor, and that growth in economic wealth requires ever new and increasingly productive applications of capital to labor. These beliefs are so widely embraced in modern societies, and universally taught in modern business schools, that we may have forgotten that their acceptance was actually slow in coming. As mentioned in a previous essay, the reluctance to accept these modern economic assertions can be illustrated by the story of Nassau Senior (1790–1864), an influential supporter and vocal advocate of Adam Smith's economic theories and the first professor of economics in the long, distinguished history of Oxford University. After his appointment as the Drummond Professor of Political Economy, Senior articulated these pro-capitalist assertions in his 1826 inaugural lecture before an audience of his fellow Oxford faculty members, a group of scholars and literary masters who would have been more at home with the humanist writings of the time, the social and economic commentary of Thomas More's *Utopia*, and the philosophical writings of Erasmus than with

Adam Smith. As Professor Senior continued with his lecture, it is recorded that the learned Oxford scholars "walked out one-by-one, leaving him [Senior] only with the Vice-Chancellor."[25]

The industrial age, however, was fundamentally changing this natural relationship between work and property, regardless of the opinions of Professor Senior's Oxford peers at the time. While the industrial revolution brought in a wave of technological advances, it also fundamentally altered the idea of economic commodities. With the advent of the industrial revolution, the world came to be presented with the highly institutionalized modern economic abstractions of labor and capital that we live in today.

Labor gradually became a commodity to be purchased and sold to the highest bidder at the local factories, landed estates, recruiting centers for armies, and civil administrations. More and more workers from rural environments migrated to the cities to find better paying employment in the rapidly expanding factory system. The final commoditization of work into labor — large-scale slavery — was almost inevitable.[26] At the same time, property was being defined more as "capital," and reorganized in various English, French and Dutch "charter" companies, essentially 16th and 17th century versions of investor supported stock companies and other modern corporate bodies.

The rise of labor and capital as the primary economic forces, during and after the Industrial Revolution, ultimately resulted in what economist Karl Polanyi (1886–1964) calls the birth of "fictitious commodities."[27] To Polanyi, throughout history, economic exchange was based upon products and services that were actually created for the purpose of exchange. Shoes, clothes, hats and bread and other trade goods are natural commodities, created for exchange and consumption. Farm crops are grown for exchange and consumption. However, the industrial revolution and capitalism ushered in three new commodities, land, labor, and capital, that were never meant to be commodities. These commodities of the modern age, Polanyi labeled "fictitious commodities," and as "fictitious commodities" the exchange of these commodities significantly undermines the self-regulating economic system that had developed around these "fictitious commodities." In *The Great Transformation*, Polanyi also discussed the idea of "substantivism," where economics actually has two meanings. The first is the rational model of modern neo-classical economics. The second, and perhaps a more important meaning, is the "substantive" meaning or how economic individuals interact with the society and nature that surrounds them.

While labeling the modern concepts of land, labor, and capital as "fictitious goods" may be accurate given both natural law and the history of pre-industrial economics, another important behavioral change was taking place that Polanyi and others generally overlook. From a phenomenological point of view, individuals started to perceive themselves differently. As more and more people started working in the great factories around the world, competing and selling their labor for wages, they naturally started to perceive themselves, and others around them, as just commodities rather than complex, productive, and spiritual humans operating in a natural world. From a phenomenological perspective, the conscious and unconscious mind was forever altered, and the historical "self-in-the-world" perspective was rapidly changing. Individuals were now being treated as commodities by both other individuals, and the broader socio-economic system in general. No longer was the world surrounding them "human centered" where work and property were somewhat synonymous in the natural order, rather individual time and labor become a commodity with a clear market price determined by the supply and demand conditions of the labor market. Ultimately the world was being viewed as nothing more than a grand dehumanized commodities exchange. This was the new human experience of value and worthiness.

Whole new societal institutions started to appear — labor unions, labor movements, labor parties, and governmental departments of labor — that further institutionalized, albeit perhaps with good intentions, the fictitious nature of the labor commodity. By the 19th century, a popular theme in fine art, sculpture, political cartoons, and public murals became labor, scenes of workers toiling in mass in factories, shipping docks, or vast agricultural estates.[28] Diego Rivera's murals commissioned by the Detroit Institute of Art and Edsel Ford in 1930s epitomizes this theme. Scientific management, with a focus on breaking labor activities into incremental movements, with the specific intention of reducing time in assembly operations, became the norm in early business schools.

The history of the labor movement is indicative of this change. In early medieval times, peasants and serfs tended to be viewed, and treated in a somewhat respected manner within Feudal society, as appropriate within the context of the spiritual nature of work. However, with the rampant inflation of the 13th century in Europe, the resulting devaluation of the coinage by various rulers, and the famines and plagues of the 14th century, the income gap between the working peasants and the rich nobility in Europe increased dramatically starting around 1450.[29] This resulted in an increasing number of peasant revolts. However, these peasant revolts were primarily instigated by regional food security issues, frustration at increased taxation, and as retaliatory acts against the abusive behavior of certain landed nobles.

The later labor movement, and the various labor upheavals, labor strikes and labor actions, on the other hand, were fundamentally different. These were based primarily upon the assumption of the fictitious commodities of wage labor, and ultimately centered around job safety and more importantly determining the fair market price of wage labor in conflict with employers. And in the extreme, the labor movement often became socialist or Marxist in nature, ultimately focused on a desire to internalize the other fictitious commodities of capital. In fact, one might argue that the abysmal failures of Marxist thought in actual practice is its underlying effort, as articulated in Karl Marx's *Das Kapital* and by subsequent Marxist thinkers, to glorify the fictitious commodities of labor — which can only be effectively managed on a large scale by bureaucracy and dictatorship — while vilifying the other false commodity of capital without recognizing that both are still fictitious commodities.

Capital was also becoming commoditized in several important ways. Money become much more available, sophisticated capital markets developed, and new institutions evolved to manage the availability, storage, and accounting of capital. The natural, symbiotic humanistic relationship between work and property was torn. This ultimately evolved into the commodification of other, previously human centered activities — education, culture, language, ethnicity, medicine, religion, and family. The phenomenological transformation of human experiences was complete in how a person perceives both themselves and others.

World "Experiences" and the Modern Entrepreneur

We argue, however, that entrepreneurship brings the person's work (skills, effort, and time) back into connection with the production process. Entrepreneurship in modern society is one of the few activities that breaks the mentality of fictitious commodities, and synergistically combines a person's work and property back into a natural relationship. This relationship has an important phenomenological implication. A dominant line of thought in phenomenology holds that the phenomenal character of a mental activity consists in a certain form of awareness of that activity, the experience itself creates a perception. Classical phenomenologists like

Edmund Husserl (1859–1938) and Maurice Merleau-Ponty (1908–1961) argue for a broad view of the phenomenal characteristics of experiences. Husserl, for example, talks extensively about the "lived-body," that a person sees the world as a field of sensing and experiences.[30] If individuals toil and live within the inhuman market and institutions of "fictitious" commodities on a daily, intimate basis this naturally will become their frame of world reference for their personal thoughts, actions, and behaviors.

A related argument is seen in the philosophy of language. A linguistic relativity argument, often called the "Sapir-Whorf" hypotheses, posits that the structure of a person's language largely determines, or at least affects, the speakers' perception of the world about them. A strong version of linguistic relativity, referred to as "linguistic determinism" argues that language fundamentally determines a person's perceptions and thought. The weaker version of linguistic relativity argues that language at least influences human perception and thought. Modern empirical research in cognitive linguistics appears to support, at least, the weaker version of linguistic relativity.

Under this framework, the language of modern economics actually influences people's perception of economic relationships. Teaching modern economics, finance, and business in terms of labor and capital factor inputs, with expansive and detailed lectures and case analyses of labor rate determination, the workings of labor and capital markets, the importance of scalability, and the continuous reliance on financial and accounting statements creates a language for students, corporate managers, the media, and government alike that makes these fictitious commodities seem very real. People then perceive, and ultimately treat, others in the world based upon the reality created by the language of these underlying fictitious commodities. This is perhaps one of the most serious, but least understood, issues of the modern world.

The actual entrepreneur, like the tradesman of old, however, personally produces a "non-fictitious" commodity, a real product or service that is specifically designed for the marketplace. An entrepreneur is not simply selling labor or capital as a commodity; rather the entrepreneur is creating a transformative value of inputs (physical and intellectual) in the traditional sense. In addition, the entrepreneur brings back the close relationship between property and work — entrepreneurs personally own the tools of their trade, even if it is a high technology, modern start-up. Entrepreneurs personally impart their work effort for the creation of value. And entrepreneurs have a financial stake, and thus the owner's capital is internalized and transformed into property. This relationship is particularly true for the tradesman and small entrepreneurial efforts that aren't obsessively driven by the world of entrepreneurial "jargon" such as quick scalability, valuation multiples, and exit strategies, but rather focus on value creation by the innovative application of work and property. In a sense, the entrepreneur brings back the natural symbiotic relationship between work and property. The language, world experiences, and ultimately world perceptions are still, to some extent, human based for the modern tradesman and small entrepreneur. This argument does not imply that the entrepreneur need not worry about finances, or the need to live in a world of labor and capital, but rather they understand the non-human context, institutions, and language of the world they live in.

Humanistic behavior has important psychological characteristics, a perspective that clearly emphasizes empathy. But it is difficult to express empathy in a world of fictitious commodities. Entrepreneurship in its core meaning, by definition, allows individuals to experience the human side of property and work, and thus, hopefully regain the lost world view of the symbiotic nature of human experience.

Endnotes

1. This thesis is developed in C. Stiles, C. Galbraith and O. Galbraith IV, "Thomas More's Utopia: Origins of Modern Images of Labor and Capital," *Journal of Markets and Morality* 22, no. 2 (2020), 281–303. For a discussion contrasting Jean Bodin and Karl Marx see G. Sabine, A *History of Political Theory*. (New York, NY: Holt, Rinehart and Winston, 1961).

2. J. Schumpeter, *History of Economic Analysis* (London, UK: George Allen & Unwin, 1954), 72.

3. See. B. Koehler, "The Economics of Property Rights in Early and Medieval Christianity," *Economic Affairs* 37, no. 1 (2017), 112–124. Koehler clearly shows that Schumpeter, and other economic historians are in error in this respect regarding the history of economic thought. Our discussion of this topic draws from this analysis.

4. For a discussion of how various Church Fathers of this era considered this issue see H. Dean, *The Political and Social Ideas of St. Augustine* (New York, NY: Columbia University Press, 1963); R. Dyson, *The Pilgrim City: Social and Political Ideas in the Writings of St. Augustine of Hippo* (Woodbridge, UK: Boydell Press, 2001) and D. MacQueen, "St. Augustine's

Concept of Property Ownership," *Recherches Agustiniencces,* 9 (1972), 187–228.

5. M. Cicero, *Cicero. De senectute, De amicitia, De divination,* transl. W. Heinemann (Cambridge, MA: Harvard University Press, 1938), Book 1: 42, 150–151.

6. See H. Applebaum, *The Concept of Work: Ancient, Medieval, and Modern* (Albany, NY: State University of New York Press, 1992), 95–96.

7. See Ambrose, *Some of the Principal Works of St. Ambrose,* transl. H. De Romestin (Oxford: J. Parker & Co, 1896), 471.

8. Applebaum, *The Concept of Work,* 193.

9. This Franciscan belief in non-property ownership is clearly seen in how the Franciscan missionaries in California developed the mission properties specifically as a "trust" for the native population that the native population would later inherit. This attitude was always made clear in the writings of the mission's friars; for example, as late as 1827 Frs. Zalvidea and Barona of Mission San Juan Capistrano wrote to the Governor Echeandia of California, "all these lands did and do now belong to the Indians (Letter, 12/22/1827). The notion of a land "trust" for the native population was supported under the laws of Spain as codified in the *Recopilacion de leyes de los Reynos de las Indias,* 1680. For a discussion of these issues see C. Galbraith, C. Stiles and J. Benitez-Galbraith, "Economics and Spirituality in the Entrepreneurial Development Strategy of the Franciscan California Missions: The Historical Case of San Diego," *Journal of San Diego History* 56, no. 4, (2010), 233–256.

10. *Ad conditorem canonum* (1322); *Quia quorundam* (1324); *Cum inter nonnullos* (1324), and *Quia vir reprobus* (1329). A good analysis of the development of medieval thought regarding the relationship between property rights and "natural law," given the "imperfections of mankind" are found in S. Swanson, "The Medieval Foundations of John Locke's Theory of Natural Rights: Rights of Subsistence and the Principle of Extreme Necessity," *History of Political Thought* 18, no. 3 (1997), 399–458; H. Chroust and R. Affedlt, "The Problem of Property According to St. Thomas Aquinas," *Marquette Law Review* 34, no. 3 (1951). 152–182; and P. Booth, "Property Rights and Conservation," *The Independent Review* 21, no. 3 (2017), 399–418.

11. A. Lustig, "Natural Law, Property and Justice: The General Justification of Property in John Locke," *The Journal of Religious Ethics* 19, no.1 (1991), 119–149.

12. See, for example, J. Rollo-Koster, "Mercator Florentinensis and Others: Immigration in Papal Avigno," in *Urban and Rural Communities in Medieval France: Provence and Lanquedoc, 1000–1500,* ed. K. Reyerson and J. Drendel(Brill: Leiden and Reyerson, 1998), 73–101.

13. In medieval times, there were certainly domestic serfs, who simply served in the households of the Lord — these were generally considered the lowest class of serfdom, see P. Boissonnade, *Life and Work in Medieval Europe* (Westport, CN: Greenwood Press, 1964).

14. These farm instruments, particularly the flail and axe, would many times become the weapons of the lower-class medieval foot soldier when called to war by their feudal masters.

15. For a good discussion of work, and role of serfs in Medieval Europe see R. Fossier, *Peasant Life in the Medieval West*, transl. J. Vale (Oxford: Blackwell, 1988) and G. Duby, *Rural Economy and Country Life in the Medieval West,* transl. C. Postan (Philadelphia, PA: University of Pennsylvania Press, 1998).

16. See Stiles *et al.* "Thomas More's Utopia."

17. B. Mansfield, "Erasmus and More: Exploring Vocations." in *A Companion to Thomas More* ed. A. Cousins and D. Grace, (Madison, WI: Fairleigh Dickinson University Press, 2009), 155.

18. See both D. Herlihy, "The Economy of Traditional Europe," *The Journal of Economic History* 31 no.1, 153–164 (1971) and W. Gilbert, *The Renaissance and the Reformation* (Lawrence, KS: Carrie, 1998). for good, detailed analyses of the economies in medieval Europe.

19. In his discussion of sixteenth-century economics, Gilbert, *The Renaissance,* defined capitalism as a system in which enterprises are not controlled by those who supply the labor.

20. Much has been written on both the enclosure movement in England, and the Highland Clearances in Scotland. Less has been written on similar movements in other countries. For a good discussion of the enclosure movement in France, see A. Rozental, "The Enclosure Movement in France," *The American Journal of Economics and Sociology* 16, no. 1 (1956), 55–71.

21. J. Schumpeter, "The Crises of the Tax State," in The Economics and Sociology of Capitalism, ed. R. Swedberg (Princeton, NJ: Princeton University Press, 1991), 109.

22. K. Marx, *Capital: Volume 1: A Critique of Political Economy,* transl. B. Fowkes and D. Fernbach (New York, NY: Penguin Publishing Group, 1976), 880–881. Original work published 1867.

23. Schumpeter, *Crises,* 109.

24. Marx, *Capital,* 876.

25. P. Oslington, "John Henry Newman, Nassau Senior, and the Separation of Political Economy from Theology in the Nineteenth Century," *History of Political Economy* 33, no. 4 (2001), 828.

26. Although both the Catholic Papacy and various Protestant factions continuously fought the idea of slavery, the Portuguese started large scale slavery from Africa in the early 1600s, just as the notion of labor as a commodity

was being institutionalized. In this essay, we have discussed "European" philosophical thought primarily from the dominant Christian and institutional European history, however much of Southern Spain (Iberia) was controlled by various Islamic rulers from their invasion and complete destruction of the existing Visigoth civilization in the 8th century. From this period, to the final Spanish "*Reconquista*" in the 15th century, slavery of Christians and other groups appeared common, which led to several revolts. In fact, the great Islamic palace and fortress (Alhambra) preserved in Granada, Spain was built primarily by thousands of Christian slaves, in a period of severe economic distress. See R. Irwin, *The Alhambra* (Cambridge, MA: Harvard University Press, 2011).

27. See K. Polanyi, *The Great Transformation: The Political and Economic Origins of Our Time* (Boston, MA: Beacon Press, 2001), Ch. 6, 71–80. Original work published 1944.
28. For a discussion of economically based themes in visual art see C. Galbraith and O. Galbraith, "Metaphors of Economic Activity in 19th and 20th Century Western Art," *International Journal of Management* 21, no. 1 (2004), 16–24. This study examined thousands of paintings and found that while labor themes were typically praised, themes related to capital, industry, and management were degraded or vilified.
29. For a discussion of the historic trends in income inequality, see G. Alfani and F. Ammannati, "Long-term Trends in Economic Inequality: The Case of the Florentine State, ca. 1300–1800," *Economic History Review* 70, no. 4 (2017), 1072–1102, and G. Alfani and T. Murphy, "Plague and Lethal Epidemics in the Pre-industrial World," *Journal of Economic History* 77, no. 1 (2017), 314–343.
30. See E. Husserl, *Ideas: A General Introduction to Pure Phenomenology,* transl. W. R. Boyce Gibson (New York: Collier Books, 1963). From the German original of 1913, originally titled *Ideas Pertaining to a Pure Phenomenology and to a Phenomenological Philosophy*, First Book. Newly translated with the full title by Fred Kersten. Dordrecht and Boston: Kluwer Academic Publishers, 1983. Known as *Ideas I*; and M. Merleau-Ponty, *Phenomenology of Perception,* transl. D. Landes (London and New York: Routledge, 2012. Original work published 1945.

10

The Meaning of an Entrepreneurial Pilgrimage

A quick search of the internet indicates that many entrepreneurs often refer to their entrepreneurial experiences as a sort of pilgrimage, a deep and somewhat mysterious adventure. As entrepreneur and blogger, Skip Walker, notes, "all of us who become entrepreneurs are joining the long tradition of the entrepreneurial pilgrimage."[1] The British consulting group, N[2] Accountancy correlates the entrepreneurial experience with walking the Camino de Santiago de Compostela (the Way of St. James) in France and Spain. They note that the Camino de Santiago de Compostela is "an ancient pilgrimage that draws on the same entrepreneurial skills of the modern businessperson and demonstrates entrepreneurial success in action."[2] While perhaps attempting to be somewhat poetic in description, the use of the term "pilgrimage" to describe the entrepreneurial experience actually underlines something much deeper about the nature of entrepreneurship. It separates in several important ways the entrepreneurial experience from other career choices and economic activity.

Pilgrimages in Time and Space

In this essay we explore the underlying nature of the term "pilgrimage" throughout history, and what it means at the personal level. A pilgrimage in the traditional sense is, in fact, something quite serious and represents an activity that is fundamentally different from other human activities. Pilgrimages, almost by definition, are meant to be extremely difficult and often deadly, but at the same time pilgrimages can lead to something immensely rewarding at the personal level. Pilgrimages are not the human equivalent of animal migrations and spawning events but are rather something uniquely human that requires a deeply personal commitment of time, effort, and thought. Nor are they simply "bucket list" vacation excursions or trips to medicinal hot springs. Instead pilgrimages are something somewhat spiritual in nature, an activity that elevates the human experience in a significant manner. And not all individuals who embark on a pilgrimage are able to complete the journey.

Pilgrimages also have a long tradition in history. In Ancient Greece we know of important pilgrimages to the main sanctuaries of Delphi, Epidauros, and Olympia, as well as the less well-known oracles of Didyma in Asia Minor and the Isthmus of Corinth.[3] The Roman empire had its pilgrimages. In Islam, it is expected that all able-bodied Muslims attempt the pilgrimage to Mecca and visit the Masjid al-Haram Mosque at least once in their lifetime. In Japan, a popular pilgrimage is the Kumano Kodō on the Kii Peninsula to the Kumano Sanzan temple complex. The Char Dham in India is widely revered by Hindus and takes pilgrims to four different sacred sites. In Buddhism, pilgrimages focus on Kapilavastu where Gautama Buddha began his life, Benares where he opened his sacred mission, and Kasinagara where he died. And to Christians there are historically hundreds of pilgrimage sites around the world.[4] Well-known pilgrimages are to travel the Camino de Santiago de Compostela in France and Spain, following St. Paul's trail in Turkey or St. Patrick's path in Ireland, and pilgrimages to the Basilica of Our Lady of Guadalupe in Mexico, the Church of the Holy Sepulchre in Jerusalem, the Metropolitan Cathedral of Iași in Romania, and the Seven Station Basilicas of Rome. While certainly representing different cultures and religions, pilgrimages share some important characteristics. And it is important that we understand these characteristics as they relate to the entrepreneurial pilgrimage experience, and ultimately the notion of humaneness.

To investigate the idea of the entrepreneurial journey as a pilgrimage, we will start by examining the nature of pilgrimages in the early medieval period, a time when pilgrimages were seen as a critically important function of human life. This was also the period when, from an economic perspective, human work and property were viewed as intertwined with nature and the entrepreneurial tradesman held a special position in economic theory. This was the period before the final creation and institutionalization of the fictitious commodities of labor and capital and the subsequent phenomenological impact of viewing humans as mere commodities within a larger, non-humane economic system. And this was a time when pilgrimages were time consuming, difficult and deeply meaningful, before they ultimately become thoroughly modernized as commodities themselves, to be taken as guided tours, while sleeping in Bed and Breakfast establishments, sipping café lattes, and purchasing trinkets in the gift shops of these sacred sites. It is certainly this earlier sense of pilgrimage that true entrepreneurs see most similar to their own personal economic journey.

Bishop Alexander, in 286, writes about his personal pilgrimage to the Holy Land. With the conversion of Constantine in 312, and his mother, Empress Helena Augusta's visit to Palestine and the surrounding areas in 326, pilgrimages to the Holy Land became much more frequent. Letters started to appear by the early 4th century, that read like personal travel diaries of the time, describing routes taken, sites visited, and people met during pilgrimages.[5] By the end of the 4th century, there is clear evidence of the importance of pilgrimages as seen in the writings of the influential Church leaders St. Chrysostom (347–407) and St. Jerome (347–420). A letter by St. Jerome in 386, for example, (in the name of Paula and Eustochium) to the Roman matron Marcella discusses the importance and customs of pilgrimages and urges individuals to take such journeys.

The invasion of Jerusalem, and the surrounding region, by Islamic armies in 638 made it increasingly difficult for pilgrims to venture into this region, and soon afterward other important pilgrimage sites developed throughout the world.[6] Thus, the nature of pilgrimages changed from a specific location to the broader issue of a pilgrimage experience — and this is the key for the present discussion, it is the experience that is most important. Pilgrimages became so important that they were discussed in medieval manuals. As John de Burg notes in 1385, "contra acediam, opera laboriosa bona ut sunt peregrinationes ad loca sancta," which loosely translates as "against laziness, laborious effort is good when travelling to holy places."[7]

Characteristics of a Pilgrimage

The word pilgrimage itself stems from the Latin word, *peregrinum* which represents the idea of wandering over a distance with an underlying purpose. We suggest that there are six key elements of a pilgrimage, and that these elements are also key to understanding the entrepreneurial experience at a personal level.

Condition 1. Purpose. There is a purpose to the experience at a personal level. Pilgrimages have a specific purpose, and inevitably they have a purpose of expanding a sense of a person's humaneness. This can be defined as a religious, or spiritual purpose depending on one's life orientation, but it is inevitably a sense of purpose to understand and appreciate the meaning of one's life. It is important to note that pilgrimages are not simply adventures. The word, "adventure" stems from the 12th century French root word, *aventure,* which means "happens by chance or accident." By the 14th century, the word adventure started to take on an additional element of "risk or danger", thus being presented as a novel or particularly exciting experience — which is essentially the current meaning of "adventure" within the modern world. Pilgrimages certainly have an adventure component embedded in the experience, but adventure is not the purpose of a true pilgrimage. One can achieve adventure by climbing mountains, white water rafting, or sky diving. To some, joining the military represents an adventure.[8] And many will walk the Camino de Santiago de Compostela as an "adventure" without experiencing the true nature of the pilgrimage. But true pilgrimages have a more important overriding purpose, a more existential purpose.

Condition 2. Difficulty. Pilgrimages are meant to be difficult, combining physical effort with mental effort. The physical hardship of a pilgrimage is by design. Within early medieval philosophy, there was an important spiritual component to the act of physical effort, particularly when that effort is productive in nature. In fact, early pilgrimages were often taken as a form of atonement, where the hardship associated with the pilgrimage was, itself, a sanctifying process. It takes passion, an absolute commitment by the individual to complete the pilgrimage. In medieval times, pilgrimages could also be dangerous, if not deadly, as pilgrimage routes were favorite spots for bandits, shysters, and in some routes, by invading armies. This creates a motivation, determination, and sense of purpose that often exceeds normal capabilities.

Condition 3. A Path of Decisions. Pilgrimages have a starting point and an ending point. But along the way, pilgrimages contain significant and important decision points. These decision points may be as simple as selecting what route to take, how to deal with bad weather on a mountainous path, or whether to form a joint venture with other pilgrims. Other decision points may be more significant, such as how to deal with injury and sickness, and ultimately whether to simply quit.

Condition 4. High Sensory Experience. Pilgrimages are sensory experiences; they involve a multi-sensory involvement of the locations visited and traveled through. Pilgrims eat, drink, rest and sing along the way. They walk, rest, and sleep on the route. Pilgrims typically view some of the most beautiful scenery in the world as they hike over mountain paths, navigate lakes and rivers, and cross natural obstacles. They immerse themselves into the architecture, artifacts, and art of the different towns, shrines, monasteries, and museums along the pilgrimage route. Research examining the artistic depictions of pilgrimages, in paintings, tapestries, and stained glass, underlines the sensory nature of pilgrimages. Human senses become an important fabric of a pilgrimage.[9] Early pilgrimages were not only multi-sensory in nature, but highly corporeal. Pilgrims expected to not only view various holy relics, but also encouraged to touch them. When analyzing the stain glass panes at the tomb of St. William in York, art historian Emma Wells notes, "pilgrims are seen kneeling within the shrine niches, touching and kissing the reliquary caskets, and even licking the shrine…"[10]

Condition 5. Sense of Accomplishment. At the end of the pilgrimage, participants clearly feel a sense of accomplishment. They have endured a variety of hardships, they have made crucial decisions during the journey, they have visited historically significant landmarks, and perhaps through this journey they have also uncovered a deeper meaning to their lives. Interviews with pilgrims indicate not only a sense of accomplishment, but other, even higher emotions such as elation, spiritual contentment, introspection, and heightened level of sensory acuteness.

Condition 6. A Significant Life Event. Pilgrimages are significant, non-trivial life events, undertaken perhaps only once in a person's lifetime. Planning and preparation are critical for a successful pilgrimage. Pilgrimages are physically and emotionally exhausting. Some individuals, however, can manage multiple pilgrimages, sequentially in time.

It is clear, however, that the fundamental purpose of pilgrimages was soon corrupted by some, particularly as the potential for commercializing these activities became apparent. By the 11th century, indulgences, particularly for the affluent and aristocracy, became intertwined with pilgrimages. Hospices started to develop along the routes, travel maps were published, and early versions of tour guides arose. By the late medieval times, even the actions of a few holy sites along popular pilgrim routes became more of a business, where some monasteries and sanctuaries would often compete with each other for alms and customers, promoting that their "relics" were more important or "miraculous" than others. By this time, it was obvious that a few pilgrims had lost the sense of what a true pilgrimage was all about.

As the English Dominican monk, John Bromyard, writes in 1522, "There are some who keep their pilgrimages and festivals not for God but for the devil. They who sin more freely when away from home or who go on pilgrimage to succeed in inordinate and foolish love — those who spend their time on the road in evil and uncharitable conversation may indeed say *peregrinamur a Domino* — they make their pilgrimage away from God and to the devil."[11] And of course, Erasmus makes a satire, albeit certainly exaggerated, of this abusive behavior in his 1526 colloquy *Peregrinatio religionis ergô*, or "Pilgrimage for Religion's Sake."

While the corrupting nature of commercialization has certainly occurred over the centuries, the laxity of modern life has led to another, perhaps even more insidious devaluation of the deep meaning associated with a true pilgrimage. A search of university catalogs for courses about pilgrimages, for example, clearly reveals this dangerous and simplistic way of modern thinking. Almost all of these courses appear to suggest that a simple ritualist activity that involves some short-term, temporary period of physical or mental effort rises to the level of a "pilgrimage." Thus, to the modern mind, an annual family vacation to Disneyworld, or a 2-hour hike to a mountain overlook, now constitutes a pilgrimage. One university course syllabus even suggests that a short meditative tea party in one's backyard can be considered a pilgrimage.

The Entrepreneurial Pilgrimage Experience

The true entrepreneur knows the difference, however. When an entrepreneur speaks of their endeavors as a pilgrimage, it has a much deeper meaning analogous to the true nature of a pilgrimage. The entrepreneurial experience involves a long-term process of deep emotional, financial, and physical commitment. It involves a birthing process of creation, that has a beginning and end, whether the end is an IPO exit, or simply the realization that the venture has been successful. The entrepreneurial process involves periods of extreme stress, uncertainty and anxiety combined with periods of satisfaction, happiness, and even elation. The entrepreneurial experience forces the individual to realize that they are human, and what it means to be human with very human physical and emotional limitations. And many people do not complete the difficult pilgrimage, giving up before its natural end. The entrepreneurial experience, in many respects, parallels the six characteristics of a true pilgrimage. It has deep personal purpose, it is a lengthy and difficult process, it is an existential path of critical and revealing decision points, it is highly sensory, and if completed, there is a true sense of accomplishment. The entrepreneurial experience is not at all like a family vacation, two-hour hiking excursion, or backyard tea party.

Perhaps the pilgrimage most universally recognized in the modern world comes from the *Lord of the Rings* films, where the Hobbit Frodo Baggins, having been given the Ring of Power by his cousin, Bilbo Baggins, sets off to remove the ring from the Hobbit shire on the advice of the Wizard Gandolf. He gathers companions along the way. It is a long journey, where the travelers are assaulted by various temptations, the most serious being triggered by the actions of evil character Sméagol/Gollum. Along the way, the travelers need to confront and survive a variety of severe physical and emotional dangers. Decision points are always presented, and there are periods of deep anxiety mixed with happiness, friendship, and comfort. The party of travelers have different abilities and moral perspectives, and at the end when the Ring of Power is thrown into the volcano at Mount Doom, there is an extreme sense of accomplishment. And the accomplishment is not only physical in nature, but also spiritual, represented by the death of evil Sméagol/Gollum at the same time. While the film version obviously overlays a somewhat shallow, Hollywood, perspective on the journey, the author, J. R. R. Tolkien clearly meant the Lord of the Rings as a pilgrimage of deep spiritual meaning, or in Tolkien's own words, it is a saga of life, temptation, and immortality. The published versions of the *Lord or the Rings* book(s) written between 1937 and 1949, are also filled with a number of high sensory components, such as maps, calligraphy, drawings, and poetry. Not surprisingly, some entrepreneurship faculty have used the Lord of the Rings journey as an analogy to the entrepreneurial process. A popular entrepreneurship magazine in India even published an article on the analogy, noting,

J. R. R. Tolkien's The Lord of The Rings is considered by many as one of the greatest mythologies of all time, and like others (such as the Ramayana, Mahabharata etc.), it is a storehouse of knowledge and strategies which can be applied to the present day. More useful are the analogies that if given a thought, work perfectly for an entrepreneur struggling with his/her startup.[12]

Positive Psychological and Sociological Outcomes

But what are the benefits of a pilgrimage? Certainly, as discussed there are a variety of possible spiritual and existential outcomes, but research has also indicated additional beneficial psychological and sociological outcomes of a pilgrimage. One research study published in *Psychological Medicine* found that those individuals completing a traditional pilgrimage resulted in both a short-term and long-term reduction in anxiety and depression.[13] Another study found that pilgrims reported a significant improvement of their quality of life, and that the experience assisted in increasing their sense of togetherness and community.[14] Other studies report similar psychological and medical benefits of traditional pilgrimages. Research has also indicated other therapeutic benefits from a pilgrimage. For example, an empirical study of pilgrims walking St. Olaf's Way in Norway, found a variety of benefits, including "improved mental, physical, spiritual and social health, personal health assets, and a more positive outlook on life."[15] There may be other more sociological and anthropological benefits associated with a pilgrimage experience. Anthropologists Victor Turner and Edith Turner's classic examination of pilgrimages, *Image and Pilgrimage in Christian Culture*, indicated that pilgrims often have a transformation from an individual orientation at the start of a pilgrimage, to one of "brother" and "neighbor" during the pilgrimage.[16] Others have found that traditional class structures are often dissolved during a pilgrimage process as people interact with others of different classes, ultimately focusing their orientation on other, more meaningful aspects of life.

While a number of underlying psychological, sociological and theological explanations have been offered to explain these benefits, there is certainly clear evidence that the act of a completing a true pilgrimage, in its entirety, with all of the trials, tribulations and characteristics described above, results in not only a number of psychological benefits at the personal level, but also an increased sense of community, togetherness, and charity, all key elements of a humane way of thinking.

Does the true entrepreneurial experience, as a form of a pilgrimage, make an individual more humane? Both the theoretical arguments and empirical evidence, at least, appears to suggest this might be the case. If the entrepreneurial experience is, indeed, a real pilgrimage as argued by the many individuals that have followed the path, it might represent the economic analogy of a Camino de Santiago de Compostela, a Hajj to Mecca, or the Tibetan path to Lhasa. Just like a true pilgrimage, the entrepreneurial experience combines an outward action of a severe physical journey with an internal act of deep intentions. And all the evidence suggests that if the entrepreneurial experience is a type of pilgrimage, then it offers the experiential framework and conditions to perceive the world in a more humane manner, both from the personal, psychological, and quality of life benefits of a pilgrimage-like experience, as well as the increased broader perspective of community, togetherness, and charity.

Endnotes

1. https://skipwalter.net/2020/07/27/emails-to-a-young-entrepreneur-joining-the-entrepreneurial-pilgrimage/.
2. https://msquaredaccountancy.co.uk/2019/02/01/the-camino-pilgrimage-an-entrepreneurs-lesson/#.
3. For a good description of the various pilgrimages in Ancient Greece see M. Dillon, *Pilgrims and Pilgrimage in Ancient Greece* (New York: Routledge, 1997).
4. It is important to note a distinction between the nature of Christian pilgrimages and most other Religions. Islam, Buddhism, and other religions that are centered on a single individual tend to focus their pilgrimages to the birthplace (or death) of that individual, such as Mecca for Islam. While Christianity is also focused on Jesus, and not surprisingly popular Christian pilgrimages are to Bethlehem and Jerusalem, the universal nature of Christianity has also resulted in hundreds of locations around the world, where there are sacred relics, sites of special spiritual experiences, important monasteries or churches, or the prior travels of spiritual individuals and Saints; many of these have become the focal points of various pilgrimages that are all equally important in Christianity. Thus, it is the pilgrimage experience that is most important, not the location. This is why we use the early Medieval period of pilgrimages as the analogy to the entrepreneurial experience — the focus is on the nature of the experience.
5. One such description is reflected in the aptly named "Bordeaux Pilgrimage" written in 333, often considered the oldest known Christian interarium (like a travel guide). Another pilgrimage process is described in the "Peregrinatio Silvise", written around 367. By the end of the 6th century, there were perhaps dozens of pilgrimage stories and guides to the Holy Land.
6. One of the major reasons behind the Crusades was to re-establish pilgrimage routes in the area.
7. Pupilla oculi, fol. LXIII, referenced at https://www.catholic.com/encyclopedia/pilgrimages.

8. Both authors enlisted in the military when young, one in the Marines and one in the Army, partly motivated by a sense of adventure.
9. The sensory nature of pilgrimages and medieval art has been explored in a number of studies, such as E. Wells, "Making 'Sense' of the Pilgrimage Experience in the Medieval Church," *Peregrinations* 3 no. 2 (2011), 122–146; V. Turner and E. Turner, *Image and Pilgrimage in Christian Culture* (New York: Columbia University Press, 1978); R. Nelsonand and N. Bryson (eds.), *Visuality Before and Beyond the Renaissance: Seeing as Others Saw* (Cambridge, UK: Cambridge University Press, 2000).
10. Wells, "Making Sense", 135.
11. "Summa Praedicantium", Tit. Feria n. 6, fol. 191, Lyons, 1522. https://www.catholic.com/encyclopedia/pilgrimages.
12. A. Balbir, "Some Startup Strategies Entrepreneurs Can Learn from The Lord of the Rings," *Entrepreneurship India Magazine*, July 20 (2016), 1. Accessed at https://www.entrepreneur.com/article/279411, August 30, 2022.
13. P. Morris, "The Effect of Pilgrimage on Anxiety, Depression and Religious Attitude," *Psychological Medicine* 12, no. 2 (1982), 291–294.
14. J. Klimiuk and K. Moriaty, "The Lourdes Pilgrimage and the Impact on Pilgrim Quality of Life," *Journal of Religions Health* 60, no. 6 (2021), 3775–3787.
15. J. Eade, T. Ekeland and C. Lorentzen, "The Processes, Effects and Therapeutics of Pilgrimage Walking the St. Olav Way," *International Journal of Religious Tourism and Pilgrimage* 8 (2020), 33–50, 33.
16. See Turner and Turner, *Image and Pilgrimage*.

11

Internalizing Moral Markets: Solving the "Smith Problem"

By the very individualistic nature of entrepreneurship, true entrepreneurs internalize the normal separation between market activities and social activities. This is a key issue in understanding how the entrepreneur, versus other business decision makers, can incorporate a humane perspective within the larger context of the modern economic world. Although Adam Smith is often considered the father of modern economics, he really did not explore in detail the nature of entrepreneurial action, and its role in innovation and economic growth. Smith, however, does spend an extensive amount of time on the idea of human beneficence, and the impacts that the human characteristics of virtue, charity, and sympathy have upon economic behavior.

Adam Smith, in *The Theory of Moral Sentiments*, first published in 1759, notes that compassion is primarily a limited social activity and not necessarily a fundamental market activity. In a famous passage regarding the hypothetical scenario of China being swallowed by an earthquake, Smith discusses the limits of compassion.

Let us suppose that the great empire of China, with all its myriads of inhabitants, was suddenly swallowed up by an earthquake, and let us consider how a man of humanity in Europe, who had no sort of connection with that part of the world, would be affected upon receiving intelligence of this dreadful calamity. He would, I imagine, first of all, express very strongly his sorrow for the misfortune of that unhappy

125

people, he would make many melancholy reflections upon the precariousness of human life, and the vanity of all the labours of man, which could thus be annihilated in a moment. He would too, perhaps, if he was a man of speculation, enter into many reasonings concerning the effects which this disaster might produce upon the commerce of Europe, and the trade and business of the world in general. And when all this fine philosophy was over, when all these humane sentiments had been once fairly expressed, he would pursue his business or his pleasure, take his repose or his diversion, with the same ease and tranquility, as if no such accident had happened.[1]

Smith is not being insensitive, but simply recognizing the human limits of compassion. In a broader sense, over time and through his various publications, Adam Smith appears to present two, and apparently conflicting perspectives of humaneness, charity, and efficient economic behavior. In this essay we look at this issue from the perspective of Smith's major treatises, *The Theory of Moral Sentiments*, published in 1759, and his later, more well-known and cited work, *The Wealth of Nations*, published in 1776. We also reference an important, yet less cited collection of Smith's lecture notes from the early 1760s, *Lectures in Jurisprudence*.[2] This short essay will examine Smith's perspective of human virtue within the context of 18th century life, its role in economic decision making, and some of the aspects of the classic "Smith Problem." We argue that entrepreneurial activities and small business, in many respects, resolves the conflicting aspects of charity and humaneness at a more practical level.

The Smith Problem has been examined from a number of different perspectives over time. Some authors have considered the Smith Problem within an evolutionary context, that Smith's philosophies changed significantly over time. This was a particularly common theme among Smith commentaries published in the 19th and early 20th centuries. Many of these historians suggest that that Smith underwent a radical theoretical change when visiting France in the mid-1760s, after publishing the first edition of *The Theory of Moral Sentiments* in 1759, but prior to publishing his *Wealth of Nations* in 1776. However, the discovery of student notes of Smith's lectures from 1762 and 1763 at the University of Glasgow suggests that many of Smith's economic ideas that ultimately ended in the *Wealth of Nations* were evident prior to his trip to France.[3]

In addition, Smith actually produced six editions of *The Theory of Moral Sentiments*, some with significant revisions such as the 2nd edition in 1761 and the 6th edition in 1790 some fifteen years after the publication of the *Wealth of Nations*.[4] These two facts alone make the pure "radical change in theoretical perspective" argument difficult to support. The evidence seems to support, at least in Smith's mind, that his two famous treatises should be read and understood as companion pieces, each focusing on different components of human activity. This perspective appears to the most typical approach when addressing the Smith Problem at the present time. For example, James Otteson, in an oft-cited essay, looks at the Smith Problem by examining the nuances of Smith's understanding of individual sentiment and sympathy with the nuances of Smith's "self-interest" economic framework presented in the *Wealth of Nations*.[5] The key to this approach, however, seems to focus on the "nuances" of Smith's statements, and the fine tuning of Smith's notion of sympathy and human sentiment in markets in order to explain the compatibility between the *Wealth of Nations* and *The Theory of Moral Sentiments*.

While certainly in agreement with the more "companion" oriented perspective of *The Theory of Moral Sentiment* (particularly with its revisions in the 6th edition) and the *Wealth of Nations*, argument, we argue that resolving the Smith Problem is not found just by debating the nuances of sympathy and sentiment, but rather in the problems of business structure and human experiences. For example, in prior discussions of the Smith Problem, there is almost no analyses of the impact of organizational size, institutional giantism and the human experiences of individuals within an increasing industrialized economy, and world primarily understood in terms of labor and capital. This is the thesis of this essay, that entrepreneurial action, combined with the community of small proprietors and "tradesmen", directly addresses the Smith Problem from both structural and phenomenological perspectives.

Charity and the "Smith" Problem

The starting point seems to be Adam Smith's general perspective of poverty, and the role of charity. There is no doubt that Smith was very interested in the notion of distributive justice, and how to address what seems to be an endemic problem of poverty and class structure. Adam Smith was born 1723, in Fife, Scotland. He grew up in a somewhat professional family and graduated at an early age from the University of

Glasgow. By 1748 he was giving lectures at the University of Edinburgh, and later earned a professorship at the University of Glasgow.

Scotland during Smith's life was in a period of a major transition, buffeted by a number of different social, political, and economic forces. Agricultural reform, and the introduction of sheep first into the Scottish Lowlands region, then soon afterward into the Scottish Highlands and Islands, resulted in the infamous "Highland Clearances," a process that is considered to have started in the early-1700s, and continued to the mid-1800s in different phases. This inevitably involved an "enclosure" process of the land-owning gentry and aristocracy fencing off their large estates for the raising of sheep, the breaking up the Highland clan structure of small crofts and townships that had existed for centuries, rapidly increasing land lease rates, introducing more modern farming techniques, and in some cases more draconian actions, such as forcibly evicting small peasant farmers and their families. Seeking employment, these displaced Scots quickly joined the rapidly growing poor neighborhoods in the industrial cities of Western Scotland, such as Glasgow and Paisley or in the eastern Scottish city of Dundee; some enlisted in the famous Scottish regiments fighting in various colonial wars; and many, like the ancestors of one of the authors of this essay, ultimately immigrated to the Americas, particularly North Carolina and Canada for a better life. Some historians have noted that the rural Scottish family and clan systems, both in the Lowlands and Highlands, were actually the entrepreneurial, social, and productive backbone to the Scottish agricultural regions, and much of this individual productive and innovative spirit in Scotland was quickly lost to the Americas due to the clearances.[6]

At the same time, Scotland was also at the center of the new industrial revolution. The "Treaty of Union," which integrated the political process, financial structure, and trade economies of Scotland with England was adopted by the Scottish Parliament in 1707. The Scottish banking system, however, was less regulated than in England, and able to expand rapidly during the 1700s. Scotland has major trade ports on both the Western and Eastern coasts. And perhaps most importantly, Scotland was a center of industrial and manufacturing expansion, particularly in the linen industries. Engineering and scientific expertise was highly valued, and much of the development of steam power systems, the technological force behind the Industrial Revolution, took place in Scotland. These factors, i.e., a rapidly expanding pool of cheap labor for the Scottish factories, a historical privileged hierarchy of land-owning gentry and aristocracy, the social upheavals of the clearances, the expanding global trade in the port cities, and the industrialization of manufacturing, characterized Scotland during by the mid-1700s.

Scotland was indeed growing economically, there was expanding wealth and education that is recognized as the era of "Scottish Enlightenment," but a very large percentage of Scottish society was impoverished, still living in poor rural Highland towns or as victims of the clearances, crowded into dense urban neighborhoods and laboring if employed, for long hours at low wages in the newly industrialized factories. It was a period in Scotland of significant wealth creation, rapid industrialization, trade and banking, world class educational institutions, significant engineering and innovation, but at the same time deep and enduring poverty, an agricultural system controlled by the landed aristocracy, large population migration and a social class systems built around language (English versus Gaelic), individual wealth and education, and geographic orientation (Highlands vs. Lowlands, and industrial cities vs. agricultural regions). It was ultimately the era when the old, natural order of property and work was being rapidly being replaced by the new order of "labor, land and labor," the fictitious commodities described in Karl Polanyi's *The Great Transformation*.[7] In fact, in *The Wealth of Nations* Smith even views the role of the certain enterprising individuals as working as a "manager" intervening between the labor and capital.

Because of these upheavals, this was also a period of great private charities throughout Great Britain and Scotland. Prior to the 1700s, almost all charitable work, hospitals, and orphanages were run by religious groups. But as the legal, stand-alone corporate model became dominant in the business world, by the mid-1700s British philanthropists were also starting to band together in legal organizations for purposes of charitable work, raising funds from a much broader base of smaller donations and pooled efforts. In fact, this became the model of both religious and secular charitable organizations that we know today. This was the Scotland that Adam Smith was born into, grew up in, and wrote about. It was this world of rapidly evolving, and often competing social, political, and economic forces that influenced much of Adam Smith's theories. Smith's work really needs to be placed within this 18th century Scottish context, something that few Adam Smith commentators discuss in much detail.[8]

Throughout his first major work, *The Theory of Moral Sentiments,* Smith clearly sees individual acts of charity, kindness, love, and friendship as virtues, and that these virtues are shared by a very broad part of the population. Humans, as presented in *The Theory of Moral Sentiments*, are driven by a number of moral sentiments, emotions and forces that encourage charity and humaneness. These include a combination of human sympathy and the virtue of "self-command," a very human ability to control one's passions and desires, and to moderate selfish behavior for the benefit of others. To Smith, true beneficence cannot be coerced by individuals or society, rather beneficence is a function of an individual's personal attitudes, beliefs, and sympathies. To Smith, humans by their very nature are generous and sympathetic to others plight. Smith, however, also recognizes the importance of "mutual sympathy," where a person's charitable action might have an expectation of reciprocity. Mutual sympathy can create, under proper circumstances, an increasing consideration of charity throughout society. Smith, however, does note an important difference between human generosity and the nature of humanity. Generosity requires a self-sacrificing or altruistic action, whereas humanity is just a "feeling."

Adam Smith, Corporate Social Responsibility, and Stakeholders

Smith recognizes in *The Theory of Moral Sentiments*, as the quote about the hypothetical earthquake in China suggests, that there are indeed limitations as an "impartial spectator" to the human virtues of beneficence. This is known as the "social proximity" argument, where a person is most inclined to first assist family members, then close friends, then acquaintances, then society and country. To this extent, in *The Theory of Moral Sentiments*, Smith makes a plausible case for government intervention to assist the poor. This tentative argument for government intervention is based upon two allocative inefficiency arguments presented in *The Theory of Moral Sentiments*, the first being that poor people, particularly in British culture, tend to conceal their desperate situation due to personal shame and fear of ostracization, and second, the inefficient distribution of private charity if left simply to individual donors; donors who with the best of intentions may still be influenced by personal biases, imperfect information about the true conditions of the poor, and the problem of social proximity, as well as the occasional over ambitious effort for status and wealth that undermines personal civic duty.

But Smith also recognizes in *The Theory of Moral Sentiments* that governments can easily go too far, and ultimately infringe upon personal liberties and institutional justice. Another lesser-known work by Adam Smith, *Lectures in Jurisprudence* appears to support many of the arguments in *The Theory of Moral Sentiments* but provides some interesting legal context for these arguments. *Lectures in Jurisprudence* is actually a compilation of lecture notes by Adam Smith during the early 1760s while at the University of Glasgow. When published, *Lectures in Jurisprudence* was organized into five "Parts" with a particular focus on jurisprudence, laws, administration, and police functions.

Under these arguments, *The Theory of Moral Sentiments* appears to also make a case somewhat for a level of positivist corporate social responsibility, or CSR, where controlling managers of business can allocate corporate funds for charitable and other "moral and good" purposes. In *Lectures in Jurisprudence*, Smith makes an even stronger argument for CSR based on the commutative justice described in *The Theory of Moral Sentiments*, while adding the element of a contractual relationship between an organization, and its various stakeholders and investors. This is where Smith's notion of imperfect rights and perfect rights come into play. Similar to prior moral philosophers, Smith talks about a "perfect right" as when somebody has a title to demand something, and if refused, can then command another to perform. Perfect rights, including private property, need to be rigorously and carefully protected from the abuses of governments, corporations, and wealthy classes. An example of a corporate violation of a perfect right might be excessive executive compensation, which violates a shareholder's perfect right for dividends, or unsafe working conditions, which violates an employee's perfect right.

However, Smith also discusses the nature of "imperfect rights" as those duties that should be performed, but no one has sufficient title to compel performance. Imperfect rights, such as charity, should be upheld but cannot be enforced or coerced. Imperfect rights generally do not fall under the authority of laws. It is this combination of human beneficence/ natural sympathy and the inefficiencies of personal charitable markets/ social proximity that makes a CSR argument under Smith's "imperfect rights" arguments in *The Theory of Moral Sentiments* and *Lectures in Jurisprudence*. Under the umbrella of both *The Theory of Moral Sentiments* and *Lectures in Jurisprudence*, Smith might argue for CSR when a manager can increase the imperfect rights associated with beneficence, sympathy and charity, without violating the perfect rights of stakeholders. Smith, however, often blurred the traditional distinction between perfect and imperfect rights in his writings, making it difficult at times to exactly define Smiths view of CSR within with context.[9]

By the time *The Wealth of Nations* was published in 1776, however, Smith seems to have de-emphasized the role of both government and business as important to the distribution of charity. Here Smith argues more for efficient and competitive markets that allow all classes of people, rich and poor, to participate. Smith argues that a society made up of altruistic and beneficence-oriented individuals would also make an efficient private charity market. And due to the long-run increases in wealth created by an efficient and competitive market managed by good people operating in small enterprises, the poor ultimately would need less charity due to the increasing wealth they receive from market involvement. *The Wealth of Nations*, in fact, appears to make a much stronger argument for the stakeholder approach to charity, rather than the CSR orientation. With competitive and efficient markets, operated by fundamentally just and good people, the decreasing demand for charity is thus inevitable, and what charity is needed at any particular point in time can be more efficiently provided by an efficient private charity market.

Even in *The Wealth of Nations*, however, Smith does recognize that there are barriers to such charitable efficiencies. These barriers include the enactment of inefficient mercantile laws and institutions that protect the wealth of inefficient corporate and government leaders, idle aristocracies, and the generally unproductive classes of people; and second, in societies that don't participate in efficient and competitive markets will ultimately lag in development, and still need beneficial charitable acts. This is often referred to as Smith's "first-best" theory, and in these cases, there might be modification to a purely stakeholder argument of charity. In general, however, *The Wealth of Nations* appears to make more of an argument for a "stakeholder" approach to charity, rather than the CSR approach in *The Theory of Moral Sentiments* and *Lectures in Jurisprudence*. This apparent conflict between *Theory of Moral Sentiments/Lectures in Jurisprudence* and *The Wealth of Nations* is the basis for the "Smith Problem."

Not What It Seems

It should be noted, however, that Adam Smith's writings are often grossly misinterpreted by highly selective quotes from *The Wealth of Nations*, and inaccurately presented in humanities textbooks, liberal thinking college classrooms, and in the popular press as an amoral, or even anti-moral "egoism" model where "greed is good." This is simply not true, as recognized by a moderately careful reading of Adam Smith's works. One of the themes throughout this present book of essays, is that in all of Smith writings, whether in *The Theory of Moral Sentiments, Lectures in Jurisprudence* or *The Wealth of Nations*, Smith was a strong believer in human goodness, beneficence, charity, and sympathy, and the strong moral behavior of humans making economic decisions. In fact, a recent network-based word content analysis of *The Wealth of Nations* indicated 240 references to human virtues in relationship to societal flourishing, but only 4 references to selfishness driving prosperity.[10] In his economic arguments, Adam Smith knew that people tend to have concern and care for other people in addition to "self-regarding" behavior. This notion of "other-regarding" behavior is supported by seventeen centuries of philosophical and theological arguments, and practice by religious institutions. It is also supported by a significant amount of modern empirical economic behavior research and physiological studies.[11] But Smith also certainly recognized the workings of an efficient and competitive marketplace, and the dangers when markets do not work properly. Smith's task was to combine these powerful forces.

The modern philosopher Martha Nussbaum, in her book, *Upheavals of Thought: The Intelligence of Emotions*, recognizes the truth of Smith's emphasis on human beneficence, charity, and sympathy, and makes the case that human emotion is actually the centerpiece of moral philosophy.[12] Compassion, like empathy, regardless of its root source, is a human emotion, and something generally not seen outside humans.

Recognizing the separation of market activities and social activities often results in the knee-jerk and somewhat obvious argument for stronger and more efficient social institutions to balance the limits of compassion. Yet this can only be part of the solution as seen in the complexity of Smith's arguments. Asking larger corporations to compensate also creates issues as Nobel Laureate Milton Friedman famously notes in the title of his oft-cited 1970 essay, the "Social Responsibility of Business is to Increase its Profits."[13] To quote,

> The whole justification for permitting the corporate executive to be selected by the stockholders is that the executive is an agent serving the interests of his principal. This justification disappears when the corporate executive imposes taxes and spends the proceeds for "social" purposes.

Milton Friedman and other more libertarian, or even anarchistic economic thinkers, are often mistakenly directly associated with Adam Smith's arguments. But as we can see from the discussion above, libertarian-based theories, such as Friedman's and economists often known, perhaps incorrectly, as the "University of Chicago Economics School of Thought,"[14] offer a different perspective from Adam Smith in their understanding of the role of human virtues in economic decisions, the functioning of the institutions that participate in the marketplace, and the nature of societal flourishment.

As mentioned at the start of this essay, to a large extent Adam Smith's idea are influenced by the powerful political, social, and economic forces of 18th century Europe in general, and Scotland in particular. Smith assumes human behavior based upon many of the natural, humanistic perspectives of individual virtues of prior centuries, but develops an economic theory based on the new fictitious commodities of capital and labor. What happens to Smith's argument if the phenomenological power of viewing the modern world as a grand commodities market overshadows a sense of individual human virtues, and the historic natural, and possibly spiritual, relationship between property and work. This are important things contemplate as we consider the nature of humane capitalism, and the role of the entrepreneur.

Entrepreneurship and the Presentation of Human Virtues

This brings us to the role of the entrepreneur. While the first three essays in the section address paths in which an entrepreneur might develop a more humane, and beneficial, perspective in their economic thinking, the focus of this essay is on the fundamental conflicts associated with the "Smith Problem," ultimately a problem of virtue management in the world of business.

By the very nature of their work, entrepreneurs often ride the roller coaster of emotions. Some days are filled with the excitement of the birthing process of a new venture, the first sale, or obtaining a new patent. Other days are deep in despair, of not obtaining the anticipated financing, losing a long-standing customer, or not making that week's full payroll. But, as Nussbaum argues, emotions are a type of intelligence, they allow us to frame a better understanding of the world about us. Nussbaum's focus on the intelligence of emotions, however, is somewhat different that the phenomenologist's focus on experiences. It is this intelligence of emotions, combined with Smith's notion of human sympathy and beneficence that lays the foundation for entrepreneurial action.

As Smith certainly argues, markets are a mechanism for the human perspectives of morality and social support to be played out. Entrepreneurship, however, combines the individual's social orientation with the marketplace and brings both under the decision-making process of the individual entrepreneur. Managers with their legalistic fiduciary responsibility to maximize shareholder wealth, will always be preoccupied by the confusing analysis of who benefits, or not, from the allocation of perfect rights and imperfect rights that will always consume even the simplest of corporate social responsibility debates. This becomes a moot issue to most entrepreneurs. Many perfect rights and imperfect rights are subsumed under the same individual. Entrepreneurs are typically the primary investor and the primary employee. In this context, like any small businessperson or tradesman, they are able to combine their social, religious, ethical and moral interests, sensibilities, and behaviors into their market system decision making process, as a morally committed "tradesman" and not a wage "clerk." Pricing, product development, investments, supply relationships, labor practices, and advertising all become intertwined with the moral standards of the entrepreneur. Emotions, such as compassion, thus enter the marketplace for the entrepreneur and can become, as Nussbaum would argue, the foundation of a broader moral philosophy for entrepreneurs.

This is exactly why Smith emphasizes an economic system that is primarily made up of small, family-oriented enterprises each specializing in specific industry sectors, or what could later be called a form of "proprietary capitalism." This framework can be seen in practice to some extent in the textile industry of the 1800s in Philadelphia, known as "Quaker City," due to the large population of immigrant "Quakers" that settled in the area. William Penn (1644–1718), the founder of the colony of Pennsylvania was a member of Religious Society of Friends (Quakers). Many Quaker immigrants moved to Pennsylvania and established various economic communities. One important economic community was the textile industry in Philadelphia. By the late 1790s the Quaker textile economic community in Philadelphia was flourishing and continued strong for almost a century. As historian Philip Scranton notes, by 1880 the community had grown to approximately 850 small firms, none of which were formal corporations. This community developed highly flexible strategies for production, with an emphasis on skill, quality, and market responsiveness. The small and middle-sized firms in "Quaker Town", proved durable, effectively functioning through networks of linked specializations, with spinning, weaving, dyeing, and finishing often performed in separate establishments.[15]

Richard Turnbull refers to the economies of these early communities in Pennsylvania as "Quaker Capitalism", a system built upon several key components including (a) a strong moral and spiritual character in all aspects of life including commercial activities, (b) the focus on small family-owned and run businesses, (c) specifically avoiding aggressive expansion strategies and legalistic corporate structures, (d) developing efficient businesses with specialized single product line strategies while avoiding diversification, (e) developing business relationships within a strong community network of other small enterprises, all providing different products and services, and (f) treating employees as family, with fair wages, respect and benefits.[16] In fact, this appears to exemplify what Smith specifically outlines in the combination of *The Theory of Moral Sentiment* and the *Wealth of Nation*.

In this manner, Adam Smith's social and market systems are unconditionally intertwined for the entrepreneur. Almost by definition the entrepreneur resolves the "Smith Problem" at the personal level by merging these two systems — moral and market — into the entrepreneur's daily decision-making process. Here the CSR perspectives and the stakeholder approaches are united. But caution must be given. While small, and entrepreneurial oriented, these moral and market components are merged into a unified whole, but firms can expand and become something else. In fact, Adam Smith himself probably solved the "Smith Problem." Rather than focusing on a few selected quotes, a full reading of Adam Smith's economic theory suggests that an advancing economy, and ultimately the wealth of nations, is a function of a competitive market of small enterprises, each focusing on a particular market segment where the business owners all combine both a profit orientation and their thoroughly human, common perspective of benevolence, sympathy and charity in their economic decision making. This is, in fact, the true meaning of the oft-cited "invisible hand." Smith never conceived of the modern world of massive diversified corporate entities, competing in multiple industry sectors, managed by self-interested bureaucracies of administrators, working in concert with governments to form the industrial-government complexes that Republican President Eisenhower warned about in his 1961 presidential farewell address.[17]

Many modern definitions of entrepreneurial success, taught in business classes and popular publications, appear to promote the questionable virtues of scalability and expansion. As small firms scale up, they inevitably acquire non-related investors and wage-based employees. As these small entrepreneurial efforts become larger, they are in danger of becoming part of the problem rather than the solution. Smith's emphasis on the human virtues of sympathy, beneficence and charity in the larger, dehumanized marketplace of fictitious commodities thus becomes even more important. In developing and sustaining a humane focus, entrepreneurial scalability requires maintaining a foundation of natural law, and a continuous strategy of implementing society's rights, both perfect and imperfect in nature. This is ultimately both the entrepreneurial dilemma and the entrepreneurial responsibility.

Endnotes

1. A. Smith, *The Theory of Moral Sentiments* (Washington, DC: Regnery Publishing, 1997). Original work published 1759.
2. A. Smith, *The Wealth of Nations* (London: Penguin Books, 1986). Original work published 1776; and A. Smith, *Lectures in Jurisprudence.* Available online at AdamSmithWorks.org. Accessed at https://www.adamsmithworks.org/documents/digital-jurisprudence.
3. Smith, *Lectures in Jurisprudence.*
4. E. Matson, "A Brief History of the Editions of the Theory of Moral Sentiments," (Adam Smith Works, 2020) Available at SSRN. The 6th edition of *The Theory of Moral Sentiments* did not significantly alter Smith's emphasis on sympathy, charity and human benevolence. In fact, the most significant revisions in this edition were the addition of discussions on Theology and the Character of Virtue. https://www.researchgate.net/publication/347378807_A_Brief_History_of_the_Editions_of_the_Theory_of_Moral_Sentiments.
5. J. Otteson, "The Recurring 'Adam Smith Problem'", *History of Philosophy Quarterly* 17, no. 1 (2000), 51–74.
6. The major port of entry in the U.S. for Scottish immigrants during the 1700 and 1800s was Wilmington, North Carolina. In general, Scottish Highland immigrants quickly moved away from the more urban ports of entry in the U.S., either to farm in the Appalachian Mountains and highland areas of North Carolina, etc., or they continued to the expanding Western States. In

fact, many of the railroad engineers, bankers, ranchers, and shopkeepers in the Western United States during the 1800s were Scottish immigrants. One of this books author's direct ancestor immigrated to the U.S. from the Western Scottish Highland Loch Lomond region during the clearances, ending up as a Master Mechanic for the Union Pacific Railroad in Wyoming. Scottish immigrants who stayed in North Carolina often migrated to the Highlands and Mountains, contributing extensively to the music, language, dance and culture of the mountains. In fact, bluegrass, mountain ballads, and country music are direct descendants of Scottish music. At the same time, Irish immigration to the U.S. was also significant, particularly during the Irish Potato Famine in the mid-1800s. The Irish, however, tended to settle more in the large city urban areas such as New York, joining the expanding Irish neighborhoods that exist even in modern times. During the Civil War, whole Union regiments of Irish immigrants were formed. For an excellent, and somewhat humorous, description regarding the impact 19th Scottish immigration had upon the development of the United States see A. Herman, *How the Scots Invented the Modern World: The True Story of How Western Europe's Poorest Nation Created our World & Everything in It* (New York, NY: Crown Publishing Group, 2001). It is now estimated that approximately 25 million people in the U.S. are of direct Scottish descent, and another 30 million have Scotch-Irish/Irish heritage, combined accounting for approximately 18% of the current U.S. population. The impact (on both Scotland and the U.S.) of the Scottish clearances and migration during Adam Smith's time should not be underestimated. Surprisingly, Adam Smith makes little specific reference to these issues in his writings, but they certainly must have influenced his theoretical perspective.

7. K. Polanyi, *The Great Transformation: The Political and Economic Origins of Our Time* (Boston: Beacon Press, 2001). Original work published 1944.

8. Historian Jerry Muller is one of the few writers that discusses the historical context of Adam's life in Scotland as a driving factor behind some of his concepts. See J. Muller, *Adam Smith: In His Time and Ours* (Princeton, NJ: Princeton University Press, 1995).

9. For a full description of Smith's discussion of perfect and imperfect rights, and how these relate to Smith's perspective of distributive justice and assistance to the poor see J. Salter, "Adam Smith on Justice and the Needs of the Poor," *Journal of the History of Economic Thought* 34, no. 4 (2012), 559–575.

10. J. Graafland and T. Wells, "In Adam Smith's Own Words: The Role of Virtues in the Relationship Between Free Market Economies and Societal Flourishing, A Semantic Network Data-mining Approach," *Journal of Business Ethics* 172 (2021), 31–42 use a combination of several different

network-based content analysis algorithms on various phases and word-maps in their examination of relationships between different concepts presented in the *Wealth of Nations.*

11. For a discussion of both economic behavioral research and recent neural-economic research regarding moral sentiments and "other-regarding" behavior in economic and personal situations see P. Zak, "The Physiology of Moral Sentiments," *Journal of Economic Behavior & Organization* 77 (2010), 53–65.

12. M. Nussbaum, *Upheavals of Thought: The Intelligence of Emotions* (Cambridge, UK: Cambridge University Press, 2001).

13. M. Friedman, "Social Responsibility of Business is to Increase its Profits," *The New York Times*, September 13, 1970, 17. Accessed at https://www.nytimes.com/1970/09/13/archives/a-friedman-doctrine-the-social-responsibility-of-business-is-to.html, on August 30, 2022.

14. The reference to the University of Chicago Economics School of Thought refers to a more individual choice based economic systems. Libertarianism is perhaps more correctly associated with a range of diverse political economy perspectives than an economic foundation. Libertarianism is certainly based on a foundation of individual choice, however, not all systems based on individual choice concepts are Libertarian in nature. Not surprising, books such as *Atlas Shrugged* by sociologist Ayn Rand are considered part of the Libertarian school of thought, whereas many University of Chicago economists are not Libertarian in their thinking.

15. P. Scranton, *Proprietary Capitalism: The Textile Manufacture at Philadelphia, 1800–1885.* (Cambridge: Cambridge University Press, 2003). The Quaker textile industry in Philadelphian started to decline near the end of the 19th century due to a variety of forces, including children wanting to leave the family business and/or the Quaker lifestyle, the decline of the Quaker community network due to significant population growth in the area, and the development of cheap textiles by the large corporate textile mills and manufacturing firms. Also note that unfortunately the term "proprietary capitalism" has taken on several meanings, from notions of Libertarianism to more of an economy based on Smith's notion of small proprietors.

16. See R. Turnbull, *Quaker Capitalism: Lessons for Today* (Oxford, UK: Centre for Enterprise, Markets and Ethics, 2014). While certainly some Quaker run family businesses, such as Cadbury Chocolate, became larger over time, the vast majority stayed small and highly specialized businesses. In fact, Cadbury Chocolate stayed a relatively small family business from its founding in 1824 until the early 1900s when Cadbury constructed a new factory and 'model village' for their workers in Bournville, with more than 300 cottages, along with amenities like schools and shops. As the family were Quakers, no pubs were built in Bournville.

17. President Eisenhower specifically referred to the military-industrial complex in his farewell speech, but the broader meaning of Eisenhower's warning was the danger of large industrial enterprises working hand in hand with government agencies to not only protect and enrich these entities, but also with a strategy of making them larger and more powerful within society.

Section IV

Non-Random Thoughts on Humaneness

Section IV, titled "Non-Random Thoughts on Humaneness," provides a mix of ideas to consider. Each of these essays approach a different topic but in a novel way. The first essay, *The Power of Wise Leadership* looks at three different, and often dismissed, approaches to leadership in a different light — Frederick Winslow Taylor, Lillian and Frank Gilbreth, and the Marine Corp officer training process. Both Taylor and Gilbreth used to be required readings in early business schools but have fallen out of favor. Why is this? This essay attempts to bring these management theorists back into the forefront. Officer training in the military is often considered the peak of small group management training but is rarely discussed in university leadership classes. In *The Rise and Fall of Responsible Innovation*, we explore the history of innovation, the meaning underlying of the relatively new concept of "responsible innovation," particularly as defined by the European Union, and discuss its relevance to humane entrepreneurship. While innovation in the modern world is almost synonymous with entrepreneurship this was not always the case. This essay explores the evolution of the innovation concept and ends with a discussion as to whether the notion of responsible innovation is just another fad, supported by an interlocking network of modern "weasel words." The final essay in this section, *Beauty, Humaneness, and the Object of Economic Behavior* explores the historical development of the concept of beauty, particularly as presented in the various writings of Adam Smith. Smith has a somewhat unique perspective of beauty, something that we label, the "aesthetics of utility." Smith sees potential beauty not only in objects but also within systems and institutions. Within this context, this essay poses an interesting question as to whether the concept of beauty should, in fact, be part of the objective function in a humane economic system.

12

The Power of Wise Leadership

In this essay we look at three different, and often dismissed approaches to leadership under the lens of humane wisdom — Frederick Winslow Taylor, Lillian and Frank Gilbreth, and the Marine Corp officer training process.

Frederick Winslow Taylor: Leadership as "Initiative and Incentive"

Leadership is of central importance to any organization, from the smallest group to an entire nation. Good leadership provides vision, the source of unity and purpose among the people and the source of direction of effort. Without vision an organization is, at best, aimless and low performing. "Where there is no vision, the people perish".[1]

Along with vision, leadership provides to each individual member guidance to direct his own contribution and motivation to generate total personal commitment of effort. A leader shows his people what they need to do, *vision*, then instructs them and shows them discipline in how to do it, *guidance*, and finally makes them proud, committed, and eager to do it, *motivation*. Leadership is vision, guidance, and motivation. This is teaching. A strong leader is a gifted and committed teacher. Strong leadership shapes the personal purpose of the individual to match the purpose of the organization and makes the individual care about organization success. Wise leadership will be humane and, ideally, will lead to a true City of Health that will endure. "Without wise leadership, a nation falls."[2]

Much is written and said about leadership, but modern discussion of leadership can be repetitious and unenlightening. The problem is that leadership is typically addressed as if it were management, when in fact management and leadership are very different things. The failure to delineate the difference is furthered by the fact that the two work together. The work of management is to oversee operations, to use organization power to get things done, and the work of leadership is to provide vision, guidance, and motivation. Leadership is not at all based on power but instead makes use of non-coercive influence, the willing agreement and support of the people being led. The influence comes from the communal authority of the people being led, as they personally accord the influence to the leader. The influence must be earned by the leader and can easily be lost.

The student of business is hopefully familiar with the foundational work in the field, Frederick Winslow Taylor's *Principles of Scientific Management*, and might be pleased and impressed by the fact that the *Principles* addresses not just management but also provides some fundamental insights into the nature of leadership, an introduction to wise leadership. Taylor makes it clear that Scientific Management is largely about teaching, and teaching is the essence of leadership.[3]

The *Principles* is a very great work, said by some to be a more important work than *The Origin of Species* and according to Robert Kanigel, "the most powerful as well as the most lasting contribution America has made to Western thought since *The Federalist Papers*."[4] Taylorism, in many respects, can be said to be the most important 'ism' of the 20th century. But its important insights on leadership have tended to be lost in modern reading, because Taylor's work includes a misstep that obscures his insights on leadership and has a history of diverting the conventional interpretation onto the application of a burdensome supervisory process. His powerful emphasis on teaching becomes lost in the process.

The casual introduction that most readers get from the *Principles* focuses on the five steps in the Scientific Management process:

(1) Study the way the job is performed now and determine new and better ways to do it.
(2) Codify the new method into rules and procedures.
(3) Select and train workers whose skills match the procedures.
(4) Guide the efforts of workers in accord with the procedures.
(5) Reward performance.

The five steps have long been accepted as a foundation of management practice. Closer attention, however, suggests that (4), "Guide the efforts of workers," does not belong. The other four are true by their nature, necessarily true. How could good management not include them? But (4), "Guide the efforts of workers," does not have an obvious validity. Why must workers be subjected to guidance? After benefitting from the other steps of Scientific Management, why can they not supervise themselves?

Taylor's misstep might be understandable. He thought that generalist managers could not know everything about the planning and execution of the work. Therefore "It is necessary to provide teachers," to provide assistance to workers, and his system argued for adding a large support staff for the purpose of teaching. Taylor, in other places calls them "functional specialists," but he first, emphatically, calls them teachers. It is here that he makes the misstep. Scientific Management was built on teaching, but Taylor didn't adequately distinguish between teaching and control and thereby allowed control to intermix with teaching and confuse the true nature of Scientific Management. Taylor states that "the old-fashioned single foreman is superseded by eight different men, each one of whom … are expert teachers." He calls the first three duties to be teaching.

(1) Foreman — overall boss.
(2) The Inspector (the first "teacher") — "sees to it that he [the worker] understands the drawings and instructions…" and "teaches him how to do work of the right quality."
(3) Gang boss (the second "teacher") — "shows him how to set up the job on his machine and teaches him how to make all his motions in the quickest and best way."

Taylor does not use the word teacher to describe the remaining five.

(4) Speed boss — "sees that the machine is run at the best speed and that the proper tool is used."
(5) Repair boss — "as to the adjustment, cleanliness, and general care of his machine."
(6) Time clerk — "as to everything relating to his pay and to proper written reports and returns.
(7) Route clerk — "as to the order in which he does his work."
(8) Disciplinarian — "in case a workman gets into any trouble with any of his various bosses."

Taylor never uses the word "teacher" to describe the last five roles, because they reek of control. Teaching never implies control. The purpose of teaching is (1) to change the student and to help the student grow, (2) to transfer knowledge and experience to the student, (3) to direct the student toward productive ends, and (4) to encourage the student and leave him free to pursue the productive ends. Teaching should be seen to be the opposite of control. True teaching is never based on regulation and is not inclined to bureaucracy. In contrast, control is to enforce specified actions according to a set of rules and standards and thrives on bureaucracy.

Taylor's emphasis on teaching reveals the truth that leadership is always based on teaching, in fact is a form of teaching. Establishing the methods in a particular line of work involves management, directing human effort in that line of work. Productivity, on the other hand, comes from leadership, caring enough about the line of work to enhance the talent applied to it, to train and motivate the people to commit themselves to productivity. A worker's effort is enhanced by training in knowledge of the line of work and by distribution of effort in such a way as to give opportunity and encouragement to exercise his unique talents. A worker comes to care about the line of work and to fully commit himself to it by his acknowledgement of the value of the output of the line of work and acceptance that the output is worth his commitment. Taylor calls the working of this personal dynamic Initiative and Incentive and declares it to be the "finest type of ordinary management … in which the workmen give their best initiative and in return receive some special incentive." Initiative and Incentive is powerful because it is natural to all people and is therefore humane. It provides one half of leadership. Scientific Management provides the other half.

Anyone with the ability to be a leader/manager knows and fully accepts two truths: that all people have their own unique skills and talents and that all people love to work and are eager to use their abilities in their work. Despite this, people often do not work hard at their job and do not give it their full initiative, a fact which Taylor calls the "the mystery of work." Someone of adequate ability when put into a position of responsibility that calls for leadership may naturally apply Initiative and Incentive. *Initiative* means that the organization must draw on all skills and talents of all people and permit and encourage people to do their finest work. Every person has a large body of knowledge and ability. "The task of management is that of inducing each workman to use all of his traditional knowledge, his skill, his ingenuity, and his goodwill so as to yield the largest possible return." About *Incentive* Taylor says, "In order to have any hope of obtaining the initiative of his workmen the manager must give some special incentive to his men beyond that which is given to the average of the trade ... Under Scientific Management the particular pay system which is adopted is merely one of the subordinate elements." The set of subordinate elements of incentive that Taylor enumerates are the following: hope of promotion or advancement, higher wages, shorter hours of labor, better surroundings and working conditions, and "above all, that personal consideration for, and friendly contact with, his workmen which comes only from a genuine and kindly interest in the welfare of those under him."

This last element deserves emphasis: of the elements of incentive, above all else, above pay, is a genuine interest in the welfare of the worker. This is leadership, not management. True leadership is a difficult art because the interest must be genuine. This is easy to say, and most people who talk about leadership say it, but it is extremely difficult, and maybe rare, for a leader to have genuine interest in those under him. Only if a leader would willingly make a sacrifice for those under him, only then is he a leader. If a person in authority has any thought about pleasing a boss or bucking for promotion, such a person is not a leader. Potential sacrifice for the needs of your people is real, not the cliche of "servant leadership." Real sacrifice means willingness to cross your boss, if need be, foregoing hope of promotion, or, in some situations such as military leadership, willingness to face injury or death.

Taylor has identified the roots of leadership to lie in the combination of two approaches, his method of Scientific Management and the traditional natural method of Initiative and Incentive. The roots of leadership lie in the fact that the two approaches are not contradictory, or even contrasts, and instead they are complements that complete each other. Leadership is a union of the two approaches: Initiative and Incentive focuses on worker competence and commitment to learning the job, worker self-guidance and motivation in execution of the job. Scientific Management focuses on the leader studying the job to permit improved teaching of the job skill and the leader providing self-actualizing rewards for improved effort and output.

Taylor does not put forth Scientific Management as an alternative to Initiative and Incentive. Instead, it completes Initiative and Incentive and makes it workable. Taylor demonstrates this with the famous monolog addressing Schmidt that is central to *The Principles of Scientific Management* and is meant to seal Taylor's argument:

> What would Schmidt's answer be if he were talked to in a manner which is usual under the management of 'initiative and incentive'? say, as follows:
>
> 'Now, Schmidt, you are a first-class pig-iron handler and know your business well. You have been handling at the rate of 12 and a half tons per day. I have given considerable study to handling pig iron, and feel sure that you could do a much larger day's work than you have been doing. Now don't you think that if you really tried you could handle 47 tons of pig iron per day, instead of 12 and a half tons?'
>
> What do you think Schmidt's answer would be to this?

This does seal Taylor's argument, because of course Schmidt, any of us, would think that Taylor was just trying to force more work out of him.

Taylor doesn't highlight leadership as much as he should, because leadership is essentially the heart of the book. As powerful as *The Principles of Scientific Management* is, it would be even more powerful if it addressed more clearly its role in leadership by using his Scientific Management method to strengthen the natural and humane approach of Initiative and Incentive. Initiative would be strengthened by effort to provide training in job skills, to give the resources needed, and to teach how to use the skills and resources. Incentive would be strengthened by financial reward based on individual initiative, independence in control over the job (illustrated in Taylor's example of shoveling), and assurance of job security (also illustrated in Taylor's example of shoveling).

Taylor's monolog delivered to Schmidt could be strengthened into a monolog of leadership in the following manner:

> Now, Schmidt, you are a first-class pig-iron handler and have been handling at the rate of 12 and a half tons per day. I have given considerable study to handling pig iron and feel sure that I can lead you to become even more productive.
>
> (strengthen initiative) You can be proud of knowing your business so well and of being so productive. I can train you how to be even more productive. I will teach you how to safely handle 47 tons of pig iron per day, instead of 12 and a half tons,

(strengthen incentive) You will be able to work unsupervised and at your own pace. If you achieve the 47 tons, you will earn so much more, you will be able to afford to build that house that you are working on for your family. And you will always have a job here.

Initiative and Incentive is a powerful method because it is natural and humane. All of us have seen it used and most of us automatically choose to use it when we are placed in a position of responsibility. But as powerful as it is, alone it can fail, as seen in Taylor's monolog. If Initiative and Incentive is strengthened by Scientific Management, as in the second monolog, the union of the two becomes wise and strong leadership with a good chance of succeeding.

Frank & Lillian Gilbreth: Leadership as a Quest

In late 1924, Lillian Gilbreth published a book entitled *The Quest for the One Best Way*. It was meant to be a tribute to her husband Frank Bunker Gilbreth, the legendary theorist of efficient economic practice and "motion and time" studies, an industrial engineer and management theorist who argued that there is a correct way to do things, and that it is the challenge of the entrepreneur/leader to find it — the One Best Way.[5] But sadly, Frank died in June of that year, making the book an epitaph instead of a tribute.[6] The opening page of the intended tribute reads:

> To most of us, life is to some extent a quest, whether we acknowledge it, or even know it, or not.
>
> Many of us seek for numerous easily attained little things, — a good time; money enough to buy some small specific thing that we fancy we need or would like, — a passing interest or excitement.
>
> Some of us seek for a few big things — also attainable, but hard to get. A fortune. Fame.
>
> A few of us seek for one thing only, and that apparently forever unattainable. These few are those who dedicate their lives to a Quest.
>
> Such are the explorers, who push on and on seeking new countries and new marvels. Such are the treasure seekers, looking for real or rainbow gold. Such are the philosophers, searching out ultimate truths. Such are the astronomers, scanning the heavens for records of the universe.

These are the seekers!

The Holy Grail, — The Golden fleece, — The Fountain of Youth, — El Dorado, — and now, The One Best Way!

In the old days treasure, — divine or earthly. Today, — Knowledge.

In the old days, — leisure, beneficent or Lotus eating; hermit or sybarite. Today, — Work.

In the old days, — the knight, the cavalier, the romancer. Today, — The Engineer.

Let us follow one such in his Quest, — A Twentieth Century Adventure!

The one such that Lillian Gilbreth refers to is Frank Gilbreth, an engineer/entrepreneur, and she likens him to a Grail Knight and the Grail to The One Best Way.

A Quest is a commitment to finding something sacred, even though it will typically remain always just out of reach. Only a great hero can hope to find it. The Holy Grail is a mythological representation of something so sacred as to be almost unattainable. The Grail imagery first appeared in medieval folkloric literature and combines Catholic religious imagery with pagan fertility symbols. In literature, the Holy Grail was pursued in a religious pilgrimage by Knights. The medieval Grail literature centered around King Arthur and his Knights of the Round Table, a literature that continues into the modern era. The ultimate Grail Knight was Galahad, the Holy Innocent. He is the only knight that had the strength, endurance, and pure commitment necessary to attain the Holy Grail, but he expended himself in the quest and died. Tennyson in his 1834 poem *Sir Galahad* quotes Galahad:

My strength is as the strength of ten,
Because my heart is pure.

Lillian Gilbreth likens the Holy Grail to the One Best Way, the Grail Quest to the pursuit of complete knowledge and perfect work, and the Grail Knight to the modern engineer/manager. The Quest makes work and knowledge sacred and transforms the organization, modeled on the home, into a sacred setting. The Quest must begin from a base in culture and the family, or the questing knight will be unable to meet the high standard, will not be pure and strong enough.

The Gilbreths make leadership the center of organizations and work. Leadership is a Quest and transforms the engineer/manager into a modern Grail Knight, because leadership is heroic and a highly moral task. Therefore, leaders must have high character, because only from high character can the Leader/Grail Knight gain the needed strength and purity. "My strength is as the strength of ten, because my heart is pure."

The purity required of the leader is purity of intention. A leader's intention must focus solely on purpose, primarily on the purpose of the organization and secondarily on the purpose of each of its members. The essence of leadership, the leader's quest, is to embody the organization purpose so purely that organization members, those being led, come to see that the organization purpose is also their purpose. A leader must be selflessly committed to the purpose of the organization and of the individual members. A leader's intention must be uncontaminated by any personal agenda, otherwise the leader will be guided by his own personal outcome and will be working for his own personal advantage and will ultimately subordinate the welfare of both the organization and its members to his own.

Purity of intention is very difficult to attain and maintain. Placing the welfare of the organization and of each of its members above ones own welfare may require great sacrifice. If a person is not willing to sacrifice, to serve, the person cannot lead, and any pretense of leading may be destructive to the organization and to the individuals. Leadership requires great courage and strength of character. As a test for whether one is suitable to be a leader in a given situation, one must ask: "Is the organization purpose worth my sacrifice? Are these people worth serving? Are these people worth my sacrifice?" If ones answer is "No," then one cannot lead them.

Leadership Case: USMC and Purity of Intention

Marine Corps Officer Training, Quantico, VA, 1969. Modern Testimony from Long-held Memories:

Marine leadership training included little if any reading matter. Instead, leadership was taught directly by instructors who put the truths of leadership directly into our faces, by instructors who were selected for being themselves gifted leaders with experience practicing in combat the leadership being taught. One example of this comes to mind from long ago.

A leadership heresy (A heresy is a half-truth that, if taken literally, will corrupt and destroy the whole truth.) is that the duty of a leader is to "look after your people." This idea is heretical because it sounds both benign and inspirational and thus tends to be found in much leadership teaching material, some of merit.[7] A good leader, of course, is wholly committed to looking after his people. Leaders should be selected and trained with this expectation in mind, but this is not the primary duty of a leader.

The leader's one duty is to achieve the assigned objective, the purpose of the organization. Without the successful achievement of the objective, all effort is for naught, and anything that lessens the likelihood of achievement contributes to failure and pointlessness. If the likelihood of failure is too high, the effort should not be made at all. The heresy of putting the interests of personnel first, as any leadership heresy, contributes to the likelihood of failure.

Attainment of the objective is the first and primary duty of the leader, but his responsibilities of course include secondary elements. One of the important secondary elements is the conservation of resources, which is an abstraction for "looking after the welfare of your people." It is an element that is so important, it should not require much effort to impress itself on a leader. But it is not the primary duty of the leader.

The following incident is reconstructed from a long-ago memory of infantry training in preparation for service in Viet Nam by one of the authors of this book. It is one example of Marine Corps efforts to drive home the danger of this heresy to a class of young officers in training. We were being taught tactics by an officer instructor who was a veteran of combat in Vietnam with experience leading Marines in stressful and dangerous challenges and who inspired us all with awe. We had spent long, exhausting hours assaulting a hill, being shown all the proper tactics. Toward the end of the exercise, the instructor gathered us around him for a face-to-face grilling, a Marine Corps teaching technique, to put leadership directly to us in the exact context. Instead of asking us questions about tactics, about such things as fire and maneuver or the use of supporting weapons, he simply asked, "What is the primary duty of the leader?" Someone quickly said, "to look after the safety of your people." The group of officer trainees, about thirty of us, promptly nodded in agreement, and there were some echoes of "Yes, to look after your people." Marine Corps training had obviously taught us that principle well. Groupthink being what it is, we all seemed to agree, until one lonely voice said "That can't be true. Our primary duty must be to take that hill.

Otherwise, why are we even here, and why expose our Marines to any danger at all?"

The instructor replied with force, "Exactly." He continued with a bit of condescension, "Well. It appears that we have one leader in this group, and the rest of you might make up a good flock of sheep. Your duty, your only duty at this moment, is to take that hill. And this isn't just extreme Marine Corps callousness to human life. This is unassailable logic. Logical, because if your primary duty as an officer and a leader is to look after the safety of your men, you wouldn't even expose them to the obvious dangers of the assault. You would turn your platoon around and lead them out of here, and the battle would be lost. So, most of you guys don't even think very clearly. You are arguing for cowardice and retreat without even realizing it. You are arguing for hesitance and timidity. And this is in the relative safety and comfort of our exercise. Wait until you have before you the lives of actual men in your platoon who you know and admire.

Your sacred duty as an officer and a leader is to use all the courage and expertise at your disposal to try to help your men, even at the risk of your own life. But that is a secondary duty and can be addressed only after you have addressed the primary duty, to inspire your men to give their full commitment, everything that they have, including their lives, to taking that hill. Their degree of commitment must be inspired by your degree of commitment. Any hesitancy on your part will erode their confidence, doing a disservice both to them and to the Corps. This is a hard truth, but it is leadership. If you don't understand that, you don't understand leadership. If you can't grasp that, then you have no place among us. There is no place here for sheep."

Endnotes

1. Proverbs 29:18.
2. Proverbs 11:14
3. F. Taylor, *Principles of Scientific Management* (New York: Harper & Brothers, 1911).
4. R. Kanigel, *The One Best Way* (London: Abacus, 1997), 11.
5. L. Gilbreth, *The Quest for the One Best Way* (Chicago, IL: Society of Industrial Engineers, 1924).
6. The well-known book, *Cheaper by the Dozen* was actually written in 1948 by their son, Frank Gilbreth Jr., and daughter, Ernistine Gilbreth Carey,

describing their somewhat humorous upbringing in Frank and Lillian Gilbreth's household.

7. E. Hess and K. Cameron, *Leading with Values* (Cambridge, MA: Cambridge University Press, 2006). This book contains Marine Corps examples, although neither of the authors appear to have been Marine Corps leaders themselves.

13

The Rise and Fall of
Responsible Innovation

In modern vocabulary, the term entrepreneurship has become almost synonymous with the term innovation. By the 20th century, economist Joseph Schumpeter brought the combination of entrepreneurship and innovation to the forefront of economic theory. More recently, given the rapid up-tick in the rate of technological innovations, there has been an increasingly loud call for "responsible innovation," or RI. The purpose of this essay is to examine the evolution of both concepts, entrepreneurship and innovation, and see if the call for responsible innovation, can add to our parallel interest in humane entrepreneurship.

The concept of innovation has become one of the most critical components in understanding modern economic development and is constantly called upon by government entities as a primary mechanism to increase positive economic activity. The 4th edition of the *Oslo Manual* written as a joint effort between the OECD's Directorate for Science, Technology and Innovation and the various European Commission members, to assist government entities in defining and measuring innovation data, offers a fairly typical and modern definition. With a focus on commercial innovation, the manual defines innovation as, "a new or improved product or process (or combination thereof), that differs significantly from the unit's previous products or processes and that has been made available to potential users (products) or brought into use by the unit (process)."[1] Within this manual, the OECD offers a number of characteristics of innovation: the outcome of innovative activity is uncertain; investments are required to achieve a level of innovation; innovation involves either developing new knowledge or combining existing knowledge in a new manner; innovation provides various positive spillover effects to society; innovation may have an element of property rights attached to it such as patents, and innovation generally provides the person who can use it with a competitive advantage in the marketplace.

The term, "innovation" is derived from the 14th century Latin root word, *innovationem* which is the noun from the *innovare*, or creating something "new". The term was used extensively by the Italian Renaissance writer, Niccolo Machiavelli in his 1513 discussion of administrative action, *The Prince*.[2] In *the Prince*, Machiavelli sees innovation as a political process, as a way of taking the initiative, when things become too predictable. This is reinforced in Machiavelli's *Discourses on Livy* where in 1517 he discusses political renewal, and the role innovation has in political renewal. As Machiavelli scholar Ero Arum points out, "to 'renew' (*rinnovare*) is to make something as if new, but it is also to recommence, to begin again, and thus to 'innovate' (*innovare*), or introduce something for the first time. If any distinction could ordinarily be drawn between 'renewal' (*rinnovazione*) and 'innovation' (*innovazione*), Machiavelli blurs the difference by using the terms interchangeably … Machiavelli uses *rinnovare* and *innovare* as synonyms."[2]

It is a way of taking quick action in a daring, and perhaps risky manner to achieve an end. Francis Bacon also discussed the nature of innovation in many of his writings, such as his 1625 *Essays or Counsels, Civil and Moral,* which contains a whole treatise on innovation, and the more philosophical work, *Novem Organum* published in 1620 which discusses scientific reasoning, and the rate of innovation. Like Machiavelli, Bacon also views innovation under a somewhat socio-political lens, as a way to accomplish something that needs to be done. But Bacon also recognizes the importance and benefit to humankind of scientific, intellectual, and artistic innovation, and that time is probably the greatest force behind innovation.[3]

Both Michiavelli's and Bacon's discussions of innovation recognizes that innovation has multiple elements. One element is that innovation is not only desirable, but necessary for the advancement of society, whether society is defined narrowly or broadly. Another element is that innovation should always be considered within the context of space and time and needs to be developed in the appropriate manner given the situation. And finally, both Machiavelli and Bacon imply that there is an "ethical" component to innovation, that it is something that needs to be properly thought out and implemented by the individual innovator.[4]

Whereas the earliest discussions of innovation up to the 19th century often framed innovation more as a process of action, incorporating elements of risk-taking, more recently the term is used more in combination with technological developments and advancements in science.

When examining the issue under a technology or product-development lens, innovation becomes a different process from the inventive process. While invention involves a creative component of idea generation, establishing "proof of concept" and possible protection of intellectual property through patents, innovation focuses more on the process of commercialization. Technology invention is generally the realm of scientists and design engineers. While these inventive individuals can also be innovators, the notion of innovation brings an element of management, finance, and business to the definition. There are many inventions in the world, but few of these are ever brought to the marketplace. The United Inventors Association in the United States reports that less than 5% of all patented inventions ever make it to the marketplace, and those that do, most will not be successful. The percentage is even lower in some industry sectors, such as biopharmaceuticals which has a 10-to-15-year pipeline of preclinical research and development, clinical trials and testing, regulatory review and approvals, and post market safety monitoring. One study for example, examined over 50,000 biopharmaceutical R&D projects, finding attrition rates close to 90% just in the preclinical stage, with the additional phases of testing and registration also showing significant attrition rates. Combining the attrition rates in each phase indicates a biopharmaceutical R&D commercialization success rate of less than 1%.[5]

Other empirical studies of R&D success rates show similar attrition. This points to an important fact that good science, while often necessary, is not sufficient for innovation. Innovation also requires a clear understanding of customer and market requirements, and the ability to obtain sufficient financing (internal or external) to continue the development and commercialization process. Innovation inevitably requires product redesign and strategic "pivoting" as user feedback is obtained through focus groups, beta-testing and field tests. It is in these activities that innovation and entrepreneurship appear to become closely connected in the modern world.

Innovation may also involve bundling a variety of other innovations and inventions into a final design. This is exactly how the Wright brothers achieved self-propelled, heavier than air flight on December 17, 1903 on the shores of Kitty Hawk, North Carolina. The Wright brothers did not invent the internal combustion engine used to power the *Wright Flyer* aircraft, nor did they invent the wing's airfoil that created lift. Instead, it was combination of these prior innovations with the 3-axis control system, something that the Wright brothers had experience with as bicycle makers, that created a successful flight.

Modern innovations in biotechnology, medicine, nanotechnology, warfare technologies, space travel, information technology, and energy have certainly taken the forefront of both interest and discussions. Not surprisingly, given the rapid rate of technological innovation (using the OECD's definition) in the modern world, and the potential for significant and large-scale negative impacts on human life, social structures and the global environment, there has been an increasingly loud debate about the idea of "responsible innovation," in both the government policy sectors and the philosophy of science literature.

Rene von Schomber of the science policy group at the European Commission, for example, has the following definition,

> Responsible Research and Innovation is a transparent, interactive process by which societal actors and innovators become mutually responsive to each other with a view to the (ethical) acceptability, sustainability and societal desirability of the innovation process and its marketable products (in order to allow a proper embedding of scientific and technological advances in our society).[6]

Discussions of "responsible innovation" are just beginning in earnest. The IEEE notes, for example, that a "decade ago, RI (responsible innovation, sometimes called RRI, or responsible research and innovation) was practically unheard of ... and the concept is still in its infancy".[7] But the community of people deeply interested in RI is growing, but this definition clearly puts the responsibility on a process of interaction, understanding and action between society, those decision makers within in society and the innovators themselves, whether individuals or entities. Given this definition of RI, why is this important for our discussion of humane economies and entrepreneurship? For two basic reasons. First, throughout recorded history economic structures, business institutions, and commercial activities are the primary driving force in most societal relationships and changes. Second, entrepreneurs, and entrepreneurial activity, are closely connected to the continuing process of innovation in the modern world.

The commonly referenced close connection between entrepreneurship and innovation is of recent origins and seems to be correlated with the rise of technological invention and R&D investment. Early references of entrepreneurship within a somewhat modern context dates to the Middle Ages, the 12th and 13th centuries when economic activity and trade greatly expanded in Europe, and large economic centers and leagues such as the Hanseatic Leage started to appear. During this period, entrepreneurial behavior was generally viewed as a "go between" trade activity that internalized or assumed much of the business risks of trade. Unlike the modern world of insurance, international letters of credit, computerized supply chain interconnectivity, limited liability organizations, and enforceable civil contracts, a person involved in trade during Middle Ages internalized most of the specific and general risks of trade. As individuals. they would personally purchase intermediate products and then assemble the finished products, own or lease the means of transporting those goods to the buyer or market (whether by ship or wagon), provide the necessary security against thievery and piracy, assume the risk of devasting weather or natural disasters, deliver the goods to the buyer, and ultimately collect the agreed upon payment in gold, silver, or barter goods for return export, and then be able to safely return with that payment without loss. Not surprisingly, early philosophical and theological discussions of entrepreneurship focused on the idea of "entrepreneurial profit" to compensate for this increased risk, something that was certainly debatable in the Middle ages where most prices (and profits) were highly regulated by royal decree, local municipal governments, large trading groups like the Hanseatic League, and particularly the powerful local craft guilds — fraternities of tradesmen who organized to set prices, manage product quality, and regulate competition within specific industry sectors. And this was a time when most Christian and Islamic theologians argued against a profit that exceeded the cost of necessary inputs.

By the 16th century, economic conditions had changed dramatically. The power of the guilds had been broken, the corporate/government charter organizational model was becoming more dominant, and the legitimacy of entrepreneurial profit had been accepted in economic philosophy.

Even by the 18th century, entrepreneurship was still not closely intertwined with the notion of innovation. Adam Smith in his various works,

The Theory of Moral Sentiment, Wealth of Nations, and various recovered lectures from the 1760s published as *Lecture Notes of Jurisprudence,* viewed an efficient economy as being composed of relatively small, proprietary businesses each specializing in a particular sector of the economy. While Smith did not specifically use the term "entrepreneur" in his writings, he did note that individuals can form businesses, and act in a somewhat enterprising manner. But Smith did not really see the idea of enterprising individuals tied closely to innovation, but rather the general functioning of the economy. In this respect, Smith took a fairly straightforward and traditional view of individuals who today we might call "entrepreneurs". Smith generally saw nations becoming wealthy, and economic growth as a function of efficient changes in the division of labor, the proper allocation of capital and labor, and trade. To Smith, an enterprising type of person can be considered, in his own words, an "individual, who forms an organization for commercial purposes." Elsewhere in the *Wealth of Nations,* Smith points out that such enterprising individuals can also provide personal capital and fund their commercial activity.[8] But there is only a hint by Smith of the tight connection between innovation and entrepreneurship that so dominants modern thinking. Smith, for example, does discuss how these individuals may have the ability to see new opportunities for products or services. But Smith, in general, saw such enterprising individuals as classic industrialists of the time, albeit with some unique characteristics of individual behavior in providing capital and sensing new demand.[9] Within this framework, individuals who act entrepreneurial can indeed contribute to economic growth and the creation of wealth, not through the power of innovation as we assume today, but more in how such an individual can impact changes in labor, and the allocation of capital and labor.[10]

The merging of the concepts of entrepreneurship with innovation really began in the 19th century. As discussed in another essay, but certainly worth repeating given our interest in the increasingly close connection between innovation and entrepreneurship, is the definitional evolution of the term entrepreneurship starting in the 18th century, leading into the 19th and 20th centuries. While Richard Cantillon in 1755 used the term "undertaker" to represent an entrepreneur that was willing to take the risks associated with developing products or services with unknown sales potential, prices, and profit, by the early 19th century, Jean-Baptiste Say, in his 1803 *A Treatise on Political Economy,* focused on a comprehensive theory of entrepreneurship and its important role in an economy. He discussed the role of the entrepreneur in slightly more modern terms, as an intermediary in both the production and innovation process, arguing that entrepreneurs are individuals who create value in an economy by moving resources out of areas of low productivity into areas of higher productivity and greater yield.[11]

According to Karol Sledzik, Say, "developed the most comprehensive concept of entrepreneurship at that time. The entrepreneur uses the ideas of a philosopher, that is new knowledge, which has not yet been applied in the economy to produce a new product. To do this the entrepreneur employs workers, capital, and natural resources to actualize the new knowledge into a tradable good."[12] While Say only touched on the entrepreneurs' role in innovation in his writings, he clearly saw an innovative component in entrepreneurial behavior. Say's work was highly influential on the founding fathers of the U.S; he maintained active correspondences with both Thomas Jefferson and James Madison and was invited to move to Virginia.

While somewhat gradual in its marriage, 20th century economist Joseph Schumpeter brought the tight relation between entrepreneurship and innovation to the forefront in economic theory. Schumpeter discusses five different types of innovation, product innovation, process innovation, market innovation (or the opening of a new market), input innovation (defining a new supply source), and organizational innovation. In Schumpeter's first major work, *The Theory of Economic Development* published in 1911, he lays out the role of entrepreneurs in an economy as developing new combinations of innovative activities, some of which are revolutionary or discontinuous. To Schumpeter, entrepreneurs draw upon inventions, and then transform these inventions or ideas into a viable product or service. Entrepreneurs, participating in a competitive marketplace, must innovate to be successful, or even survive in the long run — this creates the diffusion process of innovation through society and the economy. Some innovations are more important than others. Revolutionary, discontinuous innovations are those that are "paradigm busting," that force a significant change and re-evaluation of the prior way of doing things. To Schumpeter, this is the core of economic development. These radical types of innovation, managed by entrepreneurs, ultimately form the class of Schumpeterian "creative destruction," the key to a continuous, albeit uneven, process of economic rebirth.

Schumpeter in his later work, *Capitalism, Socialism and Democracy* (1942), and his less cited essay, *Economic Theory and Entrepreneurial*

History (1949), emphasizes the role of innovation, perhaps even more than individual entrepreneurship. In his earlier writings, Schumpeter saw the entrepreneur as an "outstanding individual," however, in his later writings, the concept was broadened somewhat; he saw entrepreneurial behavior combined with innovation as the key issue, whether this activity was performed by individuals, entities, or even countries.[13] Within this context, innovation becomes the key to economic development, and entrepreneurial behavior is that action which facilitates and encourages innovation. By the time of Murray Rothbard's 1962 treatise, *Man, Economy, and State*, and Baumol's extensive discussions of the economic role of entrepreneurship in his 1968 essay "Entrepreneurship in Economic Theory," published in the *American Economic Review*, and then later with his 2010 book, *The Microtheory of Innovative Entrepreneurship*, the conceptual and rhetorical marriage between entrepreneurship and innovation seemed almost complete.[14]

At the present time, philosophical discussions of RI tend to focus on three key issues: The philosophical assumptions of responsible innovation, the nature of responsibility when confronted by the uncertainty of the impacts of future innovations, and the way responsible versus non-responsible innovations affects perceptions, experiences, and learning. For this essay, we are primarily interested in the first issue, and how innovation is tied to the notion of entrepreneurship and a humane economy. In this respect, responsible innovation essentially moves the traditional, academic perspective of philosophy of science, to a more "action-oriented tradition" where legitimate innovation needs to be intentional, and proactively aligned with the needs of society. When implemented, RI generally includes a combination of four elements, anticipation, reflexivity, inclusion, and responsiveness as well as an understanding of both the anticipated and unanticipated impacts of research and innovation.[15] Schulff and Dijkstra reviewed the existing published literature on RI, concluding that although RI deals with important issues, the field contains perhaps too broad a set of topics. They note that if RI, "with all its elements is too complex to be realized in practice, maybe focusing on specific characteristics, dimensions or values will lead to a more complete uptake in practice."[16]

The conclusion in this essay, is that RI (or RRI) as a specific concept may suffer from the same "buzzword" phenomenon often seen in business. Driven by government bureaucracies and policy think tanks, using broad, hard to define concepts such as "inclusion" and "sustainability" to justify RI may be dangerous. A modern tendency has been to put various sensitive-sounding adjectives acting as "softening-agents" in front of activities that have taken on a more severe perception in recent times. Thus, we have "ethical" business, "sustainable" enterprise, "responsible" research and innovation, and even the focus of this book, "humane" economies and entrepreneurship. Many times, discussion of these concepts base their arguments on referencing other, equally broad, or even fallacious concepts, creating a word map of multiple "weasel words," to use Friedrich Hayek's analogy, with arrows all pointing at each other but actually devoid of real meaning upon deeper investigation. Theorists need to delve much deeper into the idea of RI and its relationship to entrepreneurship to prevent this, if it is possible.

Given that entrepreneurship and innovation are so closely related in the modern world, and humaneness is one of the components often mentioned under the umbrella of RI, it is important that we consider this issue. Hopefully, RI is not becoming just a fad or marketing scheme promoted by government bureaucracies like the EU. Like entrepreneurship, the term innovation when properly defined, is neither humane nor inhumane, but instead by its nature, may or may not contribute to the development of society. To the extent that an entrepreneur is engaged in innovation, and the commercialization of technology, RI can actually be considered an important part of our discussion of humane entrepreneurship and humane economies Afterall, a non-responsible introduction of a technological innovation, whether significant or trivial in nature, probably does not contribute to a humane economy. And just as using the notion of humane entrepreneurship simply for the purposes of marketing of a business school product, the same danger exists in using a poorly understood and unachievable definition of RI in the marketing, promotion and justification of different research and development agendas and investments.

One interesting, and perhaps legitimate exception to this observation is a suggestion by Lars Hammershøj[17] Most writers tend to look at RI as, (a) a process of inputs to the innovation process, such as individual virtues and the ethical behaviors of participants in order to increase the sense of responsibleness,[18] (b) as an output management problem which requires management of irresponsibly developed, and perhaps damaging innovations, or (c) as a demand problem where the expectation is that customers will demand responsible innovations and products in their purchasing behaviors.[19] Hammershøj, takes a different approach, and argues that innovation is affective in nature, and thus the overriding moods of the participants becomes critical. He suggests that innovation and creativity are mediated by different moods of "disturbance and enthusiasm," with creativity based upon the participants feelings of irritations (the disturbance mood) and interest (the enthusiasm mood). On the other hand, innovation is based upon the participants feelings of anger (the disturbance mood) and desire (the enthusiasm mood). Hammershøj suggests that understanding these different moods, and associated feelings, can create an ethical approach. This idea overlaps somewhat with the phenomenological approach to humane entrepreneurship suggested in a prior essay of this book. Classical phenomenologists like Edmund Husserl (1859–1938) and Maurice Merleau-Ponty (1908–1961) argue for a broad view of the phenomenal characteristics of experiences. Husserl, for example, talks extensively about the "lived-body," that a person sees the world as a field of sensing and experiences. This is the affective perspective. Moods, emotions, and desires are experiences, and thus can impact a person's view of the world, and how one ultimately acts in that world. This brings the idea of RI back to the world of experiences grounded in a phenomenological understanding, and ultimately back to our discussion of humaneness.

Endnotes

1. OECD/Eurostat, *Oslo Manual 2018: Guidelines for Collecting, Reporting and Using Data on Innovation, 4th Edition. The Measurement of Scientific, Technological and Innovation Activities*, (Paris: OECD, 2018). https://doi.org/10.1787/9789264304604-en.
2. N. Machiavelli, *The Prince*, transl. G. Bull (London: Penguin Classics, reissue edition, 2003). Original work published 1513.
3. E. Arum, "Machiavelli's Principio: Political Renewal and Innovation in the Discourses on Livy," *The Review of Politics* 82 (2020), 525–547.
4. See F. Bacon, *Essays or Counsels, Civil and Moral* (London: George Routledge and Sons, 1884). Original work published 1625. http://www.columbia.edu/cu/lweb/digital/collections/cul/texts/ldpd_7914458_000/index.html, and F. Bacon, *Novem Organum* (New York, NY: P.F. Collier & Sons 1902). Original work published 1620. Accessed at https://oll.libertyfund.org/title/bacon-novum-organum.
5. F. Pammolli, L. Righetto, S. Abrignani, L. Pani, P. Pelicci, and E. Rabosio, "The Endless Frontier? The Recent Increase of R&D Productivity in Pharmaceuticals," *Journal of Translational Medicine* 18, no. 1 (2010), 162.

6. R. Von Schomberg, "A Vision of Responsible Research and Innovation," in *Responsible Innovation: Managing the Responsible Emergence of Science and Innovation in Society,* ed. Owen, J. Bessant and M. Heintz (London: Wiley, 2013), 51–74.

7. https://spectrum.ieee.org/what-does-responsible-innovation-mean.

8. In this manner, Smith's enterprising small businessperson, or "proprietor" acts like a "proprietary capitalist", See P. Scranton, *Proprietary Capitalism* (Boston: Cambridge University Press, 2003) for a good discussion about the nature of "proprietary capitalism" versus large-scale corporate capitalism.

9. In the Smith works cited, Smith makes several claims about the character of a small businessperson that acts in an enterprising manner (although not specifically using the term "entrepreneur"). See Smith, A. (1997). *The Theory of Moral Sentiments. Washington*, DC: Regnery Publishing (Original work written 1759); Smith, A. (1986). *The Wealth of Nations.* London: Penguin Books (Original work published 1776); and Smith, A. *Lectures in Jurisprudence* (Originally delivered 1762–1763). Available online at Adam SmithWorks.org. Accessed at https://www.adamsmithworks.org/documents/digital-jurisprudence.

10. Even with the focus on how entrepreneurship can alter the allocation of labor, one can still make a significant argument that entrepreneurship can contribute significantly to economic growth and the wealth of nations under Adam Smith's economic theory presented in the *Wealth of Nations*. See S. Michael, "Entrepreneurship, Growth, and Adam Smith," *Strategic Entrepreneurship Journal* 1, no.3–4, (2007), 287–289.

11. J. Say, *A Treatise on Political Economy; or The Production, Distribution, and Consumption of Wealth* (London: Franklin Classics, 2018). Original work published 1803.

12. K. Sledzik, "Schumpeter's View on Innovation and Entrepreneurship," *SSRN Electronic Journal*, April, (2013), 92. Accessed at https://www.researchgate.net/publication/256060978_Schumpeter's_View_on_Innovation_and_Entrepreneurship, See also T. Grebel, "Neo-Schumpeterian Perspectives in Entrepreneur's Research," in *Elgar Companion to Neo-Schumpeterian Economics*, ed. H. Hanush and A. Pyka (Cheltenham: Edward Elgar, 2007).

13. See Sledzik, "Schumpeter's View on Innovation." (SSRN, 2013), https://papers.ssrn.com/sol3/papers.cfm?abstract_id=2257783.

14. See M. Rothbard, *Man, Economy, and State* (Auburn, AL: Ludwig Von Mises Institute, 1993). Original work published 1965; W. Baumol "Entrepreneurship in Economic Theory," *The American Economic Review* 58, no. 2 (1968), 64–78; W. Baumol, *The Microtheory of Innovative Entrepreneurship, (*Princeton, NJ: Princeton University Press, 2010).

15. See J. Stilgoe, R. Owen and P. Macnaghten, "Developing a Framework for Responsible Innovation," *Research Policy* 42, no. 9 (2013), 1568–11580, for an often-cited framework to consider responsible innovation.
16. M. Schuijffand and A. Dijkstra, "Practices of Responsible Research and Innovation: A Review," *Science and Engineering Ethics* 26 (2020), 533–574, 569. The authors reviewed over 50 recently published articles that addressed the issue of responsible research and innovation.
17. L. Hammershøj "Conceptualizing Creativity and Innovation as Affective Processes: Steve Jobs, Lars Von Trier, and Responsible Innovation," *Philosophy of Management* 17 (2018), 115–131. See also V. Blok, "Philosophy of Innovation: A Research Agenda," *Philosophy of Management* 17 (2018), 1–5, for a quick summary of different RI approaches. M. Hühn, "Responsible Innovation: A Smithian Perspective," *Philosophy of Management* 17 (2018), 41–57 examines the writings of Adam Smith in providing an economic perspective for responsible innovation.
18. This is the approach taken by those that see RI grounded in a Smithian sense of sympathy, charity, benevolence, and human sentiments with an economic system as described in *The Theory of Moral Sentiments*. See M. Hühn, "Responsible Innovation" and for a well-argued perspective of this nature. But without consideration of the problems inherent in both the inhumane nature of institutional giantism and the alternate world view of the human experience derived from the fictitious commodities of labor and capital in the general economy, relying on human sentiment with the marketplace, no matter how noble, this approach will still ultimately require a governmental overview of such behaviors.
19. For a demand-based argument to drive RI, see M. Schlaile, M. Mueller, M. Schramm and A. Pyka, "Evolutionary Economics, Responsible Innovation and Demand: Making a Case for the Role of Consumers," *Philosophy of Management* 17 (2018), 7–39. A stakeholder approach to RI is offered by V. Blok, "Look Who's Talking: Responsible Innovation, The Paradox of Dialogue and the Voice of the Other in Communication and Negotiation Processes," *Journal of Responsible Innovation* 1, no. 2 (2014), 171–190.

14

Beauty, Humaneness, and the Object of Economic Behavior

Beauty is not often discussed as an objective of economic behavior. Most modern economists would define economics under the commonly discussed terms of production, distribution, exchange, and consumption of goods and services. But in this essay, we will consider beauty as something to consider, particularly in combination with our focus on humaneness.

Beauty, and its conceptual partner, aesthetics has been examined since the beginning of philosophy. Aristotle was one of the first philosophers to discuss the nature of beauty, seeing it as something that creates a pleasing impression. To Aristotle, beauty was mostly an objective concept, something that existed outside a human's mind. Plato extended Aristotle's orientation and described beauty as something radiant, something clearly visible and loved. But while Plato also saw beauty as an objective characteristic, he argues that beauty also represents a relationship between the part and the whole. For example, in the dialogs described in the *Phadeo* (also known as "On the Soul") Plato notes that beauty has an opposite in "ugliness," as "just is opposite to unjust," and that something is "beautiful because it partakes of that beauty." But beauty is also put at the same level as "goodness, justice, and holiness."[1]

Plato, in fact, starts to pose one of the most perplexing issues discussed by philosophers throughout time — is beauty a function of objective characteristics? Is beauty completely subjective in nature, as the phrase, "beauty is in the eye of the beholder" might suggest. Or is beauty something in between, combining both subjective and objective characteristics? Medieval philosophers, such as Augustine, and later Scholastic thinkers, such St. Thomas Aquinas generally took a more Aristotelian approach, and considered beauty primarily as an objective reality, something that existed regardless of human senses or thinking, but was still appreciated by humans through their sensory perceptions and thought. Modern philosophers, as well as the art community in general, tend to lean more toward a subjective point of view of beauty — this allows almost anything to be called "beautiful" if a viewer has a sensory appreciation and a moving experience. Not surprisingly, as one hears often in the modern art community, there is no such thing as "bad art." American philosopher, Crispin Sartwell, explores this issue in his essay on aesthetics, part of a larger treatise on philosophical complexities his book, *Entanglements: A System of Philosophy*. Sartwell calls the objective-subjective debate a "false dilemma" that misses the complex relationship, symbiotic between the two perspectives — it is both objective and subjective; objects are always connected to a sensory experience, and they are difficult to disentangle.[2]

There are certain things that almost everybody would say are beautiful, such as the view from the North Rim of the Grand Canyon, or a radiant sunset over the Pacific Ocean. On the other hand, nobody would say, except perhaps pathologically damaged psychopaths, that a deadly car accident or mangled bodies on a battlefield are appealing or beautiful. Appreciation of beauty certainly requires the activation, range, and combination of the senses. Beauty also appears influenced by culture and time. These are the most basic problems of understanding beauty that have been discussed by philosophers for thousands of years.

The purpose of this essay, however, is not to contribute to the philosophy of art or aesthetics, but rather to consider a possible connection between beauty, economics, and humaneness. One point of note, however, is that "beauty" in most classical philosophical discussions is primarily phrased as a "noun." However, in general discussions, people often talk about something interactively complex as being beautiful, or an action being beautifully presented. This type of usage does not refer to pieces of visual art, lofty music, elegant dancing, sunsets over the Pacific Ocean, or even human attractiveness. Here the term is being applied more as an adverb or adjective, something that is associated with something else. For example, people often refer to something being beautiful when reflecting upon an elderly parent's past "good life," the intense and meaningful love a person has for another, or while viewing something, even mechanical, that appears harmonious, if not mysterious in its workings. So at least in common terminology, there seems to be something in the way a complex relationship works or presents itself, that appears to encourage a human sense of beauty.

Economies are a system of complex relationships, yet economists rarely discuss beauty within this context. While Adam Smith does not develop a philosophy of aesthetics, he does discuss beauty several times in his various writings. For example, Smith developed a series of lectures in 1762–1763 discussing the nature of language and communication. Now published as *Lectures on Rhetoric and Belles Lettres*,[3] Smith mentions the nature of beauty in relationship to language. Speaking about language, Smith seems to agree with Sartwell's perspective, that beauty stems from a complex combination of two elements, "the sentiment and the method of expressing it being suitable to the passion."[4] The sentiment element appears to be related to a sensory appreciation and pleasure when hearing the language, while the method component appears to be related to the suitability issue. Smith places much more emphasis on the second concept of suitability. Suitability, in Smith's mind, refers to how suitable the expression is for the conveyance of the sentiment. Smith argues, however, that when both concepts can be combined, then "your language has all the beauty it can have."[5]

This is an important concept since almost all discussions of aesthetics and rhetoric, both before and after Adam Smith, add other elements to their argument of beauty — most importantly, the idea of "literary tropes" (figurative language that substitutes for the more literal concept) and "rhetorical figures" (an element that gives language something more than the obvious). Zaccheus Harmon, of the *Adam Smith Works*, argues that Smith "maintains that tropes and figures of speech 'give no beauty of their own.' Instead, these literary devices 'only are agreeable and beautiful when they suit the sentiment and express in the neatest manner the way in which the speaker is affected.'"[6] The use of figures and tropes is only a 'secondary means' for conveying the sentiments or ideas of speakers in the clearest and most perspicuous way possible.[7] Whenever the use of rhetorical figures inhibits the clear expression of ideas or feelings, then these figures, far from enhancing the beauty of the composition, serve merely to deform it."[8]

Thus, Smith's understanding of beauty is one of functionality and purpose, combined with a bit of harmonious elegance. It is a beauty

grounded in the "aesthetic of utility." To Smith devices to artificially create elegance can actually "deform" the object or idea, unless these devices
can be directly tied back to the functionality. But Adam Smith's discussion of beauty is not limited to language. Smith also interweaves the
spheres of both aesthetics and ethics throughout his other writings and
goes right to the heart of his understanding of economic behavior. Eduard
Ghita points out, for example, that, "The large extent to which aesthetic
terms pervade Adam Smith's discussion of ethical issues, such as personal
duty, virtue, distinction of ranks, utility, propriety and merit would seem
to suggest, in the least, that the spheres of aesthetics and ethics interwoven
in way hardly possible to conceive in the wake of Kant."[9] But it is exactly
these virtues, particularly as expounded in Part IV of his *Theory of Moral
Sentiment* that individual small business owners, industrialists, and entrepreneurs consider in their economic decision making.

In Chapter 1, Part IV of the *Theory of Moral Sentiment* Smith also
emphasizes the utility component of beauty, something that has beauty is
a combination that has both utility or end purpose, and some objective
quality of harmonious arrangement in order to achieve this utility.[10] It is
interesting to note that many of Smith's examples in Chapter 1 are
mechanical in nature, such as a mechanical watch, and not pieces of art.
Ghita notes that, "Smith draws attention not to the utility of an object, but
to its fitness to promote a certain end ... Differently put, it is not utility
that matters, so much as the arrangement or the means which promotes
this utility."[11] Thus, it is the proper arrangement of the elements that leads
to the utility objective that is key to beauty. Smith writes, "it is the ingenious and artful adjustment of those means to the end for which they were
intended, that is the principal source of his admiration."[12] While in the
above quotes, Smith is generally referring to objects, he also extends
the arguments to "institutions." As he points out, "the same principle, the
same love of system, the same regard to the beauty of order, of art and
contrivance, frequently serves to recommend those institutions which tend
to promote the public welfare."[13] When referring to government, for
example, Smith writes, their "sole use and end" recommends the spirit of
system "a certain beautiful and orderly system." Thus, a system can,
indeed, contain elements of beauty.

In Chapter 2, Part IV of the *Theory of Moral Sentiments*, Smith
extends his discussion of beauty within the context of moral behavior and
virtuous conduct. Smith even suggests that the "characters of men," who
are essentially "repositories" of their various virtues,[14] have the ability to

appreciate beauty to a greater degree, in both their utility and design. As he writes in *The Theory of Moral Sentiment*, the "turn of mind [of the man who is prudent, equitable, active, resolute, and sober] has at least all the beauty which can belong to the most perfect machine that was ever invented for promoting the most agreeable purpose."[15] Smith is referring to the moral behavior of individuals, including economic decision makers. It is interesting to note that in Part IV of *The Theory of Moral Sentiment*, Smith discusses beauty, along with other qualities, virtues, and actions, all in the same chapter as if connected. Although not discussed much in modern economic literature, it appears that to Smith, there might be an aesthetic orientation (in combination with human virtues) that ultimately defines the oft referenced, "invisible hand."

Given this context, we believe that while Smith's discussion of beauty in language, for example, which in its most basic functional form, is simply a method of communication, his concepts of beauty can also be extended to an economy, which in its most basic form deals with production, distribution, exchange, and consumption of goods and services. Business, after all, is interested in finding a harmonious relationship between buyer and seller, it is all about the system. In Part IV of *The Theory of Moral Sentiments*, Smith makes it clear that the notion of beauty can extend to a "system." If we extend Smith's argument, the notion of beauty can also be considered intertwined with an economic system. There is a component of beauty in the virtuous "characters of men" that make up the business owner, managers, and entrepreneurial population, and there is a component of beauty in the economic system that provides goods and services. If we make this analogy using Smith's theory of beauty, however, there needs to be the economic analogy of both sentiment and suitability combined, while carefully considering the "arrangement or the means which promotes this utility." We suggest that the binding analogy, that provides sentiment and suitability, while promoting the "aesthetics of utility," is found in the notion of "humaneness" as discussed in this book, and by a small number of other economists and philosophers, such as Wilhelm Ropke and Roger Scruton. As discussed throughout this book, humaneness has meaning at both the systems level of the economy, as well as the personal, existential and phenomenological level for the entrepreneur.

An appropriate comparison is the notion of "City Beautiful." The City Beautiful movement started as a reform architectural movement in the late-1900s and early-20th century, with an objective of making U.S.

cities more beautiful in architectural design, and ultimately livability. The objective of the movement was not only to make cities, such as Chicago, Cleveland, and Detroit physically attractive after decades of unplanned, haphazard growth, but also with an understanding that beauty inspires behavioral changes, such as increasing moral actions, harmonious order, and quality of life. As Carlino and Saiz observe, "The City Beautiful philosophy emphasized the importance of improving the living conditions of the urban populace, and their physical and psychological welfare. High aesthetics were believed to imbue city dwellers with moral and civic virtue."[16] Within this context, beauty is considered a classic economic "public good," that can be enjoyed by everyone.

Understanding the tight relationship between social behavior, societal ideals, and architectural design is not new. For example, Leon Battista Alterti's 15th century treatise, *De Re Acdificatoria*, explored the integration of architecture and the humanistic culture of the times. In practice, the early Medici dynasty, patrons of the arts and architecture, not only tried to project their own wealth and status through planning and design, but also created a Florentine look at many levels that would intentionally increase both the population's quality of life and provide a higher level of humanistic and spiritual understanding.

Unfortunately, in many cities, the early City Beautiful movement often degraded into simply building monuments, rather than considering the full, inclusive, and multifaceted meaning of the word beautiful. Not surprisingly, the City Beautiful movement had it various ups and downs over the years, with critics sometimes pointing out that creating monuments should not take priority over addressing communities' various social needs. But in recent times, there has been a revival of the City Beautiful movement, with more of a focus on livability and quality of life.

The evidence certainly points to the fact that attractive cities do result in more positive spillover effects, depending on how "attractiveness" is defined. For example, in a large econometric study of 305 communities done for the Federal Reserve Bank of Philadelphia, Gerald Carlino and Albert Salz examined the relationship between certain "public goods" reflecting a philosophy of City Beautiful, and various measures of economic development. Public goods included both "objective" characteristics, such as natural and human produced amenities (proximity to ocean, historic districts, parks, etc.) and more subjective measures (architectural beauty, scenic locations, etc.) that were estimated from the rate of "geotagging" various crowdsourced photos of these communities. They found that employment and population growth were significantly higher in metro areas that were considered more "picturesque." They also found that, "beautiful cities disproportionally attracted highly educated individuals," concluding that "while the American central city generally did not come back in the 1990s and 2000s, the beautiful city within flourished."[17]

A number of more aggressive planning and zoning mechanisms, such as mixed-use communities, increased bike paths and recreation amenities, architectural design standards, historical preservation, anti-graffiti laws, landscaping requirements, and strong signage rules that eliminate ugly billboards and blinking digital signs, are now being implemented to increase the beauty, physical attractiveness, and ultimately the quality of life in urban areas. Urban communities that fail in the modern philosophy of City Beautiful appear destined for ultimate decline, population loss, and increased crime. On a more micro-level, research has shown that creating a more attractive community, such as "greening vacant lots" and "planting trees" may actually reduce crime in urban areas, as such efforts tend to increase community pride and social interactions.[18]

The above discussion points to the fact that beauty, particularly in the way that Adam Smith views it, can be a successful objective for certain types of economic decision making. Beauty, when implemented, has a number of positive direct and spillover benefits. Beauty also allows for the incorporation of virtuous behavior and ideals, one of the keys of a competitive economy as described by Adam Smith. This raises an interesting question — perhaps economics in general should incorporate Smiths perspective of beauty into its objective function. Given Smith's somewhat unique perception of beauty as an "aesthetics of utility" applied to a working system, whether that system is language, as discussed in his *Lectures on Rhetoric and Belles Lettres,* or mechanical, governmental, or human, as detailed in Part IV of the *Theory of Moral Sentiment*, can a broader economic system also be beautiful? If so, then it is reasonable to consider which economic system has the greatest potential for an "aesthetics of utility" while incorporating humans' "repository of virtues." And like the modern City Beautiful movement, focused more on quality-of-life issues versus the self-aggrandizing monuments of the 19th century (the architectural analogy of Smith's deforming rhetorical figures), it appears that systems in decline can, with proper understanding and courageous effort, be fixed. It is exactly within this context that humaneness as discussed in this book becomes highly relevant.

Endnotes

1. Plato. *Phaedo*, transl. B. Jowett. http://classics.mit.edu/Plato/phaedo.html. Original work c. 360 BC.
2. C. Sartwell, *Entanglements: A System of Philosophy* (New York, NY: SUNY Press, 2017).
3. This represents 1762 and 1763 lecture notes by two of Adam Smith's students that were discovered in 1958 at the University of Aberdeen, and subsequently published under the title *Lectures of Rhetoric and Belles Lettres*. See A. Smith, *Lectures on Rhetoric and Belles Lettres*. ed. J. Bryce. (Indianapolis: Liberty Fund, 1958). https://storage.googleapis.com/catalog.libertyfund.org/PDFPreview/Smith_LecturesonRhetoric_1684_preview.pdf. Accessed August 30, 2022.
4. Smith, *Lectures on Rhetoric*, 57.
5. *Ibid.*, 56.
6. *Ibid.*, i. 73.
7. *Ibid.*, v. 58.
8. Z. Harmon, "Beauty and Language in Adam Smith," https://www.adamsmithworks.org/speakings/beauty-and-language-in-adam-smith.
9. E. Ghita, "Adam Smith on Beauty, Utility, and the Problem of Disinterested Pleasure," *Journal of Early Modern Studies* 2 (2021), 115–130, 115.
10. A. Smith, *The Theory of Moral Sentiments* (Washington, DC: Regnery Publishing, 1997). Original work published 1759. Smith actually produced multiple editions of *The Theory of Moral Sentiment* during his life, with the last edition published in 1790. His discussion of beauty, however, did not appear to change between these editions.
11. Ghita, "Adam Smith on Beauty," 119.
12. Smith, *Theory of Moral Sentiments*, 163.
13. Smith, *Theory of Moral Sentiments*, 165.
14. See D. Reisman, *Adam Smith's Sociological Economics* (London: Routledge, 1976), 88.
15. Smith, *Theory of Moral Sentiments*, 187.
16. G. Carlino and A. Saiz, "Beautiful City: Leisure Amenities and Urban Growth," *Journal of Regional Science* 59 (2019), 69–408, 369.
17. Carlino and Saiz, "Beautiful City," 403.
18. While few in number, some studies of specific "beautifications" efforts have shown a positive correlation with reducing crime and increasing positive social behavior. See, for example, see E. Garvin, C. Cannuscio and C. Branas, "Greening Vacant Lots to Reduce Violent Crime: A Randomised Controlled Trial," *Injury Prevention* 19, no. 3 (2013), 198–203.

Section V

Humane Scale: The Structure of Humane Endeavor

Section V is titled, Humane Scale: The Structure of Humane Endeavor. Three essays are presented, all with a focus on "scale." The first essay, *Powerful Machines and Humane Growth* takes a life cycle approach, similar to humans. Over time a period of growth and development occurs and will flower into a period of maturity and maximum productivity. A healthy life will sustain the period of productivity for as long as the living person can maintain itself on its own foundation using its own resources. The productive period is inevitably followed by a period of decline characterized by both a weakening ability to produce and a lessening usefulness of both physical and intellectual output, a diminishing demand for the life's output. Decline culminates in death, always and without exception, in a state of unproductivity with no ability to produce output. Many ventures adhere closely to the human life cycle and mature and die like anything human must. From a humane beginning, corporations often grow to be organizations gigantic in size and power, often becoming inhumane in their actions. This essay looks at several case studies.

The next essay, *Managerial Capitalism: Statism and Giantism*, examines Edith Penrose's opinions on the theory of the firm. Penrose appears to reverse the traditional theory of the firm. In the traditional theory of the firm, firms identify an exogeneous demand and then acquire resources as needed to develop productive capacity to meet the exogeneous demand. Penrose theory reverses the order; the firm seeks to stimulate and generate demand in any shape, place, or time necessary to bring in revenue sufficient to feed the managerial capacity that constitutes the organization. Current demand must be kept high enough to maintain employment of the current administrative managers and bureaucracy. This creates problems of managerial statism and giantism. This ultimately leads to the various industrial-governmental complexes seen in the modern world. President Eisenhower warned the world of this problem. Unfortunately, entrepreneurship education often falls into this gigantic mode of thinking, with admiring discussions of gazelles, unicorns, and rapid salability.

The last essay, *A Humane Economy*, starts with understanding the problems of "enmassment," the giantism of virtually all institutions in society, and organizational "disembodiment." The essay then looks specifically at the humane aspects of new ventures, and provides a synthesis of how entrepreneurship, both at the institutional and personal levels, may become the path for a more humane economy.

15

Powerful Machines and Humane Growth

A new venture offers the market a new product, a new good or service, or a new method of production or distribution. Every new venture also provides an opportunity to make an economy more humane. New ventures are the seeds of change and growth, the wellspring of life of all economies whether they are large or small, advanced or primitive. They are the mechanism by which small economies become larger and primitive economies advance. The humane role of the entrepreneurial venture in change and growth is about more than just conventional business practice and, according to Schumpeter, is equally about sociology and history.

The Cycles of Corporate and Human Life

To gain an understanding of the nature of the humane, and to appreciate the role of entrepreneurial ventures, we must examine that which is natural to human beings and the nature of being human. Human life is corporeal, rooted in time and place, a product of birth and nurturing, of family and community. It is bounded in time and anchored in reality. Human life is finite, restricted in size and quantity and limited in time. It is accountable for its actions and responsible for consequences, both in the course of its life and at life's conclusion, over the arc of a life cycle, from beginning to end. While every individual life is captured by a unique expression at each stage, the stages that comprise the life cycle are always the same. A human life cycle begins with conception — desire, hope, a possibility — followed by consummation, a realization of the idea in the form of a functioning entity, a human being. Each life is established on a foundation that lays down the potential for a personal fruitfulness that will increase across time over a period of growth and development and will flower into a period of maturity and maximum productivity. A healthy life will sustain the period of productivity for as long as the living person can maintain itself on its own foundation using its own resources. The productive period is inevitably followed by a period of decline characterized by both a weakening ability to produce and a lessening usefulness of both physical and intellectual output, a diminishing demand for the life's output. Decline culminates in death, always and without exception, in a state of unproductivity with no ability to produce output. Over the arc of the life cycle, humans are called to be humane, to act with virtue appropriate to each point in the life cycle. To deviate from the acts of virtue or to weaken or break the life cycle at any point is to become less than fully human and to become less humane.

To be humane is of particular concern within a large complex market system. Personal humaneness must be played out within social and economic circumstances, and humaneness can be threatened when the individual is immersed in a large impersonal mechanism. Personal humaneness is enmeshed not only within the broader social and economic system but also at the enterprise level where the business system may impose less than humane constraints on organization members. Systemic humaneness must address the survival of personal humaneness within a mechanistic economic structure.

One of the characteristics of entrepreneurship is that the entrepreneur, as a unique individual human, is personally intertwined with the entrepreneurial effort and its offspring, the new venture. As the offspring of human effort, a new venture by its nature has some of the traits of the human. It is created from nothing, *ex nihilo*; conception begins in the mind of the entrepreneur, the vision; before there was nothing and after there is a new initiative, and consummation follows with the creation of a working entity, the new venture. Like the human that gives birth, a venture is not an abstraction but instead is grounded in the realities of its time and place and its community. It displays the humane by following a life cycle from birth through growth to decline. Many ventures adhere closely to the human life cycle and mature and die like anything human must. It produces and sells the product that was conceived and fulfills the needs of its intended consumers until its ability to do so declines, and then the humane venture will itself decline and die, some slowly and some rapidly.

Some ventures, however, do not adhere to a human life cycle and thus risk becoming inhumane.

A venture can break the life cycle by becoming something that it was not originally conceived to be. A business venture is conceived as a vision, with a clearly defined product or service, produced in a rational way, and sold to an intended consumer to meet a specific anticipated need of the consumer. In order to pursue the venture, a new organization must be built that is not part of the conception. No entrepreneur has a vision of an organization. Instead, the organization is just a necessary tool, a necessary cost that must be kept as low as possible to meet the vision, minimum capital investment and minimum expenditures on labor and materials. But once an organization is built it unavoidably takes on a life of its own. An organization is not an entrepreneurial vision but instead a set of human relationships. Human beings don't live and work within visions, they live and work within the relationships that have meaning to them, e.g., family, friends, leisure activities, self-advancement, etc. The humans that comprise the organization may not even share the entrepreneur's vision, the organization's purpose, and may work instead for pay and hopes for advancement. The crucial role of leadership is to get the people to embrace the vision. In a new venture, the entrepreneur must be an exceptional leader, but as the venture moves through its life cycle, leadership may become weaker, the vision less clear and less embraced by the organization purpose, and the people may come to pursue their own purposes. A business venture may come to pursue a life of its own that has little resemblance to the original vision and that may, in fact, be the seeds of the inhumane.

Business ventures often break the life cycle in a manner reflecting what is taught in first-year economics and business. Students are introduced to the "product life cycle," a deceptive concept that pervades business thinking, deceptive because it ignores the fact that the definition of "life" is that it must die. Students are taught that it is the job of management to attempt to extend and make permanent the growth pattern of a product by continually modifying the product, using new product technology, expanding marketing and advertising, and by attempting to attract more and different buyers. This is an obvious and conceptually easy thing for an active organization to attempt, because technology is naturally derivative, markets are easily expandable, labor and marketing services are easily purchased, and capital is perfectly fungible. If this modification process continues, the product may morph into many new products so different from that of the original business venture that they are unrelated to the initial product and produced by many different businesses in many different industries all now owned by a multi-product corporation. This is the purpose of the diversified corporate form, to permit ownership of multiple businesses and to have a lifespan not dependent on any single product. If the product modification process is effective, a corporation could grow into something barely resembling the original business venture, gigantic in size and unlimited in lifespan and the producer of anything sold everywhere. It is conceptually possible and in the nature of a corporation that it could come to be limited by nothing, an effort with no boundaries. English philosopher Roger Scruton argues that to know and to acknowledge no boundaries is the definition of being inhumane, of being unnatural to human beings. Even though friction and diseconomies will in practice prevent any organization from actually transcending all boundaries, to acknowledge no boundaries on principle is to invite indifference to humaneness.[1]

Powerful Machines

The argument that an unbounded enterprise encourages the inhumane is not a new or extravagant idea; in fact, it is an idea so obvious we were explicitly warned about its danger by the Founding Fathers of the United States. The Constitutional Convention held in Philadelphia (May–September 1787) discussed the narrow bounds placed around a business enterprise by traditional personal, local, and legal constraints and debated the possible dangers of a loosening of the traditional constraints. At issue was the corporate form of ownership whose attraction lay in the power granted by a government charter to permit an unlimited number of establishments employing great amounts of faceless and nameless "labor" spreading into endless locations, ill-defined and all-inclusive products sold to unknown and fleeting buyers, and an infinite lifespan extending far beyond the lives and aspirations of owners, workers, and buyers. James Madison was particularly fearful and distrusting of corporations, and in an argument before Congress (February 8, 1791) called them "powerful machines" that "might do a great deal of mischief if left unguarded."[2]

Madison and others within the United States expressed their concerns by drawing on their knowledge of the English experience with the corporate form. Adam Smith examined five of them in Book V of *The Wealth of Nations*, the most powerful of which became the East India Company. Established by Royal Charter in 1600, the East India Company had grown to the point of controlling almost 50% of world trade by the late 18th century. Not only did the East India Company participate in commercial activities, but also it became the dominant political and military power in the Indian sub-continent. By 1800, the East India Company's private military forces were actually larger than most countries in the world. The great British parliamentarian, Edmund Burke (1729–1797), led the effort to limit the powers of the East India Company. Like James Madison and others in the United Stated, he noted that the "bodies corporate," whether commercial, educational, political, or religious, are highly complex and formed over time. Burke, like Smith, was generally in favor of relatively free markets for economic efficiency but also understood the institutional dangers of unfettered corporate growth and power. As Burke noted in his 1786 speech at the impeachment of Warren Hastings,[3] that the East India Company had become "a State in disguise of a Merchant, a great public office in disguise of a Countinghouse." It is difficult to consider a State in disguise as a humane institution.

These late 18th century debates about corporate power in the U.S., Great Britain and other countries underline the critical connection between corporate size, growth, and humaneness. In the U.S., with the strengthening of corporate rights and powers following the 1817 Supreme Court decision in *Dartmouth College vs. Woodward*,[4] state and federal governments increasingly offered corporate charters with few restrictions on corporate behavior and power.[5] With the appearance of the railroads, chartering of corporations became a flood. The new railroad technology appeared to offer rapid economic growth and development if it were permitted to expand with no boundaries to size, location, product, or time. The subsequent history of the explosive growth of corporate power after the macro-economic expansion attributed to the growth and concentration of railroads[6] provides an illustration of the contrast between the limitations and boundaries natural to humaneness, with its qualities and conditions befitting human beings, and the unbounded growth in size and power of corporations as they exploit new technologies. All railroads began small and local to reflect personal human social and economic aspirations and hopes for local economic development. From that humane beginning, railroad corporations grew to be organizations gigantic in size and power. Railroads today are virtually unbounded, are very large, cover countless localities with a specific commitment to none and think in terms of the capitalist abstractions of "labor," "capital," and "demand." This is the pattern of birth and maturity of most new ventures in most technologies.

For example, the Union Pacific Corporation, one of the largest transportation companies in the world and the 2nd largest railroad system in the United States, retains the name from an 1862 Federal charter given for the specific purpose of building a railroad west from Omaha to link with the Central Pacific Railroad building east from Sacramento. Like almost all railroads today, the current Union Pacific Corporation resulted from the combination of these two roads and numerous other railroads, one of which was the Houston and Great Northern Railroad chartered by the state of Texas in 1866 for the specific purpose of connecting Houston to a point on the Red River. In 1872 the town of Palestine, TX sold bonds worth $150,000, an enormous sum in those days for a small Texas town, to fund construction of the railroad through the town. In return the Houston and Great Northern signed an agreement to maintain facilities and hire employees in the town in perpetuity, an agreement that was upheld by courts and regulators through all the many combinations over the years ahead that led to the current Union Pacific Corporation. In November 2019, the Union Pacific filed a lawsuit in Federal court to invalidate the agreement in the name of "modern business practice." In a published statement the mayor of Palestine, with a current population of less than 20,000, and the county judge of Anderson County protested "Union Pacific's betrayal of small-town America" and said that the layoffs would devastate the community.

> Union Pacific … thinks that because it has infinite resources, while Palestine is just a small town that can barely afford to pay a handful of public officials, it can take advantage of us and walk away with the benefits of a contractual agreement that has been repeatedly affirmed by the parties and upheld by the courts over almost 150 years.

In a press release, Union Pacific expressed its overriding interest in "modern business practice" and stated that "Union Pacific is improving operations to meet customer needs and will continue providing the same level of service to customers." This is not to indict Union Pacific, which may well be more humane than many corporations. It is simply to point out that modern business practice, improving operations, customer needs, level of service are all abstractions that could apply almost anything at any point in time to any customers anywhere. But the people of Palestine are not any customers anywhere and instead are real people, rooted in time and place in their small town who invested in Union Pacific in 1872 and made an agreement in perpetuity. Railroading is the first line of business to be regulated, for the purpose of making it more humane, but arguably regulation has only made railroading less efficient.

CSX, another large U.S. railroad corporation, was also pieced together over time by the consolidation of myriad smaller lines, each of which was once bounded by the personal aspirations of local residents who contributed significant local resources. One of the earliest local lines was the Wilmington and Weldon Railroad, chartered in 1834 by the state of North Carolina for the purpose of directing trade to the seaport of Wilmington. It was entirely locally funded with local control for a local purpose. History confirms that the uncertainty was real, the unknown potential for loss and gain was very high, and the needed commitment was total. John Henry Newman says that the essence of a true venture is the willingness to risk much, if not all, for an end not fully understood and demanding the pledge "We are able." A local historian recorded the results of Wilmington's entrepreneurial venture:[7]

> In 1835, it was determined to build the Wilmington and Weldon Railroad, and the books were open for subscription to its stock. The citizens of Wilmington, in their individual capacity, subscribed to a greater amount of the stock than the value of the entire property of the town listed for taxation, an act unprecedented in our history and never equaled so far as it is known. They were determined that the road should be built, and it was done; but very many of them beggared themselves in the effort, while others received all the benefit of the sacrifices they had made.

The Wilmington and Weldon Railroad was later absorbed into other lines and ultimately into the CSX. Local control was lost to New York banks and international investors, and Wilmington was reduced to a minor spur with a devastating impact on its economy. Like Union Pacific, the actions of CSX are likely to be as humane and its output as benign as any modern corporation. But the point is that the modern CSX actions and the output are directed at the abstraction of customer service over a large area to unknown people. The people of Wilmington are real, rooted in time and place, who once beggared themselves for a purpose natural to human beings, and who now receive little attention from CSX, nor do the people of Palestine from Union Pacific.

The human stories of Palestine and Wilmington would seem to occupy an incidental place in the mind of large corporations, where the issue is "modern business practice" for the purpose of customer needs and level of service, a commitment of the modern corporation that seemingly softens the ruthless pursuit of self-interest. The East India Company's private armies and its ultimate control over government administrative activities throughout much of the Indian sub-continent for over one hundred years until the Government of India Act of 1858, while certainly questionable behavior under today's norms, was seen by the norms of that era as simply "modern business practice." This seems to have been a problem even for Edmund Burke as he pursued the East India Company in the late 18th century. As a supporter of capitalism, modernity, and the theoretical institutional advantages of corporate bodies, he struggled to articulate the underlying causes of good forms of corporatism distinct from bad forms and the role that the "economic man" plays in this.[8]

The examples of the two railroads illustrate the dynamics behind the appearance of the large corporation detached from human scale and personal control. Despite our sympathies with the people of Palestine and Wilmington who invested their local wealth in a railroad for local purposes, it is clear that the resulting enterprise could not remain local if it were to serve the very purpose for which it was built. Much of the great power of a railroad was soon seen to lie in its ability to be linked with other railroads into a system to make the hauling of passengers and freight as seamless and low cost as possible. The fact that transportation cries out to be linked into a large system is no different from most products that grow with the benefits of scale and mass into systems of large enterprise that unavoidably becomes less humane as it extends across space and time.

The appearance and growth of the large organization followed the need to control such a large and impersonal enterprise. The large modern organization is administered by a large and growing culture of managers who have neither a financial, personal, or community stake in the organization that they manage, nor do they have any attachment to the people or the communities that they serve; they have no "skin in the game." As an organization grows larger, its managers are more detached from the people and places they serve and are attached only to the organization itself. The only skin in the game that they have is the organization hierarchy in which they serve. The organization can come to have as its purpose size for its own sake and continuous growth only for the benefit of the managers. Such organizations, forming what is called "managerial capitalism," can come to be inhumane.

Alfred Chandler in *The Visible Hand* chronicles the historical appearance and rise to dominance of managerial capitalism. He argues that once hierarchical managements prove that they are necessary to administer large and modern corporations, the managements come to run the corporations for the purpose of ensuring that "these hierarchies of increasingly professional managers might remain fully employed." Chandler demonstrated from historical experience that these managerial organizations exhibited certain proclivities. Once a managerial hierarchy had been formed and had successfully carried out its functions of administrative coordination, the hierarchy itself became a source of permanent power and continued growth. The careers of the salaried managers who directed these hierarchies became increasingly technical and professional. As the corporations grew in size and product diversity, with the ownership of more businesses, and as its managers became more professional, the management of the corporation became ever more separated from its ownership. In making administrative decisions, career managers preferred policies that favored the long-term stability and growth of their corporations to those that served customers and maximized current profits. As the large corporations grew and came to dominate major sectors of the economy, they altered the basic structure of these sectors and of the economy as a whole.[9]

Endnotes

1. See R. Scruton, "The Journey Home: Wilhelm Ropke & The Humane Eeconomy," *The Imaginative Conservative*, (2020). https://theimaginative conservative.org/2020/03/journey-home-wilhelm-ropke-humane-economy-roger-scruton-timeless-2020.html. Accessed September 1, 2022. Scruton also discusses these issues in R. Scruton, "Architecture and Aesthetic Education," Steiner Lecture, St. John's College, December 1, 2014 and R. Scruton, *On Human Nature* (Princeton, NJ: Princeton University Press, 2017).
2. S. Horton, "James Madison: Corporations and the National Security State," Lecture, University of Alabama Law School, April 14, 2011.
3. Burke led the impeachment of Hastings, the Governor-General of the East India Company, for corruption. The trial was long and politically volatile, because it centered on a political principle. Was the purpose of the East India

Company for the wealth and power of the company? Or was it for the good of the Indian people? Burke defended the Indian people as he had defended the American colonials and rebels in the decade prior. See E. Burke, "Speech on Opening of Impeachment," in *The Writings and Speeches of Edmund Burke*, (Oxford: Clarendon, 1991), Vol. 6, 282–283, 283.

4.   The Supreme Court upheld the right of Dartmouth as a corporate entity granted power by a state charter to resist political attempts by the state government to limit and control it.

5.   A. Berle, *The 20th Century Capitalist Revolution* (Harcourt, Brace and Company, 1954).

6.   R. Fogel, *Railroads and Economic Growth* (Baltimore, MD: Johns Hopkins University Press, 1964) argues that it remains unproven that the size and concentration of the railroads added anything to the growth of the economy.

7.   J. Sprunt, *Tales and Traditions of the Lower Cape Fear, 1661–1896* (Wilmington, NC: LeGwin Brothers Printers, 1896).

8.   J. Murray, "Company Rules: Burke, Hastings, and the Spector of the Modern Liberal State." *Eighteenth-Century Studies* 41, no. 1 (2007), 55–69.

9.   A. Chandler, *The Visible Hand: The Managerial Revolution in American Business* (Cambridge, MA: Belknap Press, 1977), 6–11.

16

Managerial Capitalism: Statism and Giantism

Edith Penrose in *A Theory of the Growth of the Firm*, argues that a firm, like all formal organizations, seeks to grow to make full use of its resources.[1] A firm consists of a collection of resources, financial, techno-logical, and human, with the most determining resource being human, the resource on which most management focuses. Managers exist in two forms, *administrative managers* who look to the routine operation of the organization and *entrepreneurial managers* who look to expand the boundaries of the organization. This distinction is similar to that of Sidney Sherwood in 1917 that there are two types of undertakers: those respon-sible for the *mercantile* function who take initiatives to stimulate demand and to guide product development to meet the new forms of demand, in contrast with those responsible for the *organizing* function who take initiatives to discover the "right technical combination of productive resources to procure the needed supply" of products to meet the demand generated by the mercantile function.[2] Penrose's entrepreneurial managers work to generate ever new demand and expanding sales growth in order to occupy the administrative managers in their work to produce products and to add more administrative managers to address the new demand. The entrepreneurial managers are the engine of growth, and the growth of interest is the growth of the organization not necessarily the increased size and prosperity of the economy and society.

Flipping the Theory of the Firm

An interesting thing about Penrose's argument is that it reverses the traditional theory of the firm. In the traditional theory, firms identify an exogeneous demand and then acquire resources as needed to develop productive capacity to meet the exogeneous demand. The business organization is built for the purpose of meeting exogeneous demand. The demand is real, and the firm is derivative. When the demand begins to decline, the organization should shrink along with it. The Penrose theory reverses the order; the firm seeks to stimulate and generate demand in any shape, place, or time necessary to bring in revenue sufficient to feed the managerial capacity that constitutes the organization. Current demand must be kept high enough to maintain employment of the current administrative managers, and if demand can be stimulated by promotion and new product variations, then the organization can afford to expand, and new administrative managers can be added. Organization expansion will necessitate an enlarged bureaucratic hierarchy, thus permitting current managers, both entrepreneurial and administrative, to be promoted. The organization and its managerial capacity are real, and demand is derivative.

This is a clear and convincing explanation of what corporate organizations are and why they relentlessly grow and embrace growth itself as their objective, their reason for being, and how managerial employment is the driving force. The revelation highlighted by the Penrose theory is the reality of continuous organizational striving for high growth in sales in order to feed a large, permanent growing managerial resource. This idea has come to be so widely embraced that it shapes our thinking. We accept growth as a norm, that it is normal and inevitable that firms will seek to grow to gigantic size and global reach, that firms should have growth as their objective, and that growth and permanence is the very reason for being of a firm. We accept this as normal even for non-business organizations, which are allowed to grow with little restraint, particularly if the organization can make a connection with the government, like universities, hospitals, and the defense industry. The idea of growth for its own sake has become an underlying principle of management taught in modern business schools and is the basis for almost all managerial rewards, both business and non-business managers. The inevitable result is managerial statism.

Managerial Statism

Statism is a managerial mechanism that works to remain in power and that manages for its own benefit, regardless of organizational and societal purpose and regardless of whether it is beneficial in a larger sense. Its primary purpose is to remain in power whatever societal circumstances may be and however the environment may change. Managerial statism is pervasive in advanced societies and economies, so pervasive as to present the spectacle of organizations becoming increasingly gigantic and concentrated. There is a threat of more and more people becoming dependent for their livelihood on the continued growth of statist organizations. The increasing pervasiveness is quiet and inexorable and might get less noticed if it were not for the glaring visibility of the "industrial complex."

Industrial complex is the name we have given the set of statist organizations that pursue endless growth and ravenous profitability from an alliance of corporations with institutions. The institution at the center of the complex is fundamental to our human society, but the organizations that serve it have become oversized, permanent, working for their own benefit, and inhumane. The statist organizations are inhumane because they distort and disfigure the real human need that the institution serves and corrupts and perverts serious commitment to the true human purpose of the institution. Statist organizations use the institution to extract wealth from consumers and usurp societal resources that are needed elsewhere.

The phenomenon was given a name and the first diagnosis was provided by President Eisenhower in his farewell address broadcast on January 17, 1961. He warned America of the "military-industrial complex" with its dangers and its irresistible growth, "We must guard against the acquisition of unwarranted influence, whether sought or unsought, by the military-industrial complex. The potential for the disastrous rise of misplaced power exists and will persist."[3] Eisenhower had originally intended to call it "the military-industrial-congressional complex" to warn that the root cause of the problem was the flood of government money, but his aides persuaded him to cut the word "congressional" in order to avoid being too politically inflammatory.[4] That is unfortunate, because the flood of money is the source of the cancer. Now, for the first time in American history, the institution of the military became a place where one could make a lucrative career and possibly get very rich. Military organizations, which by their nature should be lean and focused and built upon the call for sacrifice, morphed into organizations that are top heavy with bureaucracy, have become famous for waste and self-indulgence, and provide careerists with a comfortable life and a lucrative retirement, with vast wealth and political power awaiting those at the top of the bureaucratic hierarchy. The flood of government money provided high profits to corporations supplying the military, with the corporations becoming huge in size and with an assurance of continuing high profits. Maybe more seriously, the military-industrial-congressional complex distorted and disfigured the clear and simple purpose of the military institution to provide national security for the people. Instead, the institution became a large and growing complex, working for its own benefit, and therefore inhumane.

The military-industrial complex is a subset of the larger and more inclusive government agency-industrial complex, for which the government collects taxes and increases the national debt to fund a proliferation of agencies which hire more and more people to work for wages and benefits that exceed those in the private sector. Baumol points out that the entrepreneurial mindset can find particularly rich opportunities for personal advantage within the domain of government by pursuing what is often unproductive or even destructive entrepreneurship.[5] Casual empiricism confirms the existence of large and powerful industries of lawyers and lobbyists, a vast and expanding bureaucracy, and the spectacle of very many government careerists, including career politicians, getting very rich. Baumol's government entrepreneurs are a variation on Penrose's entrepreneurial managers.

There are many other industrial complexes that are widely talked about, one in almost every valued institution of life. The institutions display a great variety, but they all have in common the fact that the institution is assaulted and distorted by a flood of money, essentially money from the government either in the form of direct expenditures by the government to a myriad of establishment-government relationships or in the form of the insertion of money into the economy of the institution. There are countless forms of industrial complex in almost every institution of modern life. A few examples, some intimidating, some sad, and some amusing: The intimidating include, along with the military-industrial complex, the medical-industrial complex, the science-industrial complex, the higher education-industrial complex, the political-industrial complex, the art and culture-industrial complex, the journalism-industrial complex, and the religion-industrial complex, among many others. The sad include the poverty-industrial complex, charity-industrial complex, and even the skid row-industrial complex. The amusing includes the wedding-industrial complex, the eulogies for celebrities-industrial complex, the outrage-industrial complex, and even the climbing Mount Everest-industrial complex.[6]

The workings of the industrial complex phenomenon can be illustrated by the gigantic higher education-industrial complex, an incestuous complex of statist organizations that feed off each other and expand together, government, corporations, and schools, the schools once mostly non-profit, both private and government, but increasingly for-profit. This is the industrial complex that many of us are most familiar with. The educational institution that the older among us entered decades ago, lean and with a clear purpose, a little like the military institution described above, is barely recognizable today in the massive and growing industrial complex that it has become. The change, as is typical, began when the government began to overwhelm the various educational establishments with huge amounts of money and assured the continuous flow of the money by pumping up demand by calling for every American to have a college degree, all without any standards or clear performance measures. The natural desire of every human being to learn, most efficiently and in a subject that is most interesting and useful to each of them, has become an unnatural and inhumane industrial complex which continually expands, and off which multitudes get rich.

The organizations that constitute various industrial complexes tend to become inhumane, not necessarily because of the ethical decisions of organization leaders, but rather because of the underlying forces placed on establishments as they exist within the modern economic and social structure. It is the structural nature of the problem that is inhumane. A symptom of the inhumane nature of statist organizations and industrial complexes is the fact that they tend to grow uncontrollably to an, often, enormous size, an affliction known as "giantism." The systemic nature of the problem of giantism is what allows a small, often tiny, new entrepreneurial venture to act as an antidote.

The Modern Passion of Giantism

Instead of seeing giantism as a pathology, statist organizations typically make the case for their importance by emphasizing their giant size and reach, often citing their size as the mark of their legitimacy. For example, Union Pacific in its promotional material and annual reports proclaims the fact that it has 32,200 miles (about 51,820 km) of track in 23 states and 37,000 employees, and CSX proudly notes that it has 21,000 miles (about 33,796 km) of track in 20 states and 21,500 employees. But is gigantic scale a virtue? These two corporations talk as if it is, but this giant scale takes them a long way from the humans in smaller communities.

Proclamations of giantism permeate all areas of society. Whenever a modern corporation receives bad press, the immediate corporate response is likely to be to proclaim how large and important they are, and above all, how many people they employ and serve. Universities cite their size and growth as a measure of their success and importance, without addressing whether organization size furthers the work of the education institution. The "too big to fail" mentality permeates far more than just bailouts of auto manufacturers and Wall Street banks — we find it throughout our economy.

Entrepreneurship education often falls into this gigantic mode of thinking. Entrepreneurship students are constantly being taught how to "scale-up" fast track enterprises or obtain high "multiples" on their venture investments. The case studies dissected by students in entrepreneurship classes are inevitably firms such as Microsoft, Apple, Amazon, and Facebook that were once fledging start-up ventures but have now grown into huge and arguably monopolistic and inhumane enterprises. Students are encouraged to envy the immense fortunes gained by particularly successful entrepreneurs. The honored guest speakers at leading business programs, hailed as models of entrepreneurial success, are almost always the billionaire founders, their success confirmed by a staggeringly large financial "exit." The combined images of growth and giantism are seen as heroic.

Giantism has been so pervasive in the modern capitalist economies for so long no one seems to notice and if noticed it is accepted as normal. Few scholars seem to be concerned about it except Wilhelm Ropke, who said that with giantism and mass "all poetry and dignity, and with them the very spice of life and its human content, go out of life. Even the dramatic episodes of existence — birth, growth, and death ... We are born in gigantic hospitals;" we live in gigantic mass quarters "superimposed on each other vertically and extending horizontally as far as the eye can see;" we work in gigantic factories and offices in "hierarchical subordination;" we spend our vacations in masses, flood the universities, lecture halls and laboratories, consume the same books and movies produced in the millions; and we flock in the hundreds of thousands to the same gigantic sports stadiums.

Adam Smith gave slight attention to the effects of giantism, believing that exchange in unregulated markets would strike the right balance between healthy growth and restrained size of businesses. He based his confidence in market exchange on his belief in the enduring predominance of small, personally owned, and managed businesses as a form of countervailing power. Such businesses would always have an advantage in competing with large businesses owned by giant corporations and operated by corporate employees due to the fact that the wage laborers of a large corporate-owned business, both production labor and management labor, could never match the skill and motivation of the personal hands-on work of a small personal business.

Endnotes

1. E. Penrose, *The Theory of the Growth of the Firm* (Oxford, UK: Basil Blackwell, 1959).
2. S. Sherwood, "The Function of the Undertaker," *Yale Review* 2 (1917), 233–250.
3. D. Eisenhower, "Farewell Address." Television broadcast, January 17, 1961. https://www.archives.gov/milestone-documents/president-dwight-d-eisenhowers-farewell-address.
4. See also C. Dunlap, "The Military-Industrial Complex," *Daedalus* 140, no. 3 (2011), 135–147.
5. W. Baumol, "Entrepreneurship: Productive, Unproductive, and Destructive," *Journal of Political Economy* 98 no. 5, Pt. 1 (1990), 893–921.
6. Consider the quote, "The very mountain peaks, which Providence seems to have preserved as a last refuge of solitude, are drawn into mass civilization." in W. Ropke, *The Humane Economy: The Social Framework of the Free Market* (Washington DC: Regenery Publishing, 1960), 41.

17

A Humane Economy

John D. Mueller of the Mises Institute suggests that Smith himself inadvertently opened the door to threats to humaneness by neglect of consumer welfare and his naïve confidence (according to Mueller) that the personal self-interest of producers and exchange between free individual producers would provide protections for the human persons in their roles as labor and consumer.[1] Mueller argues that this neglect gave free reign to ignoring, first, consumption, what consumer goods would create the greatest general welfare and, second, distribution, how consumer goods should be provided proportionately for the general welfare of all people. The void left by the lack of a theory of consumption and the lack of a theory of distribution was filled by makeshift approaches that Wilhelm Ropke called "anarchistic laissez-faire", the naïve belief that the chaos and clutter of market exchange will in and of itself ensure healthy enterprises and a humane society and not lead to greed and injustice.[2] In fact, in a world dominated by the industrial complex, anarchistic laissez-faire can be argued to have left the human being as both worker and consumer in a state where there is little to choose from in the face of giant corporate-institution industrial complexes.

The Massification of Life

In *A Humane Economy*, Ropke introduces the concept of *vermassung*, translated as "enmassment," the giantism of virtually all institutions in society.[3] Having accepted the economic marketplace as the only arbiter of value, every dimension of life is conceived and measured in terms of its monetary consequences and ultimately comes to be capitalized. Economic measures of output become the guides to human life, and as a result the purpose of human life is reshaped to focus on mass consumption of the measured output. Mass production and consumption in market exchange societies has led to giant enterprises that expand beyond product and market boundaries, giant enterprises that participate in the reshaping of human purpose. Ropke believed that life could become inhumane when people are guided into the economic mass. Modern humans are born in the medical-industrial complex, fed by the agricultural and food processing-industrial complex, housed by the mass housing-industrial complex, educated by the education-industrial complex, marched off to labor in mass industrial complexes regulated by the government-industrial complex, retired to the nursing home-industrial complex, and buried by the funeral-industrial complex. We have the diminishment of the individual, the centralization of all power, too-big-to-fail enterprises, and crony capitalism, all of which threaten humaneness.

Ropke was a prolific scholar whose most lasting impact has been to address the threats that enmassment poses to humaneness. He was driven by concern for the failing economy and disordered society of the Germany of his birth and the question of why its market economy succumbed so easily to the socialist economy of the National Socialist German Workers' Party. Seeing beyond the specific failures of the Nazis, he understood the larger question to be, why do people have a tendency to become so dissatisfied with market economies? He answered that they become dissatisfied because of the inhumaneness of enmassment, and they see socialism, with its talk of sharing and common ownership, as the only solution, either in the German variety of national socialism or in the Russian variety of international socialism. But Ropke knew firsthand that people are seriously mistaken in this judgement, that the real source of inhumaneness is the combination of giantism and enmassment, and that socialism always makes enmassment worse.

A few modern Futurists have also considered this issue, and what it means for society. Alvin Toffler, the renowned futurist, and author of the best-selling 1970 book *Future Shock* specifically examined the implication in a follow-up book titled *The Third Wave* in 1980.[4] He makes a persuasive argument that the industrial revolution (which Toffler labels the "2nd Wave") had an immense impact on societal relationships. Toffler argued that in the pre-industrial age, 1st Wave societies were primarily agricultural, with economic systems built around family-owned "cottage-industries". Life in 1st age societies was very human, interactive, and high touch. The industrial revolution (as also discussed many times in the present book) altered this relationship. Looking more at societal systems, Toffler notes that the industrial age not only created the problem of "giantism," but also "massification," where all of societies' activities became more generic, mass-produced and consumed. Industrial age societies even adopted the language of massification – "mass education," "mass consumption," "mass production," "mass marketing," "mass media," "mass-communication," etc. Simultaneously, the political and economic institutions of the 2nd Wave needed to re-engineer themselves to survive and prosper in this new, massified culture. For example, Representative Democracy replaced the more direct, face to face, community oriented political systems of 1st Wave Societies. Toffler even notes that the mass-education process of post-industrial societies was particularly obvious in public education — picking up young students at 8am at well-identified bus stops, quickly busing the youngsters to a large school accommodating thousands of students, immediately starting the first class when the bell sounds, later in the day giving one hour lunch breaks, then back to school until the bell rings again at 3 pm, then busing them back home — is simply a formalized training program, managed by government and funded by taxes, to teach students upon graduation to commute and work in 2nd Wave factories and offices, with the same work schedules and mindset.

Toffler notes, however, that the emerging 3rd Wave is driven by the introduction of new technologies, and many of these new technologies in robotics and communication will reduce the scale required for efficient economic relationships, thus allowing economies to go back to a more, non-gigantic, cottage-based perspective. Toffler argues that successful 3rd Wave societies will have the economic, social, and political relationships seen in 1st Wave cultures, but now on a high technology plane. He also underlines that societies that never went through an industrial revolution, such as current less-developed regions, may actually be in a better position when this happens, since their institutions are already oriented toward a more humane, less-massified, cottage-based and family perspective. The 2nd Wave institutions built around the world of gigantic scale and massified culture, such as in Western Europe and North America, will certainly fight this trend, and most of these institutions will not be able to make the transition back to a de-massified, more human society.

Disembodiment of Organizations

An organization becomes inhumane when it thinks in terms of concepts and categories rather than in terms of corporeal individuals rooted in time and place. Many of the concepts and measures of modern business practice, such standard usages as labor, capital, demand, and market share, involve a disembodiment of the human being. Dealing with a disembodied reality can lead to corporate decisions that are most definitely inhumane, even if they appear in standard economic practice to be reasonable and justified, as good business practice and the greater good for the greater number. An example is provided by General Motors' rational business decision to build in 1984 and then abandon in 2018 their Detroit/ Hamtramck assembly plant. The popular name for the plant was "GM Poletown," in memory of the Polish community that was leveled against its will to make way for the plant. Beginning in June 1980, the city of Detroit used eminent domain in a manner that would today be illegal to level at the behest of General Motors the entire community of Poletown to clear a site for General Motors to build the assembly plant. To make way for the plant, 4,400 mostly Polish Catholic people were displaced along with 1,500 homes, 144 businesses, 16 churches, and 1 hospital. The Catholic Archdiocese of Detroit joined the industrial complex with General Motors and the city of Detroit — a big business, big government, big religion-industrial complex — to accomplish the destruction of Poletown. Then, in 2018, General Motors decided, for sound business reasons, to abandon the plant, and the site now lies vacant. The justification for displacement of Poletown to build the plant was the promise of jobs and taxes. General Motors delivered the jobs and taxes, but their abstract nature clouded the reality that they may not have been as many as promised, were not offered primarily to Poletown residents, lasted only about thirty years, and have now gone elsewhere, both jobs and taxes unrooted in time and place. The city of Detroit must now endeavor to find a use for the abandoned and empty site. General Motors and the GM Poletown plant are gone with never a look back, and the City of Detroit and the Catholic Diocese of Detroit, embodied in time and place, are left to address the reality that its human citizens with their businesses and their human parishioners with their churches are now gone. The sterile emptiness and disembodied nature of this inhumane episode brings to mind the phrase used by the Roman writer Publius Tacitus to describe the extermination of the primitive Scottish tribe called Caledonians in 83 AD amidst the globalist expansion of the Roman Empire: Where they expand "they call it empire; and where they make a desert, they call it peace."

The Humane in New Ventures

In *A Humane Economy*, Ropke argues that both unrestrained private enterprise and socialist enterprise always lead to an inhumane economy, because both result equally in enmassment. Both systems, in fact, encourage enmassment, because both are focused on supplying mass produced goods to a mass stimulated demand. Mass is the ideal of the modern economy, both private enterprise and socialist. If both systems make a virtue of mass employment of labor and mass consumption of goods, then it does not matter which way a society chooses to offend against the humane. If both ways lead to enmassment, then both ways are equally inhumane.

So, what might the solution be? At various times, scholars have warned of the dangers of enmassment, Ropke's *vermassung*, calling for people to return to a human scale life and to human scale work. There are the Ordoliberals (c. 1930–1950) in Germany (e.g., Wilhelm Ropke and Walter Eucken), the Catholic Social Distributists (c. 1890–1920) in England (e.g., G.K. Chesterton and Hilaire Belloc) and the Southern Agrarians (c. 1930–1940) in the United States (e.g., Allen Tate and Richard Weaver). More recently, economist E.F. Schumacher again warned about the dangers of unfettered growth and inhumane production, publishing his views in the appropriately titled, *Small is Beautiful: Economics as if People Matter.*[5]

Our thesis is that every new venture represents a possible antidote to enmassment and disembodiment. This is the key to humane entrepreneurship from the perspective of process, providing a countervailing power against statism. In fact, the natural inclination of people to engage in human-scale business activity, their propensity to "truck, barter, and exchange," was put forth by Adam Smith in Book 1, Chapter 2 of *The Wealth of Nations* as the psychological foundation of his entire explanation of competitive economics. In some people this psychology will focus itself as an entrepreneurial propensity to create new ventures. The existence of the propensity is confirmed by the never-ending stream of new ventures that continually appear, even in modern advanced societies that display enmassment in every institution of life, economic and noneconomic. The stream of new ventures confirms that the entrepreneurial mind set must be natural to humans, because it persists even when discouraged by the world of enmassment. We must look beyond the mechanics of our mass economy and see the entrepreneurial personality that continually renews the mass with new ventures. If we seem to be daunted by industrial complex giantism, it is because we have let it obscure the humane role of the entrepreneur. "The dehumanization of theoretical economics necessarily includes a human devaluation of the entrepreneur. As against the physics of the economy, we have to underscore its psychology, ethics, intelligence — in short, its human elements."[6]

Entrepreneurs nurture humaneness in the economic system when they create new ventures. To make an economy more humane, entrepreneurs must be encouraged, and the economy must be structured so that entrepreneurship can flourish. The natural force of entrepreneurship offers a powerful defense of humaneness in the world of work. New ventures by their nature start small, decentralized, and very personal. Each new venture is conceived and given vision by an individual. Each new venture, to succeed, must be nurtured by a workforce and embraced by buyers that are rooted in time and place. The material of humaneness lies in the embodied individual. Enmassment, the threat to humaneness, threatens from the outside.

At the individual level, entrepreneurs are in a unique position to consider humaneness within the context of their economic activity. Each individual venture alone cannot ensure a humane economic system, but the aggregate impact of new ventures, and the cumulative impact of the aggregate over time, holds the potential to counter the statist marks of giantism, enmassment, and disembodiment and to highlight humaneness. Each new venture, almost by definition, is born humane. It is conceived and nurtured by the commitment of the entrepreneur, embodies work and property on a human scale, provides a specific product to buyers who embrace the venture rooted in time and place, and displays a lifespan that has some of the characteristics of the human. Like a human being, new ventures inherently grow, either slowly or rapidly. Most new ventures will grow slowly and then either die or continue to function on a human scale. A few will grow rapidly to large size, and a very few will grow at an extraordinary rate to a gigantic size. These very few get too much attention, too much thoughtless admiration and too little examination of the likelihood that their giant size may lead to aspects of inhumaneness.

It instead is a warning and lament that the large size of corporations, and all organizations, may make them less humane. This is not a simple attack on corporate size, given that the life cycle natural to business organizations will lead them to grow, and some will grow large. It is a humane affirmation that, under the shade cast by the large survivors, the human propensity for creative entrepreneurship will always flower and give birth to a continuing stream of new ventures that are inherently humane. Many new ventures die, but the process of entrepreneurial creation, and the individuals making these entrepreneurial decisions, are the forces that work to ensure a humane economy.

Endnotes

1. J. Mueller, *Redeeming Economics: Rediscovering the Missing Element* (Wilmington, DE: ISI Books, 2010) particularly 1–8.
2. W. Ropke, *The Social Crisis of Our Time* (New Brunswick, NJ: Transaction Publishers, 1992), xv. Original work published 1942.
3. W. Ropke, *The Humane Economy: The Social Framework of the Free Market* (Washington DC: Regenery Publishing, 1960).
4. The *Third Wave* was published in 1980, but its arguments are equally relevant today. Other Futurists have also explored what a successful post-industrial age society might look like. See A. Toffler, *Future Shock* (New York, NY: Random House, 1970) and A. Toffler, *The Third Wave.* (New York, NY: William Morrow and Company, Inc., 1980). Toffler died in 2016 and is regarded as one of the world's most influential futurists. His books became best sellers not only in the United States but around the world. His work influenced the government policies of many of the economically expanding Asian countries. To quote one observer, "Where an earlier generation of Chinese, Korean, and Vietnamese revolutionaries wanted to re-enact the Paris Commune as imagined by Karl Marx, their post-revolutionary successors now want to re-enact Silicon Valley as imagined by Alvin Toffler", https://www.denverpost.com/2016/06/29/author-alvin-toffler-dies/.
5. E. Schumacher, *Small is Beautiful: Economics as if People Matter* (London: Blond and Briggs, 1973).
6. Ropke, *The Humane Economy*, 258.

Concluding Thoughts

A major theme in this book is that constraints to the market economy for the purposes of a common good, and to build a more humane economy, must come from a bottom-up perspective, rather than enforced by governmental top-down directives or exhorted by fancy weasel words coined by academics and business magazine writers. A humane economy must be built upon a decentralist doctrine of smaller economic communities, fueled by entrepreneurship, and guided by virtues such as sympathy, charity, and perhaps even beauty, that humankind has always cherished. Where once a person's work, property, and involvement in the economic community was viewed as part of a natural order, the rise of the industrial revolution resulted in enormous changes. The "fictitious commodities" of labor and capital became dominant, and people quickly became simple commodities in an ever expanding, inhumane economy. Modern capitalist, socialist, and Marxist political economies all universally suffer from this affliction, with various degrees of violence and governmental control. The world, in all of its natural glory and potential, soon came to be viewed primarily as a large commodities market of human labor and expanding capital, where managerial statism, giantism, and massification became the norm, if not the organizational directive of business activity. This book focuses specifically on entrepreneurship, its role of contributing to the problem, and hopefully its role in driving toward a more humane solution.

Entrepreneurship is regularly recognized by modern governments and think tanks as fueling modern economic growth, innovation, and employment. This observation has generated a number of organizations that consider these relationships in great detail. The *Global Entrepreneurship Monitor* (GEM), for example, was founded in 1997 by faculty at Babson College and the London Business School to understand and standardize the measurement of entrepreneurial activity across the globe. As the GEM's mission statement notes,

> Entrepreneurship is an essential driver of societal health and wealth. It is also a formidable engine of economic growth. It promotes the essential innovation required not only to exploit new opportunities, promote productivity, and create employment, but to also address some of society's greatest challenges, such as the United Nations Sustainable Development Goals (SDGs)... The promotion of entrepreneurship will be central to multiple governments worldwide for the foreseeable future...

Many published studies in the fields of economics, public policy, strategic management and entrepreneurship (including some by this book's authors) have indeed found that a country's rate of total entrepreneurial activity, particular entrepreneurship that is more "opportunity related" is positively associated with various indices of economic growth, such as GDP and innovative activity. Entrepreneurship appears not only to offer opportunities to venturesome individuals but also to impact societal development at a global level. Not surprisingly, entrepreneurship programs have gained a strong position within the university curriculum. In some respects, entrepreneurship has also become a growth product itself, growing almost exponentially not only throughout the education systems of the world, but in other areas as well. Entrepreneurship now has whole sections in bookstores, with literally hundreds of magazines and popular "how I did it" books written by individuals who made fortunes by raising private equity capital followed by quick "exits." Local Chambers of Commerce, Economic Development Commissions, and other government organizations regularly promote entrepreneurship in their communities. Entrepreneurial training programs abound in the consulting world. Entrepreneurial "Incubators" and "Accelerators" dominate the urban landscapes. And new reports on entrepreneurial activity are issued almost weekly by global, national, and regional government bureaucracies and private think tanks.

It is the thesis of this book that the integration of entrepreneurship concepts, whether across universities in a broad sense, or throughout society in general needs to have substance. The theoretical weight of entrepreneurship, which has heretofore had to look to economics for its theory, could be a real gift to society. However, economics as a discipline has itself been light on entrepreneurship. Why this is so takes some explaining, particularly since Joseph Schumpeter, arguably one of the greatest economists of the 20th century, made entrepreneurship the centerpiece of economic theory and made it the very force that drives growth in a dynamic economy. Without the work of the entrepreneur, an economy will be static. Schumpeter argues that the study of entrepreneurship is the study of useful economics. And it is the disciplines of philosophy and theology that must be considered when examining the impact of entrepreneurial activity on humaneness at the personal level.

As mentioned in the introduction, this book is meant to be a tentative effort to test the soil and identify the root of humaneness in economic systems, and particularly in entrepreneurship. It is believed, and it is our argument, that the entrepreneur is a humane figure, that the work of the entrepreneur is humane and has always been central to human society, that humane entrepreneurial work makes the entrepreneur a hero, that the entrepreneur has always had to fight against the inhumane forces of concentration and abuse of authority exerted for self-interest, and that the power of humane entrepreneurial activity is the life giving source of renewal and growth, over time and among rising and falling societies.

We hope that the essays contained in this book stimulate thought about this broad topic. We have approached the issues of humaneness from a number of different traditions: economic, philosophical, and historical. This has been the real challenge in writing this book — the elements of humaneness, and its association with economic systems and entrepreneurship, almost by definition, is an interdisciplinary effort that cuts across both time and disciplines.

By design we have not spent a lot of time on "solutions." Certainly, some solutions to the dilemmas discussed in this book have been touched on, or implied, in the essays. One strategy is to simply eliminate the problem, but this is a solution only if the problem is properly understood. Ultimately, the solution must lie in some form of decentralism combined with entrepreneurial behaviors drawing upon a repository of human virtues. But in complex systems, like a modern economy, and the associated impacts of "institutional inertness," "spillover effects," "externalities," and "unanticipated consequences," the solution is never that simple. Perhaps the introduction of new technologies that force a type of decentralized and de-massified society described by Alvin Toffler in *The Third Wave* is the solution. Perhaps business schools should refocus more on the humanities, and the examination of history, art, philosophy, and literature as part of management and leadership education. Perhaps entrepreneurship programs need to spend far less time on teaching aggressive private equity financing methods, designing "shark-tank" and "elevator" pitches, promoting cut-throat business plan competitions, emphasizing the importance of ramping-up and scalability, and promoting personal wealth enriching "quick exit" strategies. Perhaps we should eliminate the incentives put on business schools by both university top administrators and entrepreneurship program ranking entities, like the *Princeton Review*, on enrollment growth statistics, the salaries of graduates, and how much venture capital funding entrepreneurship alumni receive after graduation. Perhaps it is by recognizing the dehumanizing nature of organizational giantism and that governments need to disincentivize the structural problem of giantism, much like the anti-monopoly laws of the early 20th century addressed the industry concentration issue. But in doing this, governments need to have a bit of self-reflection since they also suffer from the dehumanizing nature of institutional giantism at all levels, federal, state and local. Decentralizing these government institutions at all levels seems critical to a humane economy. Perhaps it is refocusing on a deeper, and possibly more spiritual understanding of human nature. Perhaps it is all of these combined. Before any solution can be reasonably proposed, however, a clear understanding of the depth of the issues is required. That is the focus of this collection of essays.

Students of economics, whether they are formal students in a college degree program, academic professors and researchers, policy makers, or simply individuals interested in the true workings of economic systems, should understand that humans have a natural desire to discover and to create, a desire that gives rise to a propensity to venture. Humans also have a natural desire to find meaning in life, a life that by its very nature should be humane. And humans, as Adam Smith recognized in his *Theory of Moral Sentiment*, are ultimately repositories of virtues, virtues that should come to play in a person's decision-making process. If encouraged, the bold and the creative can draw on the propensity to venture. If properly educated in virtue and wisdom, the venturesome can be expected to insert life-giving change into a business world of gigantic and rigid economic systems of inefficient privilege and abuse of power.

Index

Printed in the United States
by Baker & Taylor Publisher Services